Monuments and Landscape in Atlantic Europe

D0421653

Atlantic Europe is the zone *par excellence* of megalithic monuments which encompasses a wide range of earthen and stone constructions from impressive circles to modest chambered tombs. A single basic concept lies behind this volume: that the intrinsic qualities encountered within the diverse landscapes of Atlantic Europe both informed the settings chosen for the monuments and played a role in determining their form and visual appearance. This, in part, derives from the use of local materials and the manner in which they were displayed within the monuments: for example how stone, clearly taken from the local geology, was visibly incorporated. Yet we may go further than this in some instances and propose that the nature of local landforms itself both attracted monuments, providing meaningful or dramatic settings, and offered a series of ideas which played some part in influencing the form of those monuments themselves.

Monuments and Landscape in Atlantic Europe goes significantly beyond the limits of the existing debate by inviting archaeologists from different countries within the Atlantic zone to examine the relationship between landscape features and prehistoric monuments in their specialist regions. By placing the issue within a broader regional and intellectual context, the authors illustrate the diversity of current archaeological ideas and approaches converging around this central theme. The regions represented include Britain, France, Ireland, Iberia and Scandinavia. The result constitutes a remarkable testament to the convergence of conceptual approaches to prehistoric monuments in the diverse landscapes and diverse intellectual traditions of Atlantic Europe.

Chris Scarre is Deputy Director of the McDonald Institute for Archaeological Research, Cambridge, and specialises in the later prehistory of Europe and the Mediterranean.

Monuments and Landscape in Atlantic Europe

Perception and Society during the
Neolithic and Early Bronze Age

Edited by Chris Scarre

London and New York

First published 2002
by Routledge
11 New Fetter Lane, London EC4P 4EE

Simultaneously published in the USA and Canada
by Routledge
29 West 35th Street, New York, NY 10001

Routledge is an imprint of the Taylor and Francis Group

Typeset in Bembo by
Keystroke, Jacaranda Lodge, Wolverhampton
Printed and bound in Great Britain by
Biddles Ltd, Guildford and King's Lynn

British Library Cataloguing in Publication Data
A catalogue record for this book is available from the British Library

Library of Congress Cataloging in Publication Data
Monuments and landscape in Atlantic Europe : perception and society
during the Neolithic and Early Bronze Age / edited by Chris Scarre.
    p. cm.
  Includes bibliographical references and index.
  1. Neolithic period—Europe, Western. 2. Bronze age—Europe,
Western. 3. Megalithic monuments—Europe, Western. 4. Landscape
assessment—Europe, Western. 5. Europe, Western—Antiquities.
  I. Scarre, Christopher.
GN776.22.W47 M66 2002
936—dc21   2001048692

ISBN 0–415–27313–7 (hbk)
ISBN 0–415–27314–5 (pbk)

Contents

Figures

Contributors

Chris Scarre is Deputy Director of the McDonald Institute for Archaeological Research and editor of the twice-yearly *Cambridge Archaeological Journal*. His research focuses primarily on the prehistory of Europe and the Mediterranean, with a particular interest in the archaeology of Atlantic façade (Iberia, France, Britain and Ireland). Recent publications have addressed the relationship of prehistoric monuments to their landscape setting; the use of colour in prehistoric societies; and the development and character of early state societies. He has participated in fieldwork projects in Britain, France and Greece and has directed excavations at Neolithic enclosures and mortuary sites in western France.

Lara Bacelar Alves is a doctoral student in archaeology at the University of Reading, and Research Fellow of the Fundação para a Ciência e Tecnologia – Praxis XXI (Portugal). Her doctoral thesis is on the subject of post-glacial rock art in north-west Iberia. She is currently directing a three-year rock-art research project in the Vouga basin (central-northern Portugal) sponsored by the Portuguese Institute of Archaeology (IPA). Her research interests centre upon Iberian rock art, ethnography and the anthropology of rock art.

Stefan Bergh holds a Government of Ireland Research Fellowship and is based at the Department of Archaeology, National University of Ireland, Galway. The current research project focuses on passage tombs, enclosures and the definition of ritual space in the Irish Neolithic. His research interests are centred upon Neolithic and Bronze Age landscape archaeology and he has over a number of years carried out extensive surveys and fieldwalking programmes, mainly in the west of Ireland. He is author of *Landscape of the Monuments*.

Richard Bradley studied law before becoming a full-time archaeologist in 1971. He teaches at Reading University, where he has been Professor of Archaeology since 1987. Recent publications include *Rock Art and the Prehistory of Atlantic Europe*, *The Significance of Monuments*, *An Archaeology of Natural Places* and *The Good Stones*. A new book entitled *The Past in Prehistoric Societies* will be published in 2002.

Manuel Calado has been lecturer in the University of Lisbon since 1990. He has worked in Central Alentejo since the mid 1980s, with a special focus on fieldwalking and landscape archaeology. He has developed projects involving different scales of regional analysis concerned mostly with the period between the Neolithic and the Iron Age. He is currently directing projects in the Alqueva Dam area in late prehistory, protohistory and rock art, as well as studying standing stones and their archaeological and geographical context in the Central Alentejo.

Vicki Cummings recently completed her doctoral dissertation which examined the landscape settings of Mesolithic sites and Neolithic monuments in south-west Wales and south-west Scotland. Her research interests are the origins of monumentality and the nature of the Mesolithic–Neolithic transition in the Irish Sea zone. She is currently engaged in a project supported by the Board of Celtic Studies investigating the landscape settings of Neolithic chambered tombs across Wales.

Roger Joussaume is Docteur d'Etat Es Lettres, Directeur de Recherche in the CNRS (UMR 7041 Nanterre), Lecturer at the University of Paris I Panthéon-Sorbonne and Consultant for UNESCO. He heads the Study Group for the Later Prehistory of the Horn of Africa, and has directed excavations at megalithic sites in Ethiopia and Neolithic settlement sites in Djibouti, where he has also recorded numerous rock carvings. In France, his research focuses on the Neolithic of Atlantic France, where he has excavated several megalithic tombs and a large triple-ditched enclosure. His recent publications include *Des dolmens pour les morts* (English edition *Dolmens for the Dead*) (1985) and *Tiya, l'Ethiopie des mégalithes* (1995).

Karin Ericson Lagerås studied prehistoric and medieval archaeology and art history, and now holds a position in Lund at the Archaeological Excavations Department of the Swedish National Heritage Board. During the last ten years she has participated in several commissioned archaeology projects in southern Sweden, and has a special interest in Late Neolithic and Bronze Age rituals and society, as well as in field documentation in a digital setting.

Luc Laporte is a researcher in the CNRS (UMR 6566, Rennes) and a specialist on the Neolithic, especially of western France. His doctoral thesis, completed in 1994, was a study of personal ornaments and centres of production in west-central France. He has worked on the megalithic monument or Ors on the Île d'Oléron, and since 1995 has been co-director, along with Roger Joussaume and Chris Scarre, of excavations at the tumulus de Péré at Prissé-la-Charrière. He has been involved in a number of rescue excavations and their publication, including a study of the prehistoric and historic occupation of the Charente estuary. He has also worked in East Africa and Argentina.

William O'Brien is a graduate of University College, Cork, where he completed doctoral research in 1987 on the subject of ancient copper-mining in south-west Ireland. In 1990 he joined the Department of Archaeology, National University of Ireland, Galway, and now lectures on prehistory, environmental archaeology and excavation methodology. His research interests lie in the area of Bronze Age studies, early European metallurgy and all aspects of prehistoric settlement in south-west Ireland. He recently completed a study of megalithic monuments in coastal south-west Ireland and is currently working on Copper Age metallurgy in Ireland following his discovery of the Beaker copper mine at Ross Island, Co. Kerry.

Alasdair Whittle is a Research Professor in the School of History and Archaeology, Cardiff University. He has worked extensively on the Neolithic of Europe. His current projects include fieldwork on the Early Neolithic in Hungary; a reassessment, with Michael Wysocki, of human bone from southern Britain; and an investigation, with Vicki Cummings, of the landscape settings of megalithic monuments in Wales.

Preface

The present volume owes its origins to a chance conversation at the Theoretical Archaeology Group meeting in Cardiff in December 1999. A number of speakers (including myself) had presented papers discussing the relationship of Neolithic monuments to landscape and to the nature/culture divide. It appeared to be an ideal moment to expand the discussion to include archaeologists from several different areas of western Europe, and so it was that a session entitled 'Monumentality and Landscape in Atlantic Europe' was held at the European Association of Archaeologists conference in Lisbon in September 2000. With one exception, the papers in this volume derive directly from those delivered at the Lisbon conference. My thanks go to the conference organisers, to the individual speakers, and a double thanks to Richard Bradley who helped chair the session. The final contribution to the present volume was not delivered at the conference, but Alasdair Whittle kindly accepted the invitation to provide an overview and summing-up for the papers published here.

An editor of a volume such as this owes many debts of gratitude, but I should like to reserve special mention for my colleagues at the McDonald Institute, especially Mrs Liz Farmar, and to Julene Barnes, Polly Osborn, Ruth Jeavons and the staff at Routledge who so expertly guided it through the press. We hope that the resulting volume will serve to illustrate a diversity of approaches grouped around a common theme: in what ways did the landscape of Atlantic Europe influence and inspire the forms and locations of the Neolithic and Bronze Age monuments that were built there?

Chris Scarre

1 Introduction: situating monuments

The dialogue between built form and landform in Atlantic Europe

Chris Scarre

The Atlantic coastline of Europe, from the Straits of Gibraltar to North Cape, presents for the most part a landscape of craggy granitic headlands and narrow marine inlets punctuated by low-lying basins and estuaries giving access to the interior. Traditional similarities between the coastal communities of Galicia, Brittany, Ireland and western Britain have given rise to the idea that these areas share a common heritage, linked by their proximity to the sea. This Atlantic identity – if such it is – may have been forged by millennia of maritime contact, but could also owe much to the special character of the Atlantic fringe in itself, as the land at the edge of the world, beyond which there was nowhere to go. It has recently been suggested that such factors may have induced the formation of a characteristic Atlantic mind-set as long ago as the Mesolithic period (Cunliffe 2001, 155). There are certainly archaeological parallels in such features as passage graves to suggest a measure of contact between Portugal and Scandinavia in the Neolithic, and sea-borne contacts can be pursued by archaeology into later periods through the evidence of Maritime Beakers, Atlantic bronzes and the tin trade.

Language, too, has been brought into the equation, ever since the recognition in the 18th century that the earliest attested languages of the Atlantic fringe bear a family relationship to each other. The 'Celtic' languages of Scotland, Ireland, Wales, Cornwall and Brittany are the survivors of a once more extensive series of languages which included Celtiberian and Gaulish. It is likely, indeed, that by the middle of the 1st millennium BC, the peoples living along the Atlantic seaboard from northern Scotland to the Straits of Gibraltar were speaking related languages which may for convenience be described as 'Atlantic Celtic' (Cunliffe 2001, 296). Whether this language pattern was spread by farmers from the east or through maritime contact along the seaboard (or more likely perhaps a mixture of both), remains undecided, as indeed does its antiquity, but the impact of a sense of 'Celtic' identity on recent historical and political awareness in many parts of Atlantic Europe is beyond question.

Living on the edge of the limitless ocean may have inspired and informed particular notions of cosmology and geography, both sacred and secular. While at one level this will have formed a common basis for human experience on the Atlantic fringe, it is important also to recognise the highly diverse character of the Atlantic margin. Islands and inlets, crags and moors make up a richly accentuated and often spectacular landscape, but it must not be forgotten that the lowlands of Aquitaine, fringed by long coastal sand dunes, are no less a part of Atlantic Europe than the cliffs and estuaries of the granitic massifs. Furthermore, Atlantic Europe consists of much more than a narrow coastal strip, and however significant the proximity of the sea in many parts of this broad region, traditional communities in inland and upland areas were as landlocked as any in Europe until the arrival of the railways and the transport revolution.

We must then beware of any essentialist notion of Atlantic Europe as a 'natural' entity. Its diversity in peoples, traditions and landscapes has been a feature since early prehistoric times. Yet it is also clear that the lands bordering the Atlantic were during the 5th and 4th millennia BC the setting for the construction of monuments, mainly funerary in character, which marked a visible break with the past. Long mounds in Britain, Brittany and Scandinavia, passage graves from Portugal to Sweden, rows and rings of standing stones, all mark a significant rupture with what had gone before, and the beginning of something new. Questions of origins are no longer so fashionable in archaeology as once they were, yet the transformations that lay behind the development of early Atlantic monuments remain a central focus of research. One part of the answer must be sought in the changes which European societies underwent in the course of the 6th and 5th millennia BC. These were associated with the spread of plant and animal domesticates, even though the notion that it was farming that made monuments possible may now be rejected. It is clear, in any event, that monuments in other parts of the world were not beyond the capabilities of hunter-gatherer groups. Examples range from the stone-built Inuksuit of Baffin Island, Canada, still being erected in recent times to signpost significant locations, back to the burial mound (dated to *c.*7500 bp) at L'Anse Amour on the Strait of Belle Isle in southern Labrador (McGhee and Tuck 1975, 85–94; Hallendy 2000). Aboriginal societies of Australia, too, created monumental structures for mortuary rituals or religious ceremonies: huge carved grave posts among the Tiwi of northern Australia; large earth sculptures at the 'bora' grounds of New South Wales; and settings of stone blocks, such as the 50m long line with associated circles and 'corridors' at Namagdi near Canberra (Flood 1995, 274–6). Yet in the west European context, the Neolithic monuments have no such Mesolithic antecedents. Notwithstanding rare discoveries like the line of massive Mesolithic posts in the Stonehenge car park (Cleal *et al.* 1995, 42–7), or the modest tumuli of the Mesolithic cemetery at Téviec (Péquart *et al.* 1937), there is simply nothing in Mesolithic Atlantic Europe to compare with the number, diversity and scale of Neolithic monuments.

Earlier prehistorians such as Gordon Childe invoked 'megalithic missionaries' to explain the origins and distribution of the Atlantic megaliths. Starting in the

Mediterranean, he imagined groups of sailors travelling northwards along the Atlantic coast bringing a new religion and the monumental settings that it demanded (Childe 1958, 124–34). Later interpretations have substituted marine resources for religious zeal in explaining these monuments, suggesting that the pursuit of migratory fish may have brought communities into close contact with each other in such a way as to encourage the spread of concepts and technologies (Clark 1977). Alternative perspectives have seen the shared quality of the Atlantic lands to lie in their character of periphery to a central European core. Thus megalithic monuments may have arisen independently in different areas of Europe through common response to the pressure of farming groups arriving from the east (Renfrew 1976); or through the persuasive power of a dominant ideology based on the concept of linearity embedded in the central European longhouse (Hodder 1990).

What these explanations lack is attention to the specific forms and settings of individual monuments. They in no way help us to understand why communities chose to build these particular kinds of monument, using the materials that they did. Recent studies have begun to explore this question by considering explicitly how the monuments relate to their physical surroundings. Behind this approach lies a single fundamental concept: that the intrinsic qualities encountered within the diverse landscapes of this western margin of Europe informed both the settings chosen for the monuments and played a part in determining their form and visual appearance. This in part derives from the use of local materials, and the manner in which these were displayed within the monuments: the way in which they might incorporate stone, for example, which was visibly taken from the local geology. Yet we may go further than this and propose that in some instances the nature of local landforms did themselves both attract monuments, providing meaningful or dramatic locations, and provide a series of ideas which played some part in influencing the form of those monuments.

Approaches to landscape in Atlantic Europe

The character of a particular landscape must be apparent to any archaeological field worker who has battled through rain and sun, across fields and ditches, up craggy slopes or gently shelving valleys, to locate and excavate prehistoric sites. Agricultural potential and the availability of local resources such as clay, stone or metal are frequently invoked. Yet few fieldwork reports attempt to understand the symbolic or cosmological significance of a particular location. There may perhaps be the fear that such comments would be regarded as unscientific, verging dangerously on an empathetic understanding of the past. But monuments do have specific locations and those locations would have been meaningful in a variety of ways to the communities that built them, and to their successors in both prehistoric and historical periods. The manifest difficulty of interpreting these associations should not lead to their being studiously ignored.

In southern Britain, the beginnings of archaeological fieldwork were characterised by the careful observation of several major monuments by antiquarians such as John Aubrey and William Stukeley. The plans which they prepared could be considered the first in a series of modern Western abstractions which however much they inform, may also be leading away from the monuments as they are encountered and experienced in their materiality (Thomas 1990; Tilley 1994, 75; Barrett 1994, 12ff). Stukeley, however, was fully aware of the more emotive qualities of the Wiltshire landscape:

> The strolling for relaxed minds upon these downs is the most agreeable exercise and amusement in the world especially when you are every minute struck with some piece of wonder in antiquity. The neat turn of the huge barrows wraps you up into a contemplation of the flux of life and passage from one state to another and you meditate with yourself of the fate and fortune of the famous personages who thus took care of their ashes that have rested so many ages.
>
> (Stukeley, quoted in Piggott 1985, 154)

Similar sensitivities are perhaps still more evident in illustration than prose; the early engravings of the Carnac alignments which accompanied Jacques de Cambry's (1805) *Monumens celtiques, ou recherches sur le culte des pierres*, for example, appear to show a striking awareness of close resemblances – which we may term a kind of resonance – between the built structures and the natural rock formations, albeit the latter in the form depicted by Cambry, owe a great deal to the imagination (Figure 1.1).

As archaeology became established as an academic discipline in the early 20th century, a more analytical view of landscape at a much larger scale emerged. One influential work was *The Personality of Britain* (Fox 1932), with the revealing subtitle *Its influence on inhabitant and invader in prehistoric and early historic times*. In this study Cyril Fox sought to relate patterns of prehistoric settlement to regional patterns of soils and geology, drawing the distinction between the highland and lowland zones of Britain. The development of aerial archaeology, too, encouraged the appreciation of landscapes as palimpsests of archaeological sites and monuments. At the smaller scale, there was recognition of 'archaeological landscapes' where clusters of monuments were found within a restricted compass, as for example the Avebury area, the Boyne Valley or Carnac in Brittany. Few if any of these studies, however, sought to consider in detail the meaning of the specific landscapes themselves for prehistoric and early historical communities.

The study of the relationship of individual monuments to particular features of the landscape probably arose first in the context of astronomical interpretations. It was William Stukeley, again, who in 1723 first recorded that the principal axis of Stonehenge was aligned upon the midsummer sunrise. More recently, considerations of landscape – in the shape of distant or mountainous horizons – came prominently to the fore in the surveys carried out by Alexander Thom in Britain and Brittany in the 1960s and 1970s (Thom 1967, 1971; Thom and Thom 1978). Many of these relied on the path of sun or moon at particular days of the year, and the way that the solar or lunar disc at rising or setting clipped

Pl. 3

Figure 1.1 The Carnac alignments from Cambry, *Monumens celtiques*.

the edge of a hill or a notch between mountains on the horizon. Sites such as Kintraw in Argyll were interpreted as megalithic observatories. Many of these claims do not stand up well to critical assessment; above all, the high precision alignments that Thom proposed are now generally discounted (Ruggles 1999). There remains the general principle, however, that early societies were aware of the movements of the heavenly bodies, and incorporated them into their cosmologies. These in turn will have entered into the design and placement of individual monuments. Astronomy and statistics play a key part in developing and assessing these claims; yet the fundamental question at issue is one of prehistoric belief systems, and how societies experienced and understood their surroundings be they land, sea or sky.

The study of prehistoric monuments entered a new phase in the 1990s with the development of phenomenological approaches, drawing on the work of Continental philosophers Heidegger and Merleau-Ponty. In seeking to explore the description and understanding of things as they are experienced by a (prehistoric) subject, phenomenological approaches are, by their very nature, subjective. A key contribution was Chris Tilley's *A Phenomenology of Landscape* (1994), which discussed the philosophical and ethnographic background, and proceeded to apply it to the study of Neolithic monuments in three regions of southern Britain: south-west Wales, the Black Mountains and Cranborne Chase. Tilley sought to underline 'the affective, emotional and symbolic nature of the landscape and [to] highlight some of the similarities and differences in the relationship between people and the land, and the manner in which it is culturally constructed, invested with powers and significances, and appropriated in widely varying "natural" environments and social settings' (Tilley 1994, 35). This concept of the 'numinous landscape' where places and landforms are imbued with mythological or spiritual significance is familiar from a number of ethnographic accounts and is indeed a feature of recent European folklore. It must be considered particularly appropriate to the consideration of prehistoric monuments which are thought to embody ritual practices and cosmological beliefs. The subjectivity of the phenomenological approach, however, presents considerable obstacles in methodology. Fleming, for example, has reviewed Tilley's fieldwork in south Wales and, as well as questioning some of the field observations, urges the need to consider alternative perspectives in interpreting the location of prehistoric monuments. Thus, while monuments may indeed indicate places that were held of particular mythological significance, they may have been sited so as to overlook a particular area or an important routeway. Furthermore, if we are to consider monuments in relation to natural features, these must include not only rivers, hills and rock outcrops, but vanished elements such as sacred trees or groves (Fleming 1999).

Fleming's critique highlights several of the difficulties inherent in the phenomenological approach. Yet it remains the case that, whatever the shortcomings of method, any attempt to understand a prehistoric monument which fails to consider the landscape setting is omitting one of the most salient characteristics. Here again we must distinguish between the monument, abstracted in a plan or a field report, and the monument as a visible structure, experienced within its surroundings. The holistic and integrated nature of human experience obliges archaeologists to seek to establish the original associations of meaning wherever possible. This is clearly most accessible where monuments can with some confidence be related to well-defined or prominent landscape features (such as rock outcrops, coasts, or offshore islands), and where ethnographic information can be drawn upon to increase the richness and plausibility of a particular interpretation. Thus in northern Europe, Knut Helskog has been able to draw on Saami cosmology to understand the rock-art motifs of coastal Norway (Helskog 1999). Similar cosmologies may underlie the coastal concentration of passage graves in Brittany, or on the Orkney islands.

Several Continental scholars have adopted similar approaches. Thus Boujot and colleagues have referred to the 'megalithic aesthetic' of Neolithic monuments around the Gulf of Morbihan, and its relationship to visual awareness in a landscape setting with specific qualities. 'The structures studied in coastal Brittany focus their spatial characteristics in a way which attempts to capture nature and to embed human elements in the new configuration. The burial mounds seem to emerge as a subtle representation of this capture, serving as elements which define the setting in which this developed' (Boujot *et al.* 1998, 203). In Galicia, too, studies have observed the close relationship between megalithic tombs and rock outcrops (Criado *et al.* 1994). These cases highlight the distinction between 'natural' and 'cultural' and in so doing may lay themselves open to the accusation that they are seeking to impose a modern Western frame of reference that may be entirely inappropriate to the prehistoric societies under consideration. Yet it is hard to know in what other terms we can discuss this issue.

The nature/culture dilemma is taken up in several of the contributions to the present volume. It underlies any approach which seeks to relate monuments (cultural) to landscape (natural). Landscape features may themselves have been considered cultural by prehistoric communities, or have been the focus of beliefs and practices that may not in all cases have left prominent archaeological traces:

> Arctic archaeology is concerned with the significance of unaltered places . . . These were unusual features of the natural topography – features that stood out from the surrounding country, some of which recalled petrified people and animals – but they are even more important because we know a certain amount about their significance in Saami cosmology . . . It provides a vital reminder of what they [European prehistorians] may be losing if they limit themselves to the significance of monuments.
>
> (Bradley 2000a, 14)

Which leads very naturally to the question, 'how far is it possible to study the ancient landscape when the monuments are stripped away?' (ibid., 14).

Landscape and monuments: a dialogue

It is clear that any studies which seek to explore the interrelationship between natural landforms and built monuments will focus on the contrasts and comparisons between the two. This is not to deny that nature and culture are modern analytical categories which may have been entirely foreign to the thinking of the prehistoric populations concerned. Quite the contrary, what the papers in this collection will show is how the distinctions between human and non-human elements in the landscape were frequently variable and imprecise. An old, eroded monument might easily have come to be considered part of the natural world, while at the same time we must imagine that both natural and human elements were enmeshed within a framework of myth which gave them significance in ancestral or religious traditions.

The relationship of monuments to their landscape may perhaps be envisaged as a kind of dialogue, in which communities drew upon natural landscape features or elements in a number of ways. These could include, on the one hand, the use of natural features as the focus of human activity. An example is provided by the studies of Richard Bradley and Chris Tilley on the relationship of megalithic tombs to the natural granite outcrops known as tors in the south-western peninsula of Britain (Tilley 1996a; Bradley 1998a). Bradley has argued that early populations may not have found it easy to distinguish between natural landscape features and human constructions, and may have come to confuse the tors with ruined portal dolmens (Bradley 1998a, 20). This is a phenomenon which is not restricted to the south-west of Britain, nor to the Neolithic. At Ulverston in Cumbria, for example, two Bronze Age burials had been placed in a natural sand knoll (Kinnes and Longworth 1985, 133). In the Derbyshire Peak District, the 'secondary' burial at Throwley Moor House was in a mound that consisted 'almost entirely of natural rock, the inequalities having been smoothed over into barrow form by the addition of a little earth' (Bateman 1861, 162). There is therefore good reason to suppose that natural features were sometimes mistaken for cultural constructions, or perhaps that the two were in some way regarded as equivalent where their forms coincided.

A particularly interesting example of the use of natural features for ritual or funerary activity is provided by the Glacial Kame culture of the Great Lakes region of the USA and southern Canada (Cunningham 1948). This is a glaciated landscape in which the kames are natural hills composed of sand or gravel drift, deposited by meltwater streams along the ice front and then left standing as isolated hills or ridges as the glaciers retreated. The distinctive feature of the Glacial Kame tradition, which goes back at least to the early 2nd millennium BC (Robertson *et al.* 1999, 116), was the choice of these natural mounds as places of burial. The Burch site in southern Michigan consisted of several burials at a depth of 6 feet in a round gravel hill some 150 feet across. Much larger was the Zimmerman site in neighbouring Ohio, a huge gravel kame offering views to a distance of twelve to fifteen miles. In 1931 part of the kame was quarried for gravel and yielded graves of 148 individuals, one of them a multiple interment containing three separate skeletons (Cunningham 1948, 10–12). The burials were in steep-sided shafts dug through the glacial gravel, and were furnished with shell gorgets, polished stone and occasional copper ornaments. It is interesting to note that this is the very same area in which during the following Middle Woodland period (200 BC–AD 500) the Hopewellian tradition of burial under artificial mounds was to be a prominent feature (Mason 1981). Thus it may be that a tradition of burial in natural hills and ridges was transformed over time into a tradition of artificial burial monuments which in their low rounded form replicate the shape of natural glacial features.

In both the Cornish and the Glacial Kame examples it is evident that a particular landscape feature was being referenced or exploited, and we may deduce that the rocky tors or the prominent gravel hills were in each case places endowed with a special significance within their respective landscapes. Coastlines and islands may attract similar significance, as places where earth, sea and sky meet, and where the twice-daily ebb and flow of the tides successively drowns and exposes the foreshore. If boundaries and liminality were of particular concern to prehistoric communities, then coasts and islands are the clearest natural instances of such zones. In many cases, the sea as a provider of marine foods and a medium of maritime communication may in itself explain the frequency with which prehistoric sites cluster along shorelines; but it is important to consider the cosmological significance of such settings by careful consideration of individual site locations.

Coastal landforms might sometimes be directly referenced in the form of the built monument. One example is Petit Mont in southern Brittany. Recent excavations (1979–89; Lecornec 1994) have shown this to be a four-phase monument. The first phase (*c*.4500 BC) consisted of a low earthen mound, measuring 49m long and 19m at its widest, but only 1.6m high. This initial long cairn had a menhir at its south-western extremity and was carefully positioned to follow and accentuate the general orientation of the promontory on which it stands. The same orientation was retained in phase 2, when the low earth mound is replaced by a taller and squatter structure of stone, rectangular with rounded corners. Again, the orientation relates to and emphasises the projection of the promontory. In phases 3 and 4, however, the orientation of the long mound, parallel with the main axis of the promontory, was suppressed when Le Petit Mont was transformed in several stages by the addition of three passage graves (*c*.3900–3800 BC: Lecornec 1994). The stone mound of phase 2 was entirely engulfed in the later structure, and its orientation was lost. But the striking feature of the final mound is the way in which it conforms to the shape of the headland on which it stands; it has the same roughly pentagonal shape. This must surely be interpreted as the cultural elaboration of a natural landform. It is all the more impressive for the prominent situation of Le Petit Mont at the entrance to the Gulf of Morbihan; a natural landmark for sailors. This significance is enhanced by its being built largely of local materials, blending to that extent with its geological and topographical surroundings.

Alongside the forms of the monuments we must also consider the significance of the elements of which they were made. In simple terms these might be listed as timber, earth and stone, but this masks a wide diversity in choice and manipulation of elements. The widespread deployment of large slabs or blocks which has given rise to the term 'megalithic' has attracted particular attention since at least the time of the early antiquaries in the 17th century. Alongside scientific debate they have also attracted considerable folklore, much of it citing supernatural or mythical beings or events. This in itself illustrates the evocative power of the large blocks. One recent interpretation has suggested, by analogy with ethnographic evidence from Madagascar, that the hardness of stone was symbolic of the fixed nature of the ancestors and may have been seen in opposition to the softer more mutable qualities of wood used in structures for the living (Parker Pearson and Ramilisonina 1998).

The materiality of the stone deserves particular emphasis in the present perspective. Not for nothing did early studies of megalithic monuments in English take titles such as *Rude Stone Monuments in all Countries* (James Fergusson 1872) or *Rough Stone Monuments and their Builders* (T. Eric Peet 1912), titles which draw particular attention to the shape – and indeed the irregularity – of the stones themselves. There is indeed a considerable variety in the degree to which individual elements have been smoothed and shaped. In some cases, the natural block or slab was taken as it was found, with little or no modification. In others, as for example in the Stonehenge sarsens, enormous labour was expended in the shaping of the stones. The contrast between worked and unworked surfaces would have been much more evident at the time of construction, before centuries of exposure had evened out and largely erased the differences.

In many cases, however, the use of unmodified local stones must be considered a characteristic and highly significant feature of the overall undertaking. The megalithic tombs of the Burren in western Ireland, where naturally occurring flat-faced slabs are placed upright in cracks in the limestone pavement, provide one striking example. They may be compared and contrasted with the employment in south Scandinavia of rounded boulders (glacial erratics) for the construction both of chambers and kerbs. The Kujavian long mounds of northern Poland have boulder surrounds though the burials themselves are in pit graves without megalithic elements (Midgley 1985). In the adjacent German province of Mecklenburg, the closed *Urdolmen* and the larger *erweitere Dolmen* with formal entrance are both formed of unmodified boulders, four to eight in number (Schuldt 1972). These monuments, in using local materials in this visible way, establish a powerful resonance between the built monument and the local setting. On the one hand, they express a desire for an integration between the monumental and the natural which invested the former, perhaps, with some of the special qualities of the latter. Looked at in another way, the human effort may have been intended to bring to the fore an aspect or feature which was considered already to be present, immanent, in the landscape.

Two Breton examples can be cited as illustrations. In the Carnac region of southern Morbihan, Dominique Sellier has studied the form and surfaces of the standing stones which form the alignment of Kerlescan (Sellier 1995). This consists of thirteen converging rows, each comprising between seven and forty-one stones. Study of the shapes and the differing degrees of erosion of the individual stones has enabled Sellier to distinguish between those that were already present as detached blocks and those which required only a minimum of effort to detach them from the parent rock. The distribution of the different types throughout the alignment revealed strong spatial patterning which led to the conclusion that this patterning related directly to natural erosion across the site: the detached blocks falling in the uppermost part of the site, those partly detached in the middle section, while the smallest blocks which required most work to extract and erect them lay on the lower edge of the site. This implies two remarkable things: first, that each of the blocks was raised into position very close to the point where it was found; and, second, that before construction of the alignments began, the site of Kerlescan would have presented itself as a scatter of granite blocks and outcrops: the potential for the monument would have already been visible on the ground. The builders may have considered that in raising the blocks into regular rows they were simply realising or completing a megalithic monument which was already present in nature.

Such ideas are not new. Almost a century ago, French ethnologist Yves Sébillot suggested that the Breton menhir-builders were imitating the natural stones that they saw on the surface of the ground, and that in raising these menhirs they were seeking to create structures similar to those they believed inhabited by the gods (Sébillot 1903; Cassen *et al.* 2000). Still earlier, in 1825, the Abbé Mahé had noted the suggestive parallel between a menhir on the île d'Arz and the rocks of the nearby coast.

The second illustration is from the Saint-Just area in central Brittany, where again the monuments may have suggested themselves through the natural appearance of the landscape. This is a schist upland cut through by veins of brightly contrasting quartz. The monuments make intentional use of the quartz/schist contrast in their selection and juxtapositioning of the two materials. This is seen most strikingly in the Le Moulin alignments, where two files of quartz blocks contrast with a third file comprising both quartz and schist (Le Roux *et al.* 1989; Scarre 2002). Quartz blocks are used to striking effect also in other monuments on this upland, notably in the large pillars of the Château-Bû, a passage grave reworked into an Early Bronze Age tumulus (Briard *et al.* 1995). The significance of the quartz monoliths is all the greater for the fact that they themselves are not local but were brought from sources several kilometres distant. Yet their deployment at Saint-Just must surely be considered a monumentalised reflection of the interplay between schist and quartz in the bedrock of this upland, especially as both quartz and schist are revealed in surface exposures. The special significance of quartz in traditional societies in Australia and North America – where it is seen as a material of special power, sometimes associated with the ancestors – adds further point to its deployment here.

The southern file of the Le Moulin alignments, with its hybrid use of quartz and schist, illustrates well the importance of colour in many of these monuments. A particularly striking example of this deployment of colour is the façade of Newgrange in Ireland, as reconstructed following the excavations of Michael

O'Kelly (O'Kelly 1982). Here white quartz is punctuated by inclusions of dark granite and granodiorite. Around the base of the Newgrange mound are the decorated kerbstones, many of them carved with intricate designs which may have been painted. Questions have been raised about the accuracy of this reconstruction, but it does serve the purpose of highlighting the impact that colour could have had in the appearance of these monuments.

The striking façade of Newgrange takes us a long way from the concept of monuments designed so as to reproduce or blend in with their surroundings. Yet more subtle use of coloured stone or specially selected stones may be a significant and widespread feature of megalithic monuments. On Arran, Andrew Jones has documented how the contrasting use of red sandstone and white granite has been deployed to achieve carefully planned effects in the architecture of the megalithic tombs. The red and black of the tomb architecture may indeed be related to the colours of the artefacts placed within them: red pottery and black pitchstone (Jones 1999). In north-east Scotland, Richard Bradley and David Trevarthen have studied the use and positioning of stones of different colour in the cairns of Balnuaran of Clava, and have shown a relationship to sunrise and sunset events at special times of the year (Trevarthen 2000; Bradley 2000b). In the Vǻstergǒtland region of Sweden, Chris Tilley has observed that the deployment of stones in the passage graves deliberately duplicates the layering of the natural geology. Stones of sedimentary origin are used for the passage and chamber uprights, and igneous material for the capstones, mirroring the contrast between the sedimentary plateau on which the tombs stand, and the igneous mountains visible in the distance (Tilley 1996b, 209).

The close referencing of landscape and the local materials implies a strong symbolic bond between the two, one in which qualities and powers of place were transferred to the monuments, and vice versa. It may have been the development of this particular mind-set among the peoples of Atlantic Europe – associated perhaps with myths of creation and changing belief systems – which lay fundamentally behind the espousal of these monumental architectures across this extensive and diversified region. A new way of envisioning the landscape, and people's place within it, could well have inspired, stimulated and legitimised the manipulation of local materials to create monuments that unlocked in new ways the sacred potential that was recognised to be present in natural landforms, themselves already redolent with mythological associations. Thus the monuments may be speaking to us of a transformation of meaning, running through these communities in the 5th and 4th millennia BC. Where landscape came in was in providing the visual cues on which this transformation of perception could build – both literally and metaphorically.

References

Barrett, J., 1994. *Fragments from Antiquity. An Archaeology of Social Life in Britain 2900–1200 BC.* Oxford: Blackwell.

Bateman, T., 1861. *Ten Years' Diggings in Celtic and Saxon Grave-Hills in the Counties of Derby, Stafford, and York from 1848–1858.* London: J.R. Smith.

Boujot, C., Cassen, S., and Vaquero Lastres, J., 1998. Some abstraction for a practical subject: the neolithization of western France seen through funerary architecture. *Cambridge Archaeological Journal* 8, 193–206.

Bradley, R., 1998a. Ruined buildings, ruined stones: enclosures, tombs and natural places in the Neolithic of south-west England. *World Archaeology* 30, 13–22.

Bradley, R., 1998b. Architecture, imagination and the Neolithic world, in S. Mithen (ed.), *Creativity in Human Evolution*. London: Routledge, 227–40.

Bradley, R., 2000a. *An Archaeology of Natural Places*. London: Routledge.

Bradley, R. 2000b. *The Good Stones: A New Investigation of the Clara Cairns*. Edinburgh: Society of Antiquaries of Scotland.

Briard, J., Gautier, M., and Leroux, G., 1995. *Les mégalithes et les tumulus de Saint-Just, Ille-et-Vilaine*. Comité des Travaux Historiques et Scientifiques, Paris.

Cambry, J. de, 1805. *Monumens Celtiques, ou recherches sur le culte des pierres*. Paris: Johanneau.

Cassen, S., Boujot, C., and Vaquero, J., 2000. *Eléments d'architecture. Exploration d'un tertre funéraire à Lannec er Gadouer (Erdeven, Morbihan). Constructions et reconstructions dans le Néolithique morbihannais. Propositions pour une lecture symbolique*. Chauvigny: Association des Publications Chauvinoises.

Childe, V.G., 1958. *The Prehistory of European Society*. Harmondsworth: Penguin.

Clark, J.G.D., 1977. The economic context of dolmens and passage-graves in Sweden, in V. Markotic (ed.), *Ancient Europe and the Mediterranean*. Warminster: Aris & Phillips, 35–49.

Cleal, R.M.J., Walker, K.E., and Montague, R., 1995. *Stonehenge in its Landscape*. London: English Heritage.

Criado Boado, F., Fabregas Valcarce, R., and Vaquero Lastres, J., 1994. Regional patterning among the megaliths of Galicia (NW Spain). *Oxford Journal of Archaeology* 13, 33–47.

Cunliffe, B., 2001. *Facing the Ocean. The Atlantic and its Peoples 8000 BC–AD 1500*. Oxford: Oxford University Press.

Cunningham, W.B., 1948. *A Study of the Glacial Kame Culture in Michigan, Ohio, and Indiana*. Ann Arbor: University of Michigan Press.

Fleming, A., 1999. Phenomenology and the megaliths of Wales: A dreaming too far? *Oxford Journal of Archaeology* 18, 119–25.

Flood, J., 1995. *Archaeology of the Dreamtime. The Story of Prehistoric Australia and its People*. Sydney: Angus & Robertson.

Fox, C., 1932. *The Personality of Britain*. Cardiff: National Museum of Wales.

Hallendy, N., 2000. *Inuksuit. Silent Messengers of the Arctic*. Vancouver: Douglas & McIntyre.

Helskog, K., 1999. The shore connection. Cognitive landscape and communication with rock carvings in northernmost Europe. *Norwegian Archaeological Review* 32, 73–94.

Hodder, I., 1990. *The Domestication of Europe*. Oxford: Basil Blackwell.

Jones, A., 1999. Local colour: megalithic architecture and colour symbolism in Neolithic Arran. *Oxford Journal of Archaeology* 18, 339–50.

Kinnes, I.A., and Longworth, I.H., 1985. *Catalogue of the Excavated Prehistoric and Romano-British Material in the Greenwell Collection*. London: British Museum Publications.

Lecornec, J., 1994. *Le Petit Mont, Arzon, Morbihan*. Rennes: Documents Archéologiques de l'Ouest.

Le Roux, C.-T., Lecerf, Y., and Gautier, M., 1989. Les mégalithes de Saint-Just (Ille-et-Vilaine) et la fouille des alignements du Moulin de Cojou. *Revue Archéologique de l'Ouest* 6, 5–29.

Mason, R.J., 1981. *Great Lakes Archaeology*. London: Academic Press.

McGhee, R., and Tuck, J.A., 1975. *An Archaic Sequence from the Strait of Belle Isle, Labrador*. Ottawa: National Museums of Canada.

Midgley, M.S., 1985. *The Origin and Function of the Earthen Long Barrows of Northern Europe*. Oxford: British Archaeological Reports.

O'Kelly, M.J., 1982. *Newgrange: Archaeology, Art and Legend*. London: Thames & Hudson.

Parker Pearson, M., and Ramilisonina, 1998. Stonehenge for the ancestors: the stones pass on the message. *Antiquity* 72, 308–26.

Péquart, M., Péquart, S.J., Boule, M., and Vallois, H.V., 1937. *Téviec: Station-nécropole mésolithique du Morbihan*. Paris: Archives de l'Institut de Paléontologie Humaine 18.

Piggott, S., 1985. *William Stukeley. An Eighteenth-Century Antiquary*. London: Thames & Hudson.

Renfrew, C., 1976. Megaliths, territories and populations, in S.J. de Laet (ed.), *Acculturation and Continuity in Atlantic Europe*. Brugge: De Tempel, 198–220.

Robertson, A., Lovis, W.A., and Halsey, J.R., 1999. The late archaic hunter-gatherers in an uncertain environment, in J.R. Halsey and M.D. Stafford (eds), *Retrieving Michigan's Buried Past: The Archaeology of the Great Lakes State*. Bloomfield Hills, MI: Cranbrook Institute of Science, 95–124.

Ruggles, C., 1999. *Astronomy in Prehistoric Britain and Ireland*. New Haven and London: Yale University Press.

Scarre, C., 2002. A place of special meaning: interpreting pre-historic monuments in the landscape, in B. David and M. Wilson (eds), *Inscribed Landscapes: Marking and Making Place*. Honolulu: University of Hawaii Press.

Schuldt, E., 1972. *Die mecklenburgischen Megalithgräber. Untersuchungen zur ihrer Architektur und Funktion*. Berlin: Deutscher Verlag der Wissenschaften.

Sébillot, Y., 1903. *Histoire du peuple breton depuis son arrivée en Armorique jusqu'à nos jours*. Paris: Maisonneuve.

Sellier, D., 1995. Eléments de reconstitution du paysage prémégalithique sur le site des alignements de Kerlescan (Carnac, Morbihan) à partir de critères géomorphologiques. *Revue Archéologique de l'Ouest* 12, 21–41.

Thom, A., 1967. *Megalithic Sites in Britain*. Oxford: Oxford University Press.

Thom, A., 1971. *Megalithic Lunar Observatories*. Oxford: Oxford University Press.

Thom, A., and Thom, A.S., 1978. *Megalithic Remains in Britain and Brittany*. Oxford: Oxford University Press.

Thomas, J., 1990. Monuments from the inside: the case of the Irish megalithic tombs. *World Archaeology* 22, 168–78.

Tilley, C., 1994. *A Phenomenology of Landscape. Places, paths and monuments*. Oxford: Berg.

Tilley, C., 1996a. The power of rocks: topography and monument construction on Bodmin Moor. *World Archaeology* 28, 161–76.

Tilley, C., 1996b. *An Ethnography of the Neolithic. Early Prehistoric Societies in Southern Scandinavia*. Cambridge: Cambridge University Press.

Trevarthen, D., 2000. Illuminating the monuments: observation and speculation on the structure and function of the cairns at Balnuaran of Clava. *Cambridge Archaeological Journal* 10, 295–315.

Part I

Atlantic Iberia

Introduction

The Iberian peninsula at the south-western extremity of Europe is a large and diverse land mass connected to the remainder of the Continent by a relatively narrow neck of land that is itself obstructed by the Pyrenean mountain chain. The Atlantic zone comprises Portugal and northern Spain, from the Algarve to Galicia and Cantabria. The early importance of maritime connections along this coast is suggested by the shell middens of the major Portuguese river systems, and the layers of shell detritus and fish bones in the cave sites of the Asturias and Cantabria. Fishing and foraging may have continued in some areas for several centuries after the introduction of farming in other parts of the region (Arias 1999; Zilhão 2000).

The megalithic monuments of Iberia have been well known since the surveys conducted by Georg and Vera Leisner from the 1930s to the 1960s (Leisner and Leisner 1943; 1956–65). These documented the wealth of surviving material, with particular emphasis on passage graves, which brought Iberia clearly within the broader west European family of megalithic monuments. Other categories of site received less attention, and it is only within the last thirty years that the significance of standing stones and stone settings, including many with carved motifs, has come to be recognised. At the same time, greater attention has been directed to the diversity of the funerary monuments, with the excavation in particular of mounds containing sealed chambers (rather than passage graves) in Portugal and Galicia. A third trend, which is represented in many other parts of Atlantic Europe, is the greater interest in survey and settlement evidence, which seeks to place the Neolithic monuments in their broader context.

The three papers in this section of the volume cover different categories of monument and adopt a number of theoretical approaches. In central Portugal, inland from the Mesolithic shell middens of Muge and Sado, Manuel Calado presents new evidence from the Central Alentejo which highlights the importance of standing stones (which occur both singly and in settings) at the very beginning of the Neolithic. The spatial relationship between standing stones and the growing number of Early Neolithic settlements discovered by field survey suggests that the two belong together and that menhirs may have played a role in the Neolithic transition of this region. There are parallels with the evidence from Brittany, where recent evidence likewise suggests that standing stones should be placed at the very beginning of the Neolithic monument sequence, and that the motifs carved on them are symbolic of the new relationship between people and their surroundings engendered by the Neolithic transition.

Rock art is another feature which ties Iberia into the broader west European Neolithic tradition. Simple designs such as cup-marks are present from Portugal to Scandinavia, but Iberia also has a rich heritage of more complex motifs including representations of humans and animals (Bradley 1997). In the third contribution to this section, Lara Bacelar Alves focuses on the Schematic Art tradition, and its placement in caves and rock shelters. She compares this with the distribution of art in megalithic monuments, and highlights the case of El Pedroso, a cave that resembles a passage grave in certain respects, and where the transition from natural to cultural is carefully elided in the sequence of carvings from entrance into the interior. Thus rock art becomes a way of enculturating natural features, turning them into monuments.

The second contribution moves away from art and funerary contexts to consider a very different kind of site: the hilltop enclosures of north-east Portugal. Traditionally regarded as defensive locations or elite residences perhaps associated with early metallurgy, these structures are presented by Vítor Jorge and colleagues as monuments in their own right, that were designed as statements within the landscape. In chronological terms they follow the megalithic tombs of the Middle Neolithic, and may in some respects have assumed similar roles. Once again, it is landscape setting which provides the crucial insight; only by considering these enclosures within the topography and geography of local settlement can their significance be understood. Thus these three chapters together illustrate the diversity of monument forms – encompassing standing stones, rock-art sites and Chalcolithic enclosures as well as the more customary megalithic tombs. They are also united in their common concern with the progression from the study of individual monuments towards a broader understanding which places their significance within prehistoric landscapes of meaning.

References

Arias, P., 1999. The origins of the Neolithic along the Atlantic coast of Continental Europe: a survey. *Journal of World Prehistory* 13, 403–64.

Bradley, R., 1997. *Rock Art and the Prehistory of Atlantic Europe*. London: Routledge.

Leisner, G., and Leisner, V., 1943. *Die Megalithgräber der Iberischen Halbinsel: der Süden*. Berlin: De Gruyter.

Leisner, G., and Leisner, V., 1956–65. *Die Megalithgräber der Iberischen Halbinsel: der Westen*. (3 vols) Berlin: De Gruyter.

Zilhão, J., 2000. From the Mesolithic to the Neolithic in the Iberian peninsula, in T. Douglas Price (ed.), *Europe's First Farmers*. Cambridge: Cambridge University Press, 144–82.

2 Standing stones and natural outcrops

The role of ritual monuments in the Neolithic transition of the Central Alentejo

Manuel Calado

The region of the Central Alentejo is a peneplain drained by the Rivers Tagus, Sado and Guadiana and enclosed by the relatively low hills of Serra de Ossa, Serra do Mendro and Serra de Monfurado (Figure 2.1). Geologically it is composed of granites or related rocks and schists (or similar metamorphic rocks); some tertiary patches are still perceptible, along with a zone of carbonated rocks (marbles and dolomites). In administrative terms, the Central Alentejo coincides more or less with the present area of the District of Évora.

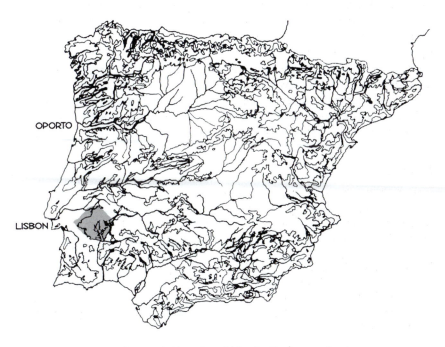

OPORTO

LISBON

Figure 2.1 Location of Central Alentejo within the Iberian peninsula.

On the map of megalithic funerary sites (mostly passage graves) in the Iberian peninsula the Central Alentejo stands out clearly as the densest area of distribution (Leisner and Leisner 1959). It is also characterised by the presence of some exceptionally large monuments, among them the well-known passage grave of Anta Grande do Zambujeiro (Valverde, Évora). Somewhat surprisingly it was only in the mid 1960s, by which time Georg and Vera Leisner had already identified and published hundreds of Alentejan passage graves, that the first standing stones began to be reported. These are found either singly or grouped in megalithic enclosures, and today more standing stones are known in the Central Alentejo alone than in any other area of the Iberian Peninsula. Survey work developed over the last twenty years in the Central Alentejan region has in addition allowed the identification of a dense network of Early Neolithic settlements; these too represent a concentration of sites that is altogether exceptional in the Iberian context. With this evidence it is now beyond question that the Central Alentejo has been both the setting for activities that were of particular relevance for the regional Neolithic, and the focus for a very special form of European megalithic monumentality (Figures 2.2–2.5).

It is within their regional setting that the general characteristics of these non-funerary megalithic monuments of the Alentejo must be defined. For a fuller understanding, it is also essential to consider them in relation to other categories of site. As will emerge, they have a special contribution to make towards the broader discussion of the genesis of megaliths and the Neolithic transition in Atlantic Europe.

Standing stones and landscape

Excluding certain misleading examples, and bearing in mind that megalithic enclosures are practically unknown in the areas bordering the Central Alentejo, three principal concentrations may be distinguished among the Alentejan standing stones. In descending order in terms of both the number and size of the known monuments, these are the Évora–Montemor, Reguengos de Monsaraz and Pavia groups.

The standing stones of the Central Alentejo are exclusively of granites and their distribution in the Central Alentejan landscape correlates directly with the availability of this type of rock. This relationship does not, however, imply that the standing stones were always erected within the granite areas: on the contrary, the majority of them are located outside, although, in general, the distances are small, varying between mere tens of metres and a couple of kilometres. In the case of the megalithic enclosures, there appears to have been a clear intention systematically to avoid erecting them on granite bedrock. In fact, leaving aside the very few examples around Reguengos de Monsaraz (in particular the problematic monument of Xerez), the Alentejan megalithic enclosures are all located in the areas of tertiary deposits or in the gneiss zones bordering the granites.

In the case of the single standing stones a greater flexibility is apparent, although even where they are set in granitic terrain, locations in immediate proximity to conspicuous granite outcrops were avoided. The locations chosen for single standing stones were always open areas, free of obtrusive natural features (Figure 2.6). Some Alentejan standing stones appear to stand at the boundary between the granites and other geological zones, marking lines of separation between very distinct physical landscapes that in other contexts have been shown frequently to be special interfaces in the sacred geography (Taçon 1999, 41).

The large megalithic enclosures of the Évora–Montemor group are also found along or in close proximity to a major dividing line of the Central Alentejan landscape: the watershed between the hydrographic basins of the Tagus and the Sado. This watershed forms the junction between two worlds defined by the circulation of water and was also, in practical terms, an important natural routeway. At a more general level, the location of standing stones follows certain constants in relation to their immediate surroundings, above all their location close to the top of eastward-facing slopes. This is coupled, in the case of megalithic enclosures, with the decreasing size of the stones as one proceeds downslope.

The first settlements

Until very recently, there appeared to be no vestiges of Early Neolithic settlements in the Central Alentejo. Early Neolithic material was first found in the cave of Escoural (Santos 1971), but this in itself was such an unusual context (there being no other caves in the region) that it raised the possibility that groups bringing Cardial pottery had only been sporadically present. Even this level of activity has been questioned in one recent work, on the grounds that 'to date, no other archaeological sites of this period are known in the Alentejo interior' (Araújo and Lejeune 1995, 54). In the mid 1980s, however, archaeological work in the basin planned for the Alqueva reservoir had already brought to light the first three open-air sites attributed to the Early Neolithic, all of them close to the River Guadiana (Soares and Silva 1992). The belief current at the time was that the Early Neolithic was exclusively governed by the proximity of water resources, whether maritime, estuarine or fluvial (Arnaud 1982, 31), but by the end of the 1980s, another three settlements of the same period were finally discovered in the Évora–Montemor area (Gomes 1994).

During the 1990s, a large number of Neolithic settlement sites have been identified through the work of an ongoing regional project designed to place the standing stones of the Central Alentejo within their broader archaeological context. Many of these settlement sites have impressed and incised pottery, along with other elements (notably the microlithic industries: bladelets, transverse arrows and burins) that regularly recur in the southern Early Neolithic (Calado 1995; Calado and Rocha 1996; Calado and Sarantopoulos 1996; Diniz and Calado 1997). To these settlements, almost all located in the Évora–Montemor area, were later added others near Reguengos de Monsaraz that were discovered by new survey work in the area of the planned Alqueva dam (Calado and Mataloto 1999; Soares and Silva 2000; Gonçalves 2000). Apart from the various sites recently excavated or still under excavation in Alqueva (Gonçalves 1999, 39–40), we have only the emergency investigations (still unpublished) that were undertaken in the settlement of Patalim (Montemor-o-Novo), and the

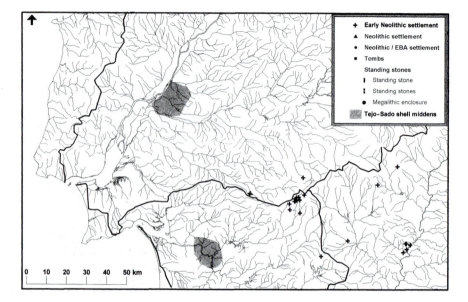

Figure 2.2 Early Neolithic settlement sites in the Central Alentejo.

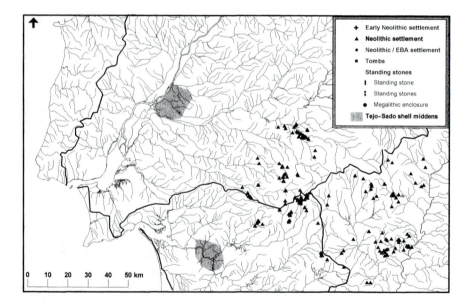

Figure 2.3 Other Neolithic settlement sites in the Central Alentejo.

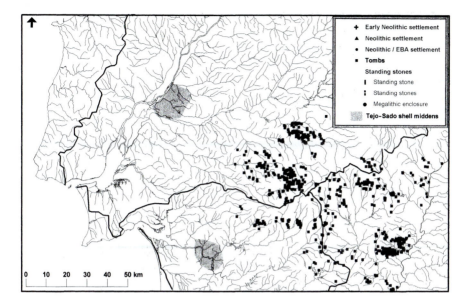

Figure 2.4 Megalithic tombs in the Central Alentejo.

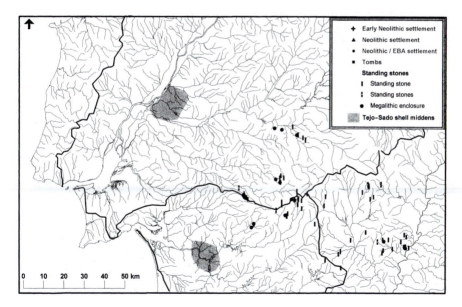

Figure 2.5 Standing stones in the Central Alentejo.

Figure 2.6 Standing stones and natural outcrops in the Central Alentejo. Left column, from top to bottom: Tojal, Almendres and S. Sebastião; right column, from top to bottom: Paicão, Vale Maria do Meio and Oliveira 5 (Early Neolithic sites).

excavations in progress at the settlement of Valada do Mato (Évora) though these are also as yet unpublished save for a preliminary report (Diniz and Calado 1997).

Like the standing stones, the Early Neolithic settlements in the Central Alentejo can be grouped into three main concentrations, in decreasing order in terms of the number of sites and, in this case, their apparent antiquity: Évora–Montemor, Reguengos de Monsaraz and Pavia. Cardial pottery is only known, at present, in the first of these groups while the Pavia sites have very little impressed ware pottery.

From the perspective which interests us here – the relationship with the landscape – this recent work raises a number of observations that must be kept in mind. In the first place, the density of Early Neolithic sites is extremely high in those same areas where the standing stones are concentrated, while at the same time they are absent in areas where standing stones are scarce. In the second place, almost all the Early Neolithic settlements are situated in locations where there are notable granitic outcrops. Some fifty years ago, the Leisners remarked upon the prominence of these outcrops: 'Throughout the whole granitic region great boulders stand out, scattered among the fields in great blocks, sometimes of strange shapes' (Leisner and Leisner 1951, 14). The Leisners themselves did not pursue this observation further, and in addition they identified virtually no prehistoric settlements. A similar observation, however, had earlier led Vergílio Correia (Correia 1921) to argue, from intuition alone, that the places marked by great granite outcrops were prehistoric sanctuaries (Correia 1921, 97–101).

The significance of special geological features is widely supported by numerous ethnographic and archaeological parallels (Taçon 1999, 40, 44; Buikstra and Charles 1999, 203; Barnes 1999, 111; Knapp and Ashmore 1999, 11, 15; Theodoratus and Lapena 1998, 23; Mulk 1998, 125; Bender *et al.* 1997; Bradley 1994, 95). Recent research on the prehistoric landscape of south-west England suggested the emergence of the phenomenon as early as the Mesolithic period, when the outcrops would have been given cultural value as 'natural megaliths'. In the ensuing Neolithic period these same outcrops were integrated into built enclosures which served as the focus of occupational or ritual activity (Tilley 1996, 165). The similarity between certain granitic tors and some of the damaged megaliths suggested another line of interpretation to Bradley, who proposed not only that the monuments were inspired by natural rock formations, but also that these formations were regarded by Neolithic people as ancestral monuments in ruins (Bradley 1998a, 20).

In the Alentejo, it is also possible that the earliest Neolithic 'colonists' appropriated places to which cultural significance had been attributed by the Mesolithic populations who were settled on the lower ground of the adjacent estuaries. The fact that the granite terrain was situated several hours' journey from the Tagus and Sado estuaries, where the Mesolithic hunter-gatherers had their primary bases, does not prevent the granite outcrops from having been the object of special significance or veneration. There are many other cases of heterotopia, where sacred places are located away from the world of daily living (Tilley 1991, 137; Bradley 1997, 6). It should also be borne in mind, first, that the estuarine landscape was totally lacking in rocky outcrops, and, second, that 'sacred sites and places are sometimes physically empty or largely uninhabited, and situated at some distance from the populations for which they hold significance' (Hirsch 1997, 4).

Waterworlds

As Patton has observed, we need not assume that a Neolithic frontier divided intrusive from indigenous populations: the communities on the Neolithic side may themselves have been indigenous people who had adopted the Neolithic way of life (Patton 1994, 288). Yet the possibility of a relationship with the Late Mesolithic populations of the Tagus–Sado shell middens is almost completely absent from Portuguese literature about the emergence of megaliths in the Central Alentejo, despite the fact that the geography of the area strongly suggests it (Arnaud 1982, 33). The principal reason for this oversight is the current model which considers the megaliths as belonging to a relatively late stage of the Neolithic transition, and supposes the existence of a previous phase, sometimes designated as pre-megalithic Neolithic (Diniz 1994), with impressed pottery and microlithic industries, but no indication of monumentality. On the other hand, the absence of concrete evidence of earlier date has led to the 'domestication' of the Central Alentejo being attributed to Middle Neolithic populations. These were bringers of plain pottery who buried their dead in proto-megalithic graves (Zilhão 1992, 162; Carvalho 1998, 55), and had no direct link with Late Meso-lithic groups. The picture has been changed by the discovery of a unambiguous inland Early Neolithic on a previously unsuspected scale, with impressed pottery including Cardial ware. It is hence essential to begin evaluating the relationship between the earliest Neolithic occupants of the Central Alentejo and the populations in the Tagus and Sado estuaries, populations who would at the very same time have been in transition towards a Neolithic way of life and to the abandonment of their traditional estuarine settlements.

The Central Alentejo is intimately connected to the estuaries of both the Tagus and the Sado through their respective hydrographic networks and across the ridges that separate them. The region may be considered a boundary area where different types of contact and interaction between the communities of both Mesolithic groups could have been performed. Clearly, if we admit the existence of links (of cooperation or of competition) between the populations of the Tagus and Sado shell middens, this implies a particular valuation of the Central Alentejo, which stands as the common hinterland for the two areas.

The Neolithic occupation of the Central Alentejo must have involved an active process of colonisation, since the region had been virtually depopulated some-where around the middle of the 6th millennium. Yet the hunter-gatherers who had settled in the low-lying tertiary terrain, without rocky outcrops, certainly made visits of a more or less sporadic nature to the Central Alentejan granites, which were situated around one day's journey away from their principal settle-ments (or half a day in the case of the Sado estuary). As suggested above, those visits may have been more for ritual than for economic purposes, considering the distances that were involved. The available data naturally allow alternative readings; it is nevertheless my view that the Mesolithic populations of the Tagus and Sado shell middens could have been responsible for the Neolithic transition in the interior. At the beginning of the 5th millennium, or a little before, the substitution of one economy by another was in progress. The transition took place in the context of a more global change and was centred in a geographic setting which, although contiguous with, was radically distinct from traditional Mesolithic landscapes. I believe that it is in this context of rupture and innovation (and, eventually, of competition between radically different ways of life) that the ferment leading to the 'invention' of the megaliths should be sought.

The evidence indicates that the earliest manifestations of the megalithic phenomenon in the Central Alentejo were standing stones and megalithic enclosures, perhaps alongside modest protomegalithic funerary monuments. It is not certain that the Mesolithic groups as such were responsible for the oldest megaliths. It is certainly possible, however, that it was these populations, or some elements of them, who in a process of profound cultural and economic change became the first megalith-builders.

Comparisons: the Central Alentejo and Brittany

As Bradley has remarked, the earliest Neolithic monuments in Brittany and Portugal may have been created while Mesolithic cemeteries were still in use (Bradley 1998b, 34). The comparison between Breton and Alentejan megaliths is not something new in Portuguese bibliography (Jorge 1977; Gonçalves 1996, 1999; Gomes 2000). In no case, however, have its implications been discussed in sufficient detail or sufficient depth; furthermore it should be noted that recognition of any relationship between the two regions is almost entirely absent from studies of the Breton megaliths. It is also curious that comparisons between the shell middens of the Tagus and Sado and those of Hoëdic and Téviec (Arnaud 1987, 63) never extended into the broader question of the relationship between the last hunter-gatherers and the first megalith-builders.

The fundamental assumption, shared by the defenders of the indigenous model and by those who supported the colonialist thesis, was that the megalithic phenomenon (which was considered only in terms of funerary megaliths) could not have occurred until the development of the agro-pastoral system had reached a mature phase. In this theoretical scheme, the existence of a pre-megalithic Neolithic had to be accepted as axiomatic. In contrast, my belief is that the idea even of pre-Neolithic megaliths should not be dismissed. We should certainly attribute the erection of some of the standing stones in the Alentejo, and in Brittany, to indigenous people engaged in a process of transition towards, or recently converted to, a Neolithic way of life.

Some years ago, reviving what was in fact a classic observation, Sherratt noted the overlap between the most important areas of European megaliths and the greatest concentrations of Late Mesolithic population, although with very little specific attention to the Portuguese evidence (Sherratt 1990, 156). In Brittany the existence of Mesolithic burials with stone structures, and with chronologies predating the arrival of the earliest Neolithic features, has inspired many authors to consider them the models for the first protomegalithic funerary monuments (Renfrew 1976; Scarre 1992, 129; Thorpe 1996, 61; Thomas 1996, 132; Whittle 1996, 251). On the other hand, the 1980s saw the discovery that certain large Breton standing stones had been re-used in the construction of megalithic and protomegalithic funerary monuments such as Er-Grah, La Table des Marchand, Gavrinis, Mané-Rutual, Mané-er-Hroëk, Le Petit Mont and Mané-Lud. This has led to the still somewhat hesitant acceptance that the non-funerary megaliths may be earlier than the funerary megaliths (L'Helgouach 1983; Le Roux 1984; Patton 1993; Thorpe 1996, 59). More recently, other observations of a chrono-logical nature have confirmed the antiquity of some of the Breton standing stones, particularly the discovery of the remains of a possible standing stone at a Villeneuve-Saint-Germain settlement (Cassen *et al.* 1998), and the socket of a possible standing-stone associated with the oldest tumulus of Le Petit Mont at Arzon (Lecornec 1994; Bradley 1998b, 56, 58).

Faced with the imprecise dating evidence for the standing stones, however, discussion of the origins of megaliths in Brittany (usually understood as the birth-place of European megalithic monumentality) has centred as a rule on the question of the relative age of the long mounds with closed funerary structures (or lacking stone structures), and the passage graves. For the passage graves there are radiocarbon dates as early as the first half of the 5th millennium BC, though these are not beyond question (Boujot *et al.* 1998a, 150). Whatever the solution to this debate, we should also consider another possibility: that it was standing stones that constituted the very first examples of megalithic monumentality, even if they coexisted with other types of monument.

When first (in 1990) I proposed an origin for the standing stones earlier than that for the passage graves, the data to support such a hypothesis were scarce. One example, however, was already known where a megalithic grave had been stratigraphically superimposed on two standing stones. Here the excavators had affirmed that 'there can be no doubt that [the standing stones] are older than the construction of the monument, because they were already fixed in the ground when the large funerary construction was built and were then included in the enormous mound which covered the whole' (Almeida and Ferreira 1971, 168). The discovery that most of the settlements with impressed pottery (Calado 1995; Calado and Rocha 1996; Calado and Sarantopoulos 1996) were in clear spatial association with the principal occurrences of standing stones, and the publication of radiometric dates for standing stones in other regions of Portugal (Gomes 1994; Oliveira 1997), even if contested (Zilhão 1998, 39–40), have in recent years added support to the proposed relative chronology. They also suggest a cultural bridge between Alentejo and Brittany.

It has been noted that in three regions, the Tagus Valley, Morbihan and the Irish Sea, there are remains of shell middens, and that the first two of these midden groups are also associated with Mesolithic cemeteries (Bradley 1997, 21). Following the same reasoning, we can add a number of further significant coincidences between Brittany and the Central Alentejo. This goes beyond the analogy between the respective Mesolithic substrates, and the antiquity of the oldest standing stones in both regions. One of the most specific parallels is to be seen in the plan of the Breton megalithic enclosures. Most of these are in the form of a horseshoe, with the opening facing the east (Scarre 1998, 59); in Alentejo, with some variation, all of the megalithic enclosures whose plan is still more or less recognisable display the same morphology (Figure 2.7).

In the decoration of the standing stones, the iconographic themes represented in Brittany and Alentejo suggest deep contacts between the communities who conceived and used them: thus the crook, the dominant motif on the Alentejan standing stones, is also present (associated with other specific themes) on the decorated menhirs of Brittany, most of which, furthermore, are carved in the same technique of low relief (Patton 1993, 90, 91). Another of the recurrent themes in the larger Alentejan megalithic enclosures (Almendres, Portela de Mogos and Vale Maria do Meio) is the lunar crescent, repeatedly associated with a quadrangular motif; the same iconographic elements occur once again on some Breton standing stones. This parallel was observed for the first time by Jacques Briard who compared the menhir of Kermaillard with one of the standing stones at Almendres (Briard 1997, 21). The same motifs, carved on the reverse of the menhir which forms the backstone of the Table des Marchand passage grave, are

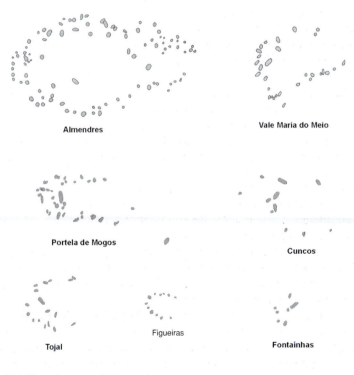

Figure 2.7 Alentejan megalithic enclosures.

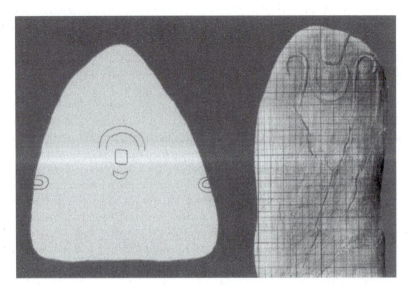

Figure 2.8 Parallel motifs on decorated standing stones: (left) the back stone of La Table
des Marchand passage grave, Brittany (originally a free-standing menhir) (from
Boujot *et al.* 1998b); (right) standing stone from the megalithic enclosure of
Vale Maria do Meio, Alentejo.

very similar to the Portuguese carvings (Figure 2.8) and were recently interpreted
as symbolising respectively the chthonic world (lunar crescent) and the earth
(rectangle) (Boujot *et al.* 1998b).

It is premature to try to establish a genetic affiliation between the Breton and
Alentejan standing stones, in one or other direction. Preferable in our current
state of knowledge is the proposal that they are generically contemporary,
although at the same time this makes explanations based on a supposed
independent parallel invention (e.g. Renfrew 1976) much less convincing. In any
event, if we accept the scenario of regular contacts between the Mesolithic
peoples of Atlantic Europe, and a specially close contact between the Breton and
Alentejan groups, innovations may well have circulated in both directions. The
discussion about the origin of the Breton Neolithic has, however, come mainly
to be centred on two opposed readings: on one side, those who seek to link it
to the groups of central European ascendancy (post-LBK) through the Paris
basin; and on the other, those who, on the basis of certain elements of material
culture, prefer to place it within a southern Neolithic with Mediterranean
affinities. In the latter perspective, the most reasonable option appears to be that
which postulates a connection with the Cardial Neolithic of Mediterranean
France through the Garonne Valley (Scarre 1992). Such a linkage may be
recognisable in some of the decorative patterns of impressed ware pottery.
Another option has been suggested by Bradley, who envisages two major axes,
one extending from the west Mediterranean around the coastline of Portugal and

Spain and into western France, the other connecting northern France and the British Isles with developments that began in the Rhineland (Bradley 1997, 23). On either reading, it is indisputable that in Brittany, Cardial and LBK influences were mingled, a confluence that is apparent in the diversity of Breton Neolithic monumentality itself. In the Central Alentejo, on the other hand, the material culture of the earliest Neolithic settlements falls, without incongruity, within a stream of cultural influence pointing generally to the western Mediterranean.

In summary, the analogies that we detect between the megaliths of Alentejo and Brittany can best be accounted for by an origin in the respective Mesolithic substrates, since in neither case do we find standing stones in those cultural contexts from which the Neolithic material cultures could be derived. In western France, Sherratt emphasised the fact that the dates attributed to sites with impressed ware pottery of southern derivation were later than those which were accepted for the first Neolithic monuments, and sought to relate these to the arrival of influences from the central European Neolithic (Sherratt 1990, 152). These influences may be responsible for the long mounds, but would be difficult to apply to the megalithic monuments, particularly the standing stones.

The symbolism of the crooks, for which many diverse readings have been proposed, is perfectly consistent with the mental ambience that characterised the Neolithic transition. The crook could have symbolised the adoption of a pastoral way of life, thus representing, in a naturalistic form, the instrument which in material terms allows the shepherd dominion over the flock (Figure 2.9) (Thorpe 1996, 59; Calado 1997, 47). The crook is almost always displayed in a prominent place on the surface of the largest standing stones and appears to imply strong affirmation of the choice of a particular way of life. It is a symbol which

Figure 2.9 Crook motif on the Monte da Ribeira standing stone, Alentejo; with (right) modern Alentejan shepherd's crook.

endures (or reappears) in later times, having gained additional complex connotations with the passage of time and in other cultural contexts. Egyptian and Christian crook symbols, for example, came to evoke the dominion (in a spiritual, but not exclusively spiritual sense) of the leader in relation to the 'flock'. It is in this context – of powerful and enduring symbols (with semantic evolution) – that I believe we should evaluate the significance of the crooks, already very stylised in form, which occur as movable objects in the Alentejan passage graves (Calado 1997, 47).

To conclude this comparison between the Breton and the Alentejan standing stones it is appropriate to consider and comment on some of the differences between the two regions. The most important and obvious is scale. Although morphologically (and in terms of raw material) the decorated standing stones of the Morbihan resemble their Alentejan counterparts, the dimensions of the former generally attain values (in length, thickness and weight) which are at least double those of the latter. This difference should perhaps be related to the different demographic potential of the two regions. We must remember that the Morbihan is a large area of considerable ecological diversity, combining the potential for agriculture and livestock-rearing together with estuarine and marine resources. The Central Alentejo is far from water and has soils much poorer for cultivation. The Neolithic acculturation of Breton Mesolithic communities did not lead to the abandonment of the region: there was a certain spread of settlement into the interior, but nothing on the scale of the movement into the Alentejo by the communities of the Tagus and Sado estuaries.

The association of the crook and the axe that is found on the Breton standing stones appears to imply a full and established Neolithic economy. By contrast, the absence of axes on the Alentejan standing stones could be explained by a less comprehensive Neolithic transition (with an economy based almost exclusively on livestock). This model is entirely in accordance with the available archaeological data.

The arrival in Brittany of cultural influences originating in the loess lands, where agriculture (and cattle domestication) is well documented from the outset, might help to explain some of the differences revealed in the iconography. The use of domesticated bovids as a source of traction for the transport and the erection of standing stones, although difficult to verify, could also explain the differences in size between the Breton and Alentejan standing stones. In the Alentejo, pastoral activity depended on the rearing of sheep and goats, as was customary in Mediterranean Neolithic societies. The representation of a bovid on a standing stone, the fragments of which are distributed among the monuments of La Table des Marchand, Er-Grah and Gavrinis, may indeed symbolise the important role of livestock. Carved on that same standing stone, at the top of the iconographic field, is an enigmatic motif currently termed the '*hache–charrue*' ('axe–plough'). Cassen and Vaquero-Lastres have recently proposed with convincing arguments that it represents a whale. This interpretation allows us to read an ordered sequence of different economic activities that were practised by the people who made the monument. From bottom to top we have the axe, the crook, the goat (?), the ox and the whale, symbolising agriculture, animal husbandry (ovicaprid and bovid) and hunting/fishing.

These categories cannot be interpreted simply in regard to their obvious economic connotations: they may reflect ideologies, conflicts and negotiations between those ways of life which, at this particular time and in this region, constituted the basic options that were available. If, however, we accept an economic reference for the symbols publicly displayed on this monument, we might perhaps better understand the magnificence of the Breton megaliths. The ecological diversity of the symbols would perhaps correspond to an economic diversification inherited from three convergent worlds: the strong Mesolithic substrate on the one hand, and the cultural influences received from the Paris basin and from the Mediterranean–Atlantic world on the other.

In the Central Alentejo, the Neolithic transition seems to have occurred in a most traumatic form: the traditional territories were abandoned, along with all the extraordinary ecological/economic potential that they offered. The mouth of the river was exchanged for its source. A landscape with water and without rocks was exchanged for a landscape that was very dry and rocky. The crook is the only symbol with an economic connotation that is clearly represented on the Alentejan standing stones, and few archaeological indicators of agriculture are found among the artefacts from the Early Neolithic sites: polished stone is rare, as are fragments of grindstones (Diniz and Calado 1997). In the Morbihan, however much the estuarine fisher-gatherer activities had declined with the adoption of the Neolithic economy and however much the whale of the 'hache–charrue' refers more to a symbolic aspect than an important economic resource, it is obvious that the builders of the standing stones had rich aquatic resources at their disposal.

We thus find a basic contrast between the two regions. In Portugal, the Mesolithic groups of the Tagus–Sado lived a considerable distance from the granite terrain, while the Neolithic groups of the Central Alentejo lived a considerable distance from the estuaries. In Morbihan, on the other hand, granite and estuary were parts of the same landscape.

The lost paradise

As has already been observed, it is difficult to interpret the analogies between Tagus–Sado and Brittany in terms of autonomous foci in the 'invention' of the megalithic phenomenon. There were, of course, differences between the developments in these two regions, but we must accept the existence of direct contacts, some of a specially significant nature, between the respective Mesolithic populations during the 6th and the 5th millennia BC. Furthermore, these contacts had an impact on the transition to the Neolithic way of life in the two areas. During a subsequent period, this framework of relations was modified and a process of diversification occurred, which is evident particularly in the different forms adopted in funerary architecture.

In the Central Alentejo, new discoveries of closed funerary monuments allow fresh comparisons to be drawn between Brittany and Portugal. Stratigraphic considerations demonstrate that some of these monuments are earlier than passage graves. These parallels may be further extended to include Galicia (Bello-Diéguez 1995, 49) and, less directly and at a slightly later date, Ireland. Within this framework, connections by sea between areas as distant as Brittany and Tagus–Sado appear most plausible (Bradley 1997), especially when we consider that the elements in common between the two regions (shell middens, horseshoe enclosures, standing stones decorated with carvings of crooks) do not exist in any intervening area. Ten years ago, I wrote that the standing stones of the Alentejo 'could thus represent the first stages of the occupation of the region by megalithic peoples, performing the rôle of appropriation and identification, at the same time as humanising elements of space'. I also observed that the megalithic enclosures of Cuncos, Portela de Mogos and Almendres are situated more or less along the line of the ridge which separates the basins of the Tagus and the Sado. Even while establishing specific parallels with Brittany, however, I did not go so far as to implicate Mesolithic peoples in the erection of standing stones. In 1993 I suggested that the standing stones could constitute the physical vestiges of the foundation rituals of sedentary settlement by groups establishing themselves apart from those communities settled on the coast and in the estuaries of the great rivers (Calado 1993, 296). Finally in 1995 I proposed that 'the abandonment of the shell middens and the eventual collapse of the economic model within which they flourished could have had their origin in the settling of the respective populations in the Alentejan interior, at the boundary of the territories traditionally exploited through a broad-spectrum economic model' (Calado 1995).

The primary problem, I now recognise, was one of scale: it was the seeking of an explanation within a perspective unconsciously limited by the frontiers of the Central Alentejo. On the opposite side of the equation, most of those authors who have been unwilling to accept the relationship between the shell middens of Tagus–Sado and the Central Alentejo have been hindered by a similar limitation of viewpoint; that is, through approaching the question from a markedly coastal perspective. My belief is that the collapse of the economic model is not sufficient on its own to explain the deep social and mental ruptures which can be detected at the regional Neolithic transition. In Whittle's words, 'becoming Neolithic may have been much more a spiritual conversion than a matter of changing diets' (Whittle 1996, 8). The crucial question with which I would like to close is, what motivated the abandonment of the estuaries and the movement into the interior, and how can this process be related to the natural features and megalithic monuments which form the title of this paper?

References

Almeida, F., and Ferreira, O.V., 1971. Um monumento pré-histórico na Granja de S. Pedro (Idanha-a-Velha). *Actas do II Congresso Nacional de Arqueologia*. Lisbon: ARP, 1, 163–8.

Araújo, A.C., and Lejeune, M., 1995. *Gruta do Escoural: Necrópole Neolítica e Arte Rupestre Paleolítica*. Lisbon: IPPAR.

Arnaud, J., 1982. Le Néolithique ancien et le processus de néolithisation au Portugal. *Actes du Colloque International de Préhistoire sur le Néolithique ancien méditerranéen. Archéologie en Languedoc, numéro spécial*, 29–48.

Arnaud, J., 1987. Os concheiros mesolíticos dos vales do Tejo e Sado: semelhanças e diferenças. *Arqueologia* 15, 53–64.

Barnes, G., 1999. Buddhist Landscapes of East Asia, in W. Ashmore and A.B. Knapp (eds), *Archaeologies of Landscape*. Oxford: Blackwell, 101–23.

Bello-Diéguez, J.M., 1995. Arquitectura, arte parietal y manifestaciones escultóricas en el megalitismo noroccidental, in F. Perez Losada and L. Castro Pérez (eds), *Arqueoloxía e arte na Galicia prehistórica e romana*. A Coruña: Museu Arqueolóxico e Histórico de A Coruña, 31–98.

Bender, B., Hamilton, S., and Tilley, C., 1997. Leskernick: stone worlds; alternative narratives; nested landscapes. *Proceedings of the Prehistoric Society* 63, 147–78.

Boujot, C., Cassen, S., Audren, C., Anderson, P., Marchand, G., and Gouézin, P., 1998a. Prélude à l'étude des tertres funéraires néolithiques d'Armorique Sud, in *Le Néolithique du Centre-Ouest de la France, Actes du XXIe Colloque Interrégional sur le Néolithique* (ed. X. Gutherz and R. Joussaume). Chauvigny: Association des Publications Chauvinoises, 149–67.

Boujot, C., Cassen, S., and Vaquero Lastres, J., 1998b. Some abstraction for a practical subject: the neolithization of Western France seen through funerary architecture. *Cambridge Archaeological Journal* 8, 193–206.

Bradley, R., 1993. *Altering the Earth. The origins of monuments in Britain and Continental Europe*. Edinburgh: Society of Antiquaries of Scotland.

Bradley, R., 1994. Symbols and signposts – understanding the prehistoric petroglyphs of the British Isles, in C. Renfrew and E. Zubrow (eds), *The Ancient Mind. Elements of Cognitive Archaeology*. Cambridge: Cambridge University Press, 95–106.

Bradley, R., 1997. *Rock Art and the Prehistory of Atlantic Europe*. London: Routledge.

Bradley, R., 1998a. Ruined buildings, ruined stones: enclosures, tombs and natural places in the Neolithic of south-west England. *World Archaeology* 30, 13–22.

Bradley, R., 1998b. *The Significance of Monuments*. London: Routledge.

Briard, J., 1997. *Les Mégalithes, ésotérisme et réalité*. Paris: Gisserot.

Buikstra, J.E., and Charles, D.K., 1999. Centering the Ancestors: cemeteries, mounds, and sacred landscapes of the Ancient North American Midcontinent, in W. Ashmore and A.B. Knapp (eds), *Archaeologies of Landscape*. Oxford: Blackwell, 201–28.

Calado, M., 1993. Menires, alinhamentos e cromlechs, in J. Medina and V.S. Gonçalves (eds), *História de Portugal*. Lisboa: Ediclube, 294–301.

Calado, M., 1995. *A região da serra d'Ossa: introdução ao estudo do povoamento neolítico e calcolítico*. Lisbon: Faculdade de Letras da Universidade de Lisboa.

Calado, M., 1997. Vale Maria do Meio e as paisagens culturais do Neolítico Alentejano, in P. Sarantopoulos (ed.), *Paisagens Arqueológicas a Oeste de Évora*. Évora: Câmara Municipal de Évora, 41–51.

Calado, M., and Mataloto, R., 1999. *Prospecções na Margem Direita do Guadiana no Regolfo do Alqueva*. Lisbon: Fundação da Universidade de Lisboa.

Calado, M., and Rocha, L., 1996. Neolitização do Alentejo Interior: os casos de Évora e Pavia. *Actas do I Congrés del Neolític a la Península Ibèrica*. Gavà: Museo de Gavà, 673–82.

Calado, M., and Sarantopoulos, P., 1996. O cromeleque de Vale Maria do Meio (Évora, Portugal): contexto arqueológico e geográfico. *Actas do I Congrés del Neolític a la Península Ibérica*. Gavà: Museo de Gavà, 493–503.

Carvalho, A., 1998. O Abrigo da Pena d'Água (Rexaldia, Torres Novas): resultados dos trabalhos de 1992–1997. *Revista Portuguesa de Arqueologia* 2, 37–79.

Cassen, S., Audren, C., Hinguant, S., Lannuzel, G., and Marchand, G., 1998. L'habitat Villeneuve-Saint-Germain du Haut Mée (St-Etienne-en-Coglès, Ille-et-Vilaine). *Bulletin de la Société Préhistorique Française* 95, 41–76.

Correia, V., 1921. *El Neolítico de Pavia*. Madrid: Museo Nacional de Ciencias Naturales.

Diniz, M., 1994. *Acerca das cerâmicas do Neolítico Antigo da Gruta da Furninha (Peniche) e da problemática da neolitização do Centro/Sul de Portugal*. Lisbon: Faculdade de Letras da Universidade de Lisboa.

Diniz, M., and Calado, M., 1997. O povoado neolítico da Valada do Mato (Évora, Portugal) e as origens do megalitismo alentejano. *II Congreso de Arqueología Peninsular*. Zamora: Fundación Rei Afonso Henriques, II, 23–32.

Gomes, M.V., 1994. Menires e cromeleques no complexo cultural megalítico português – trabalhos recentes e estado da questão. *Actas do Seminário 'O Megalitismo no Centro de Portugal'*. Viseu: CEPBA, 317–42.

Gomes, M.V., 2000. Cromeleque do Xerez. A ordenação do caos, in A.C. Silva (ed.), *Das pedras do Xerez às novas terras da Luz*. Beja: Edia, 17–190.

Gonçalves, V.S., 1996. Para além de um Portugal megalítico, por terras do mundo atlântico. *Actas dos 2ºs Cursos Internacionais de Verão de Cascais*. Cascais: Câmara Municipal de Cascais, 1, 29–40.

Gonçalves, V.S., 1999. *Reguengos de Monsaraz, territórios megalíticos*. Lisbon: MNA.

Gonçalves, V.S., 2000. O grupo megalítico de Reguengos de Monsaraz e a evolução do megalitismo no Ocidente peninsular (espaços de vida, espaços de morte: sobre as antigas sociedades camponesas em Reguengos de Monsaraz), in V.S. Gonçalves (ed.), *Muitas Antas, Pouca Gente? Actas do Colóquio Internacional sobre Megalitismo*. Lisbon: IPA, 11–104.

Hirsch, E., 1997. Landscape: between place and space, in E. Hirsch and M. O'Hanlon (eds), *The Anthropology of Landscape*. Oxford: Oxford University Press, 1–30.

Jorge, V.O., 1977. Menhirs du Portugal. *L'Architecture Mégalithique. Bulletin de la Société Polymathique du Morbihan* 104, 99–124.

Knapp, A.B., and Ashmore, W., 1999. Archaeological landscapes: constructed, conceptualised, ideational, in W. Ashmore and A.B. Knapp (eds), *Archaeologies of Landscape*. Oxford: Blackwell, 1–30.

L'Helgouach, J., 1983. Les idoles qu'on abat. *Bulletin de la Société Polymathique du Morbihan* 110, 57–68.

Le Roux, C.-T., 1984. A propos des fouilles de Gavrinis (Morbihan): nouvelles données sur l'art mégalithique armoricain. *Bulletin de la Société Préhistorique Française* 81, 240–5.

Lecornec, J., 1994. *Le Petit Mont*. Rennes: Documents Archéologiques de l'Ouest.

Leisner, G., and Leisner, V., 1951. *As antas do concelho de Reguengos de Monsaraz*. Lisbon: Instituto de Alta Cultura.

Leisner, G., and Leisner, V., 1959. *Die Megalithgräber der Iberischen Halbinsel: Der Westen*. Berlin: Walter de Gruyter.

Mulk, I.-M., 1998. Sacrificial places and their meaning in Saami society, in D.L. Carmichael, J. Hubert, B. Reeves and A. Schanche (eds), *Sacred Sites, Sacred Places*. London: Routledge, 121–31.

Oliveira, J., 1997. Datas absolutas de monumentos megalíticos da Bacia Hidrográfica do Rio Sever. *Actas do II Congreso de Arqueologia Peninsular.* Zamora: Fundación Rei Afonso Henriques, II, 221–8.

Patton, M., 1993. *Statements in Stone. Monuments and society in Neolithic Brittany.* London: Routledge.

Patton, M., 1994. Neolithisation and megalithic origins in north-western France: a regional interaction model. *Oxford Journal of Archaeology* 13, 279–93.

Renfrew, C., 1976. Megaliths, territories and populations, in S.J. De Laet (ed.), *Acculturation and Continuity in Atlantic Europe.* Brugge: De Tempel, 198–220.

Santos, M.F., 1971. A Cerâmica Cardial da Gruta do Escoural. *Actas do II Congresso Nacional de Arqueologia.* Lisbon: AAP, 1, 93–4.

Scarre, C., 1992. The Early Neolithic of Western France and megalithic origins in Atlantic Europe. *Oxford Journal of Archaeology* 11, 121–54.

Scarre, C., 1998. *Exploring Prehistoric Europe.* New York: Oxford University Press.

Sherratt, A., 1990. The genesis of megaliths: monumentality, ethnicity and social complexity in Neolithic north-west Europe. *World Archaeology* 22, 147–67.

Soares, J., and Silva, C.T., 1992. Para o conhecimento dos povoados do megalitismo de Reguengos. *Setúbal Arqueológica* 9–10, 37–88.

Soares, J., and Silva, C.T., 2000. Protomegalitismo no Sul de Portugal: inauguração das paisagens megalíticas, in V.S. Gonçalves (ed.), *Muitas Antas, Pouca Gente? Actas do Colóquio Internacional sobre Megalitismo.* Lisbon: IPA, 117–34.

Taçon, P., 1999. Identifying ancient sacred landscapes in Australia, in W. Ashmore and A.B. Knapp (eds), *Archaeologies of Landscape.* Oxford: Blackwell, 33–57.

Theodoratus, D., and Lapena, F., 1998. Wintu sacred geography of Northern California, in D.L. Carmichael, J. Hubert, B. Reeves and A. Schanche (eds), *Sacred Sites, Sacred Places.* London: Routledge, 20–31.

Thomas, J., 1996. *Time, Culture and Identity.* London: Routledge.

Thorpe, I., 1996. *The Origins of Agriculture in Europe.* London: Routledge.

Tilley, C., 1991. *Material Culture and Text. The Art of Ambiguity.* London: Routledge.

Tilley, C., 1996. The power of rocks: topography and monument construction on Bodmin Moor. *World Archaeology* 28, 161–76.

Whittle, A., 1996. *Europe in the Neolithic. The Creation of New Worlds.* Cambridge: Cambridge University Press.

Zilhão, J., 1992. *Gruta do Caldeirão. O Neolítico Antigo.* Lisbon: IPPAR.

Zilhão, J., 1998. A passagem do Mesolítico ao Neolítico na costa do Alentejo. *Revista Portuguesa de Arqueologia* 1, 27–44.

3 Castanheiro do Vento and the significance of monumental Copper and Bronze Age sites in northern Portugal

Vítor Oliveira Jorge, João Muralha Cardoso, António Sá Coixão and Leonor Sousa Pereira

Archaeological research on the prehistory of northern Portugal began in a scientific manner only some twenty-five years ago. The region, comprising the three provinces of Minho, Douro Litoral and Trás-os-Montes e Alto Douro, is an immense territory covering over 20,000 km² from the Galician border in the north to the municipalities (*concelhos* in Portuguese) on the left (southern) bank of the River Douro in the south. Research since 1975 has focused on three principal domains: megalithic tombs and cemeteries; 'settlements'; and rock-art sites. This work has established the general framework of the Neolithic, Copper and Bronze Ages, both in chronological and distributional terms. The entire time period covers more than 4,000 years, from the end of the 6th millennium to the beginning of the 1st millennium BC. It is clear, however, that an enormous task has still to be accomplished to compensate for the lack of research before the mid 1970s. A particularly urgent requirement is the establishment of closer connections between the evidence from northern Portugal and that from Galicia and the Northern Meseta, the adjacent areas of Spain. The prehistory of north-west Iberia needs also to be placed more clearly in its palaeoenvironmental setting.

One of the most promising aspects of recent research is that which attempts to combine tombs, 'settlements' (sometimes walled and in prominent locations, sometimes not), and rock-art sites in the same enquiry. Such studies consider the developing dialogue between communities and the natural and built environment in terms of monumental behaviour throughout the lengthy 'domestication' of the landscape during late prehistory, from the introduction of herding and agriculture to the consolidation of ranked societies in the Iron Age and Roman periods. This leads us to ask why communities in certain periods invested so much labour in 'burial' places, and how these related to 'living' sites. On the other hand, while settlements were practically invisible in certain periods, in others they were conspicuously monumental. This dichotomy between burial and living sites, however, was probably meaningless in prehistory. More interesting is to look at the territory as a whole, with its natural geomorphological characteristics, and the transformations that human action produced on it through time, by adding new features to those already existing.

In certain periods, or in certain aspects, these transformations were minimal; at other times, or in other activity domains, the desire to build a cultural landscape was considerable. From a social and cognitive standpoint, we must consider the possible meanings of these different cycles of human action in the landscape. What was the significance of the 'graphic behaviour' of communities that marked certain outcrops with different motifs? What kinds of mental map were being elaborated and negotiated at each point of time and space, and what was their social role in the creation and legitimation of a new social order, or in the maintenance of the status quo?

These important questions may not be solved in the short term, but must nonetheless constantly be kept in mind. Our immediate concern is to approach monumental sites with the minimum of academic preconceptions. The focus in the present study is hilltop enclosures of the Copper and Bronze Age. Their duration in time, the considerable input of energy they represent (not only in their construction, but in the constant maintenance they required), their promi-nent position in the landscape – everything suggests that these sites were in some way 'central places', performing a broad variety of roles. As archaeologists, our first task is to reconstruct the specific architectural history of each enclosure. As social scientists, our ultimate goal is to seek to understand their contribution to the continuously negotiated process of the structuration of communities. What role did these sites play in the construction of landscapes, in the creation and recreation of cognitive maps, and, finally, in the broader world-vision of these communities? Architecture, as monumental behaviour, was then, as it is now, a way of creating an enduring order, a microcosmos articulating with a general model of the cosmos. To build was to repeat a creative act, but was also to experience (both physically and psychically) a significant environment.

It is against this background that we may turn now to the example of a specific archaeological zone.

The study area

Some twenty years ago, one of us (ASC) began a systematic archaeological survey of the Freixo de Numão area; later, this research was extended geographically, first to the territory of the municipality of Vila Nova de Foz Côa as a whole and, in the 1990s, beyond that. One of the consequences of this work was the discovery in the late 1980s of the prehistoric sites of Castelo Velho (near Freixo de Numão) and Castanheiro do Vento (near Horta do Douro). Both are located on prominent hills in an area of schist geology, and are visible from afar. Before excavation, the surface of these sites was covered by large numbers of small stones and other indications that appeared likely to be related to significant underlying remains of stone structures such as walls. Together with the presence of prehistoric pottery, these observations suggested that these were the first obvious 'fortified settlements' of the Copper Age to be recognised in the north of Portugal.

The Portuguese Cultural Heritage Institute (IPPC, now IPPAR) judged that these sites deserved to be studied and protected, and so invited Susana Oliveira Jorge of the Faculty of Arts, University of Porto, to undertake research at Castelo Velho in 1989. This was a fortunate moment to begin the study because it prevented these sites – or at least their summits, the parts with the most obvious monumental remains – from being extensively trenched for the planting of eucalyptus, a practice which has caused the destruction of archaeological evidence on an enormous scale all over Portugal.

Eleven campaigns of excavation have so far been carried out in Castelo Velho. A better future now seems to be promised for the site, since the former owner (the Swedish company CELBI) donated the land to the Portuguese state in 2000. IPPAR has now taken charge of it, and a new programme of study and restoration is in preparation for 2001 and beyond.

In 1998 the original project – focused mainly on Castelo Velho and the Freixo de Numão area – was reviewed, and a revised programme approved by the Portuguese Institute of Archaeology (IPA). This included the excavation of Castanheiro do Vento, to provide comparison for the richness of the evidence recovered at Castelo Velho. Although the material conditions have only allowed us to spend the equivalent of a month of research there between 1998 and 2000, Castanheiro do Vento already deserves to be more widely known by the archaeo-logical community. Its huge surface area, and the good state of preservation of many structures, clearly indicate that its study, conservation and restoration (together with that of Castelo Velho) will be an important landmark in the knowledge of the later prehistory of the Portuguese Upper Douro.

The aim of this research is to understand the functions of these monumental places, going beyond the traditional military clichés suggested by the expression 'fortified sites', in order to establish how the territories of the local Copper and Bronze Age communities were organised. We hope then to integrate into this general picture other archaeological features of the landscape: for example, smaller sites, settlements, rock-art sites, statue-menhirs and standing stones. Our ultimate objective is to understand how the region was successively occupied by communities of hunter-gatherers, cultivators and herders – how it was connected to the more general world of the interior of the Iberian Peninsula, and the Douro basin in particular. But in the meantime, at a more practical level, another important goal is the presentation of Castelo Velho and Castanheiro do Vento as places that will attract specialist and non-specialist visitors alike. It should be noted that these sites – and others currently being studied by other archae-ologists – are in the vicinity of the well-known Côa Valley rock-art complex (the only Portuguese archaeological monument classified by UNESCO as a World Heritage Area). Visitor itineraries, including places of interest other than the Palaeolithic and Iron Age rock engravings, are essential for the develop-ment of cultural tourism in a region which is still often seen as being off the beaten track.

Portugal is a country in which people and resources are excessively concentrated near the coast rather than inland. In our view, the development of archaeological knowledge can be joined to issues of development in general as the dual inextricably intertwined goals and justifications for this work, which is being undertaken both in and for the Portuguese interior.

Castanheiro do Vento

Castanheiro do Vento is in the *freguesia* (parish) of Horta do Douro, in the municipality of Vila Nova de Foz Côa, Guarda district (coordinates: 41° 3′ 49″ North; 7° 19′ 18″ West Greenwich) (Figures 3.1 and 3.2). From it, one has views across a wide landscape, which includes the Ribeira da Teja (an important watercourse and tributary of the Douro) to the east, and to the north some significant landmarks on neighbouring elevations, such us the Castelo de Numão (a walled medieval village where prehistoric objects are often found) and Senhora do Viso, a peak with a chapel, where potsherds of Bronze Age type have been unearthed.

The site is located next to the village of Horta do Douro, on the upper part of a roughly circular schist hill at *c.*730 metres above sea level. For convenience it can be considered to lie within the curve of the 720 metre contour, which means that it probably extends for more than 200 metres north–south. It is crossed by several tracks used by local farmers, but fortunately these have avoided the core of the northern part, the most monumental and stoniest area of the site (Figure 3.3). The southern part has been extensively disturbed by agriculture, and potsherds, fragments of granite grindstones and other artefacts are frequently found on the surface, but we do not know the real magnitude of the destruction, nor from where exactly all these dispersed materials came. There do not appear to be any important stone structures in this southern area, such as walls, but they may have been partially or totally eliminated by ploughing and digging. At the southern edge of this plateau there is a geodesic landmark (723 metres).

The higher of the two monumental areas, at an elevation of *c.*724–730 metres, is the northern one. Relatively flat, it is covered by shrub vegetation, with at certain points considerable accumulations of small stones, clearly the result of the destruction and removal of ancient structures. At first sight there appears to be a large subcircular enclosure with a diameter of approximately 100 metres. Remains of walls or other linear structures made of superimposed schist slabs are visible from outside the area (i.e. viewed from the zone now disturbed by ploughing). The contour curves on the topographic plan show clearly that the northern side would have been the most monumental: that is, it could have included some sort of 'façade', conceived to impress those who looked at or approached the site from the north. This hypothetical feature will be the object of research in future excavation campaigns. Inside the 'enclosure', at one of its highest points, there is a particularly substantial accumulation of stones and slabs, elliptical in shape and measuring *c.*10 × 7 metres. Its archaeological significance is unknown, but it may correspond to the remains of a kind of tower, like the one known at Castelo Velho.

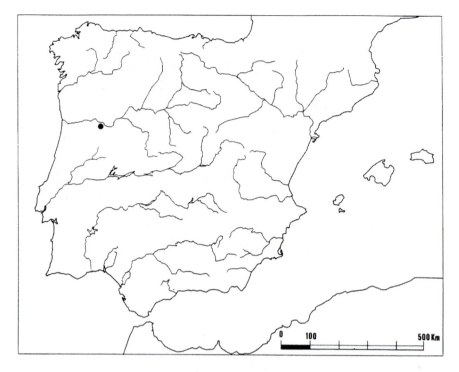

Figure 3.1 Map of the Iberian Peninsula showing location of Castanheiro do Vento.

Figure 3.2 Castanheiro do Vento, from the north-west.

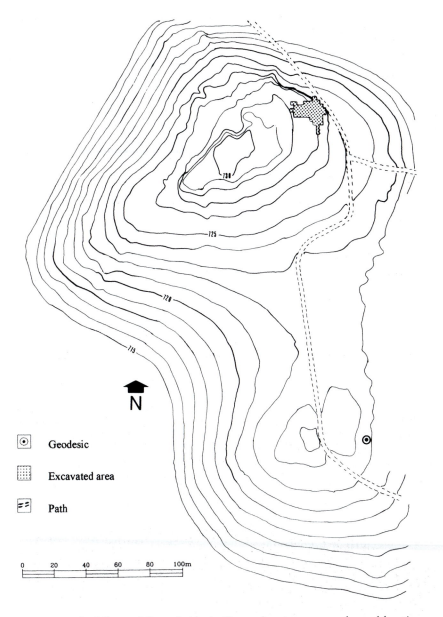

Figure 3.3 The hilltop of Castanheiro do Vento showing topography and location of excavations.

The ground around this summit has been considerably disturbed, particularly through the experimental planting of eucalyptus. We shall never know the original surface area of the monument, and to what extent it covered the slopes around. This means that it is impossible to estimate its visual effect on those who looked up at it from the valleys or from the hills below the site. Fortunately, one of us (ASC) was able to intervene at the last minute, stopping the machines just at the moment when they were about to do here what that they have done elsewhere – completely remove every vestige of past human occupation.

It is nonetheless clear to us that Castanheiro do Vento was designed to be seen at a distance, and acted as a material device to show to everyone the importance of those who lived there, and/or the activities, daily or occasional, which were carried out there. That effect would have been most striking for those looking at it from the east and north-east. It is also obvious that the site visually dominated the fertile land of the Ribeira da Teja valley. To the south-west, the valley of the Torto river (another tributary of the Douro) lies quite close (*c*.2.5km), allowing easy access to the river in that direction, but arguments for a special connection between the site and the Torto basin must be considered tenuous, since to the north-west of Castanheiro do Vento a chain of hills neatly separates the site from the rest of that basin.

Preliminary results

As excavations began only in 1998, the study of this large site is still in its early days. The methodology adopted is open area excavation, exposing the stone structures beneath the surface in order to understand the general design of the architecture, its 'history' and its transformations over time. Deeper excavation only takes place once this first study has been completed; for the moment, this second stage of the work has only been applied to the two 'bastions' (rounded structures associated with a wall) that will be described below. As a result, we have not yet been able to identify a clear Bronze Age occupation layer (such as is present at Castelo Velho), distinct from those of the Chalcolithic (Copper Age) period. We believe nonetheless that the site was occupied during the Bronze Age, on the basis of artefacts that have been recovered, including pottery, but the exact chronology of Castanheiro do Vento has still to be defined.

The potential archaeological area has been surveyed and marked out in a rectangle of 37,500 m^2 (250 m N–S × 150 m E–W), giving 9,375 excavation units (squares) of 2 × 2 metres. Of those units, only a small percentage (*c*.0.61 per cent) have so far been studied (1998–2000: 58 units = 232 m^2), all of them located in a single area in the north-eastern corner of the site, beside the track which leads up the hill (Figure 3.4). In the majority of those units that have been studied, work has been limited to clearance of the vegetation cover and removal of the topsoil.

The roots of a variety of holm-oak which cover the site penetrate deeply to the base of the archaeological deposits and are very difficult to remove, often destroying or seriously damaging the more superficial structures. It is thus very hard to clean a single excavation unit in order to record the stone elements that

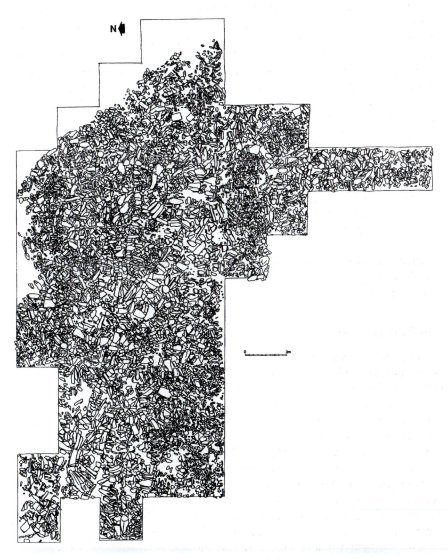

Figure 3.4 Plan of the excavated area at the end of the 2000 campaign.

it contains. In addition, the schist used in the construction is fragile, especially when the clay that was employed as a kind of mortar has disappeared through erosion. The loss of this clay bonding element, coupled with root action, has caused structures to break up and their constituent parts to be scattered. This means that only the more monumental structures are likely to be preserved, and it is these that attract our attention, deflecting it from other aspects which could be equally valuable for an understanding of the site as a whole in all its complexity.

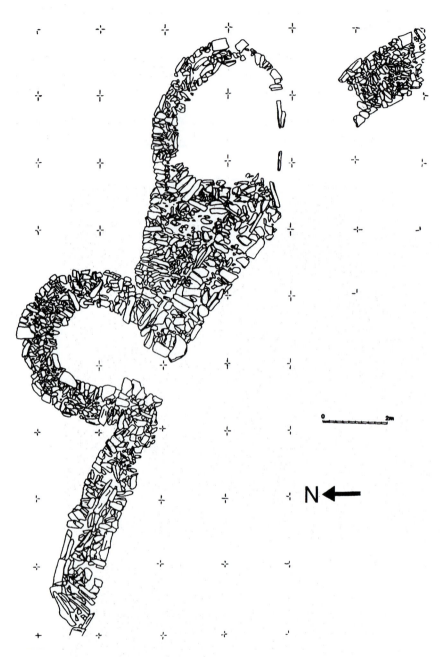

Figure 3.5 The principal structures within the excavated area: bastions A and B and dry-stone wall.

The most important structures revealed in the excavation area (Figure 3.5) were as follows:

- A long wall of Chalcolithic date, with an average width of only 1.2 metres, running north–east/south–west. This wall may correspond to the external boundary of the main enclosure of this part of the site, but it is still too early to be certain.
- To the north of this wall, and close to it, two Chalcolithic bastions, some 3 metres apart: bastion A to the west and bastion B (Figure 3.6) to the east.

Figure 3.6 Excavations in progress (2000), with bastion B in the foreground.

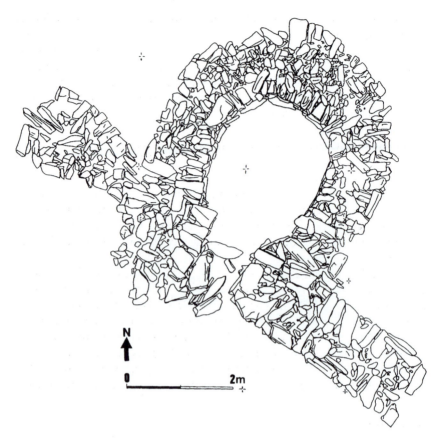

N

0   2m

Figure 3.7 Plan of bastion A.

The former is certainly connected to the wall, and the latter may also be connected. Bastion A has a regular, elliptical outline (Figure 3.7); its entrance to the south corresponds with a break in the long wall mentioned above. Bastion B is more irregular than A, and has clearly undergone several transformations. Within it were a number of 'stelae', aligned and facing east. The excavation of this bastion is still in progress, but it is already certain that its present state is the result of works which extended over several periods. Beneath the stelae was a layer which appeared to underlie the floor of the bastion.

- In a subsequent stage, bastions A and B were linked by a new linear alignment of stones, and by a massive structure starting from the northern edge of bastion B and covering the eastern end of bastion A. This shows that bastion A was already partially ruined (or was partially demolished) when the new structure was built. This massive structure completely fills the triangular space thus created between the two bastions and the wall. In fact, this modification seems to be part of a different design from that of the wall and bastions, and was probably undertaken at a time when they were no longer considered important.

- The transformations which affected bastion B are also noticeable on its southern edge. Both the edge of the bastion and the part of the 'boundary wall' which should be present there are difficult to recognise, probably because the area was used as a kiln or furnace: many of the schist fragments have been altered in colour and texture by heat.

Among the artefacts recovered at the site are abundant quantities of handmade pottery. Some of this has parallels in the vessels from both the Chalcolithic and Bronze Age occupation at Castelo Velho. Pottery decorated with wavy line motifs executed with a multi-toothed, comb-like instrument (*decoração penteada*) is very common, and may be dated to both periods. In general, however, Chalcolithic and Bronze Age pottery differ considerably from each other. It is only in the Bronze Age, for example, that there is plastic decoration, the use of handles, and flat bases.

Other finds include clay 'loom weights', granite grindstones (both querns and rubbers), and quartzite river pebbles (for heating, or as hammers). Quartz hammers were probably used for shaping the schist during construction. On the other hand, polished stone is rare, as are beads and flaked stone: there are no arrowheads, no blades, and no microliths, though some cutting tools were made of quartz. There may also have been some metallurgical activity: fragments of schist had been exposed to temperatures intense enough in extreme cases to alter the stone completely, suggesting that these fragments formed part of a furnace.

Conclusion

Those unfamiliar with this particular area and its archaeology may consider the description of the results given above to be overly detailed. They do, however, form the background of our main concern, that is, the interpretation of general processes of development. Our long-term aim is to understand the logic of the occupation and the transformation of the territory by human communities. But we should not confuse that major goal with the evidence currently available, which despite a decade of work on the region remains relatively meagre. It is not possible to generalise from locally established facts as if they might be applied to an entire region; nor do we propose to use what are only hypotheses, based on inference, as certainties in order to reach a higher level of interpretation.

In a seminal paper, it was shown how fragile is current knowledge of the so-called fortified settlements of the Copper Age in the Iberian Peninsula (Jorge 1994). From highly heterogeneous data, prehistorians have repeated general interpretations which themselves were not based on sound evidence, or which were based on an oversimplification of the available evidence. These sites have successively been interpreted as colonies established in indigenous territory by metal prospectors, or as local fortresses designed to protect an elite (those able to control the metal resources) from their poorer neighbours. They have always been the focus of researchers' attention, as if the Chalcolithic landscape was composed only of famous rocky sites, poised in prominent positions. Even if we accept the 'colony model', or the 'fortified settlement model', both imply that only a minority 'lived' in these prestigious places, and it remains therefore to be established where the everyday settlements of the majority of the population are to be found. To our knowledge, only one person in Portugal – the late Nuno C. Santos – has explored this dimension, scanning the territory of Portuguese Estremadura in search of all available information on Chalcolithic occupation.

It is obvious that no firm conclusions will be possible until an entire region – such as the area south of the Douro, between its tributaries the Torto and the Côa – has been studied in detail, with documentation of all types of sites presumed to date from the Copper Age, a period of roughly 1,000 years' duration. Considering the whole of this territory and its Chalcolithic occupation (in the broadest sense, including all the material remains of human activity of this period), it is clear that Castanheiro do Vento and Castelo Velho should be regarded as exceptions rather than the rule, i.e. as extraordinary sites, not only by virtue of their prominent position in the landscape, but also in the input of energy needed for their conception, construction and maintenance. The majority of the population certainly lived lower down near the valleys, taking advantage of the proximity of abundant water, fertile soil, wild fauna and flora, and, moreover, of more favourable weather (we know from our field experience the discomforts associated with the uplands!). Lower-lying locations have been more affected by modern activity, and are therefore less visible in the archaeological record, but we have discovered some traces, and more would appear if survey effort were increased. If monumental sites like Castanheiro do Vento and Castelo Velho were not places at which to live, save for a minority in charge of their conservation; if they were not walled villages or hamlets; if we assume that societies did not exist in a state of endemic war that forced them to take permanent refuge in these upland locations; why then was so much architectural effort concentrated in works that apparently served no purpose?

To understand the context, we must step back a little from such a primarily functionalist view and realise that some questions are too simplistic to be useful, being only projections into the past of our practical mentality of today. We need also to recall that, throughout history, humankind has always reserved its greatest effort for 'non-utilitarian' works such as passage graves, burial mounds, megalithic monuments, pyramids and churches. When we look at monumental enclosures like Castanheiro do Vento we need to rid ourselves of what we could call the 'medieval castle syndrome' – the idea, common in children's stories, that the only solution for a menaced community was to seek refuge behind walls and endure a siege, whether short or prolonged. It is clear that defensive enclosures could only have any practical utility in relation to other military and logistic practices, where they were just a part of a whole technical and social context of managing states of war or conflict. In fact, most enclosures have more to do with the symbolic division of space, between domestic and wild, between settlement and nature, between inside and outside, or between a secure domain and an insecure one – but in a psychological sense.

It is easy to forget that we are dealing with the results of actions by symbol-using individuals like ourselves – people with a reflective consciousness, a system of values, a need to organise the entire space around them, both at the material and at the explanatory levels. That is the 'function' of architecture, be it minimal (using mainly the natural topography) or monumental (involving considerable projects of transformation): to install an order in nature, an order which is in accordance with a representation of the world and of society. Outside that order, we are lost.

Thus the answer to the simplistic enquiry as to why such effort was expended could be that monuments such as Castanheiro do Vento were communal symbols of wealth, marks of identity in the territory, places where people joined together at certain times of the year. It is probable that an elite lived there, or controlled the actions that could take place there, or assured the safe-keeping of goods held there, including stored food or prestige items. In periods of conflict, these enclosures could have been used to assemble those who felt themselves menaced. But this was not their permanent role. They were material devices, points of reference, to be seen at a distance, just like the parish churches of recent times – announcing both to locals and to strangers that they were in a particular territory.

In certain ways, furthermore, these Chalcolithic monuments assumed the 'identity function' of the former megalithic cemeteries of the Middle and Late Neolithic (5th–4th millennia BC); and indeed that is the main reason that we do not find important (monumental) funerary monuments in this region during the Chalcolithic. Visible tombs and settlements are mutually exclusive, because they accomplished different roles: in the Middle and Late Neolithic, tombs were to be seen and to be enduring features, settlements to be perishable structures. In the Chalcolithic the opposite was the case: the tombs (at least the majority) were invisible, as were ordinary settlements; the exceptions were the idealised, monumental 'settlements', placed in elevated positions, again so as to be seen in their impressive settings. The ideology had changed; the locus of the monumental had turned from the dead (or *some* of the dead: the ancestors) to the living, from after-life to 'daily' life – not the daily life of the common people, but probably an idealised life connected with the elites, or with chiefly ancestors.

This also implies a significant difference in terms of architectural effort and planning. A megalithic cemetery like Aboboreira (Porto district) or Castro Laboreiro (district of Viana do Castelo) has an additive logic; that is, the monuments in it were built one by one. The cemetery was certainly not randomly formed, but it did not have a strictly pre-established plan or design, concentrated in a continuous, limited space, such as we find at Castanheiro do Vento or Castelo Velho. Thus, while considerable further work must be undertaken before we can progress further in interpreting this type of Chalcolithic site, we believe that they deserve henceforth to be regarded as an important step in the history of monumental effort and creative imagination in south-west Europe. They are very impressive places; it is unfair to condemn them to oblivion, increasing decay, or even rapid destruction – fates that have already befallen too many of them.

References

Jorge, S.O., 1992. An approach to the social dynamics of northern Portugal's late prehistory. *Bulletin of the Institute of Archaeology* 29, 97–120.

Jorge, S.O., 1994. Colónias, fortificações, lugares monumentalizados. Trajectória das concepções sobre um tema do Calcolítico peninsular. *Revista da Faculdade de Letras do Porto, II^a série – História* 11, 447–546.

Jorge, S.O., 1998. Regional diversity in the Iberian Bronze Age – on the visibility and opacity of the archaeological record. *Trabalhos de Antropologia e Etnologia* 36, 193–214.

Jorge, S.O., 1998. Later prehistoric monuments of northern Portugal: some remarks. *Journal of Iberian Archaeology* 0, 105–13.

Jorge, S.O., 1998. Bronze Age settlements and territories on the Iberian Peninsula: new considerations, in *Gods and Heroes of the Bronze Age: Europe at the Time of Ulysses.* London: Thames & Hudson, 60–4.

Jorge, S.O., 1999. Castelo Velho de Freixo de Numão (Vila Nova de Foz Côa, Portugal). Geschichte der Interpretationsversuche. *Madrider Mitteilungen* 40, 80–96.

Jorge, S.O., 2000. Domesticating the land: the first agricultural communities in Portugal. *Journal of Iberian Archaeology* 2, 43–98.

Jorge, S.O., 2001. Castelo Velho (Freixo de Numão, Vila Nova de Foz Côa, Portugal) et la problématique des "habitats fortifiés" de la Péninsule Ibérique, *Communautés Villageoises du Proche-Orient à l'Atlantique* (dir. J. Guilaine), Paris, Errance, 241–52.

Jorge, S.O., and Jorge, V.O., 1997. The Neolithic/Chalcolithic transition in Portugal. The dynamics of change in the third millennium BC, in M. Díaz-Andreu and S. Keay (eds) *The Archaeology of Iberia: The Dynamics of Change.* London: Routledge, 128–42.

Jorge, V. O., 1995. Late prehistoric funerary mounds in northern Portugal as indicators of social complexity, in K.T. Lillios (ed.), *The Origins of Complex Societies in Late Prehistoric Iberia.* Ann Arbor: International Monographs in Prehistory, 29–43.

4 The architecture of the natural world: rock art in western Iberia

Lara Bacelar Alves

Prehistoric rock art has long fascinated scholars by its spectacular visual display and the opacity of its intrinsic meaning. Research on Iberian rock art has hitherto been heavily dominated by study of the formal characteristics of the depictions (whether paintings or carvings), by discussions over chronology and terminology, and by an exhaustive effort to build rigid typological frameworks. Although the accurate recording of rock art and the documentation of its formal traits are crucial for the understanding of individual sites, interpretation must go well beyond such issues. Rock-art recording needs to be seen as the foundation of a complex construction, built on layered platforms of interpretation and framed by a diversity of theoretical pillars. Such a procedure will induce a more idiosyncratic approach to the essential constituents of the phenomenon – iconography, style and techniques – and their relationship with the natural backdrop.

Recent years have seen the emergence of innovative theoretical approaches to Iberian rock art (e.g. Bradley 1997; Bradley *et al.* 1995). The introduction of landscape archaeology has been paramount in widening the range of questions to which our object of study can be subjected. This approach is sustained by methodological procedures that incite a view from above, located at a considerable distance from questions related to the formal 'act' upon the rock-face. They privilege the analysis of distribution patterns, the relationship between the siting of the rock art, the spaces of the living and the dead, land tenure and access to natural resources. In addition, attention is paid to the way in which the physical attributes of the terrain, such as the position of geomorphological features or pathways of movement across the land, interact with the rock art to create an intelligible landscape.

The present study aims to achieve a more holistic approach by complementing the 'view from above' provided by the external variables used in landscape archaeology with a 'view from within' which incorporates concepts and inferences commonly used in rock-art studies based on informed methods of analysis (Chippindale and Taçon 1998, 6–7). The objective is to switch the focus from the most visible element of the phenomenon – the depiction – to aspects that have hitherto been peripheral to Iberian rock-art studies. Recent research outside western Europe, particularly in areas where the ethnohistorical record assists in understanding the origins and contexts of the rock art, indicates that the 'archetype' of rock art resides not in the imagery itself but in the physical space where it is found. Rock art is thus not randomly located in the landscape, and understanding the reasons behind the selection of particular rock formations for decoration must be considered as important as questions concerned with the formal analysis of individual motifs. Iconography may have been replicated on perishable materials, but rock art is anchored in the natural world: that is to say, it is deep-rooted in nature. Rock art thus becomes inherent to nature, although it is culturally generated.

What is presented here should be regarded primarily as a theoretical essay where Iberian rock art is subjected to various interpretative scenarios. Legitimation of the approach will require further empirical observations and systematic fieldwork at a regional level. The aim is to propose a conceptual platform of interpretation that can guide, if only partly, subsequent studies of Iberian rock art. This should contribute to the development of a closer definition of the structure and organising principles underlying the practice of depicting signs at particular places in the landscape (Bradley 1999, 65).

The natural setting of rock art

It has been widely recognised that the implantation of rock art in the landscape obeys fundamental codes, independent of its style, geographical setting, chronological attributions and other conventional categories or classificatory devices used by scholars in their attempt to create a consistent interpretational platform for research. It can be argued that at a regional level of analysis, different groups or traditions of rock art might form exclusive patterns of distribution and landscape location. Leaving aside its distinctive characteristics, however, and taking the rock art in its atemporal and universal dimension, the significance of the locations appears to reside in the symbolism of the natural place that was selected to receive a layer of humanly made depictions.

To understand such locations as 'places of special significance' might be subjective at first glance, as it relies on the individual experience of the archaeologist and the kind of analysis carried out in the field. This seems to be the case in the majority of European rock-art studies and contrasts with studies undertaken in parts of the world where the ethnohistorical record provides support for empirical observations. In western Iberia, however, inferences about the symbolism of particular natural features might be substantiated by a rich oral tradition, which reiterates prevalent cosmological concepts in relation to the perception and experience of the landscape. A widespread belief that particular natural formations enclose special properties has prevailed in the collective memory of peasant societies of western Iberia that still maintain their essential links with the land (Alves 2001, 72–4).

The social space of these non-urban communities is punctuated by references to a transcendental world of spirits and fantastic creatures inhabiting specific places in their territory. These are not necessarily located outside the domestic sphere, but are part of the daily-experienced space, which may explain why they have continued to play an important role in cosmological beliefs that are perpetuated in oral narratives. Although many of the natural landscape features associated with such legends coincide with the location of archaeological sites – including prehistoric settlements, burial monuments or rock art – others are apparently ordinary natural formations, devoid of evidence of past activity. Furthermore, the same stories are applied at some length to particular sections of rivers, to caves or rock shelters, to prominent landforms and rocky outcrops, and to minor river valleys or hilltops. These locations are seen as portals to a supernatural world, the world of the spirits, though this world is inaccessible to the ordinary human being. Some of these sites have been reinterpreted in the light of Christian beliefs. There are several examples where caves or rock shelters have been christianised through a belief in the apparition of a saint from a rock fissure. These natural places were – in fact still are – seen as hierophanies.

In a recent paper on Australian sacred landscapes, Paul Taçon has pointed out that particular landscape features invoke special feelings of wonder, respect and reverence, which are universal to humans (Taçon 1999, 36–7). First among them we may consider those generated by 'great acts of natural transformation' like mountain ranges, gorges, steep valleys; second, 'junctions or points of change between geology, hydrology and vegetation'; third, distinctive landscape features such as caves or prominent peaks; and finally, places that command extensive views across the landscape (Taçon 1999, 37). This idea is paradigmatic as it seems that there are basic principles which underlie the human conceptualisation of space. Social order has always partly, or entirely, originated from preliminary notions inserted in topological space. As Ingold observes, territories are appropriated through the attribution of a structure of meaning to the physical world (Ingold 1986, 145–6). Topographic features are set upon a network of cognitive structures, which later constitute symbolic references in the collective memory of the people that is maintained, almost unaltered, through time. In other words, landscape is conceptualised through the symbolic values attributed to specific formations, both natural and humanly made – particularly those whose creation is not fully understood or is difficult to perceive within a conventional temporal framework. Prehistoric rock-art sites might have also played an important role in cognitive constructions through time and are still considered significant locations in the landscape. Their importance is attested by the attribution of place names and by the legends that ultimately provide the only 'vivid reference' to otherwise mute, inanimate sites.

The symbolism of natural features may be illustrated by considering one particular prehistoric rock-art tradition in Iberia – Schematic Art – in an attempt to understand the significance of its placement in the landscape.

Schematic Art in Iberia

Schematic Art is traditionally regarded as a Mediterranean prehistoric rock-art tradition which spread across southern Europe, adapting to local sociocultural features and therefore breaking down into regional variants. In the present discussion, the focus is on the character of Schematic Art towards the western limit of its distribution, in Iberia (Figure 4.1). Although there is a long tradition of rock-art research in Iberia, beginning with the studies of Henri Breuil early in the 20th century (1917; 1932–33), there is no recent synthesis of the subject based on innovative theoretical approaches. Regional monographs have, however, provided a more accurate overview of the phenomenon and, simultaneously, have involved a necessary, though massive, accumulation of empirical information.

In Iberia the distribution of Schematic Art runs obliquely from southern Spain to north-eastern Portugal, across the Spanish Meseta. Current knowledge suggests that Schematic Art avoids the far north-western and south-western regions of Iberia. Towards the north-western limits of its distribution, Schematic

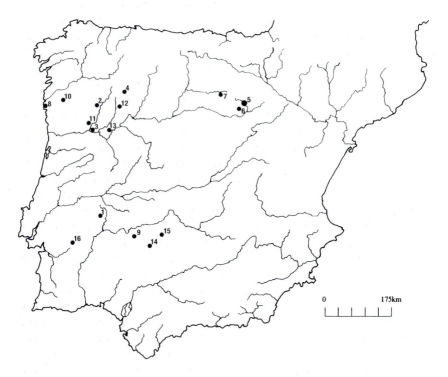

Figure 4.1 The location of Iberian Schematic Art sites or groups of sites mentioned in the text. Key: 1. Serra dos Louções (Arronches, Portugal); 2. Regato das Bouças (Mirandela, Portugal); 3. Cachão da Rapa (Carrazeda de Ansiães, Portugal); 4. El Pedroso (Zamora, Spain); 5. Oteruelos and Monte Valonsa-dero (Soria, Spain); 6. La Peña de los Plantios (Soria, Spain); 7. Cubillero de Lara (Burgos, Spain); 8. Montedor (Viana do Castelo, Portugal); 9. Charneca Chica (Badajoz, Spain); 10. Gião (Arcos de Valdevez, Portugal); 11. Pala Pinta (Alijó, Portugal); 12. Penas Roias (Miranda do Douro, Portugal); 13. Casal dos Mouros (Freixo-de-Espada-à-Cinta, Portugal); 14. Cueva del Bercialejo (Peñalsordo, Spain); 15. Buitres IX (Peñalsordo, Spain); 16. Escoural (Évora, Portugal).

Art converges with the so-called Atlantic Art tradition (Bradley and Fábregas 1998). In chronological terms it is usually placed between the Neolithic and the Late Bronze Age (e.g. Collado Giraldo and Fernández Algaba 1998; Acosta 1968; Gomes 1989).

Schematic Art is primarily painted, and is typically displayed in rock shelters or small caves. It is mainly monochrome, the application of red ochre being widespread, although white, black and some purple-red pigments are introduced at a later stage of the sequence (Collado Giraldo and Fernández Algaba 1998, 217–18). It is a predominantly iconic tradition, in which the human figure is frequently represented. The great majority of depictions are, however, geometric patterns – ladders, angular lines, zig-zags, crosses, meanders, hand prints and grids. It is usually, though not exclusively, found on the vertical faces of rock outcrops or rock shelters. Of particular interest is the fact that, in rock-shelter paintings, the iconography is rarely organised into complex compositions. The distribution of motifs is either sparse, consisting of a handful of figures painted at particular places in the rock surface, or motifs are scattered in an almost chaotic manner throughout the rock shelter.

As regards their physical setting, Schematic rock-art sites are usually found in modest concentrations and occupy dramatic locations in very specific parts of the landscape, or scattered along particular geomorphological units. In north-west Iberia they occupy cliffs on the edge of small valleys, overlooking a river course or stream. Open-air Schematic Art carvings are frequently found in physically enclosed spaces such as natural amphitheatres or basins. Moreover, it is not unusual to find Schematic Art sites closely associated with prehistoric settlements dated to the Copper Age, notably the painted rock shelters of Serra dos Louçóes (Gomes 1989, 229), Regato das Bouças (Sanches and Santos 1989, 15–17; Sanches 1996, 222–3) and Cachão da Rapa (Santos Júnior 1934). This same relationship may be attested at El Pedroso (Esparza Arroyo 1977) where the rock art found in two separate chambers within a prominent rock outcrop consists of rock carvings that may be included within the scope of Schematic Art (Figure 4.2).

The concept of Schematic Art has been restricted by its immediate identification with the paintings found in rock shelters or shallow caves. Recently, several authors have emphasised the need to widen the range of examples that should be included under this term, or that should at least be considered within the context of Schematic Art. This includes some of the art found on the slabs of megalithic tombs, since the imagery and techniques employed find their closest parallels in rock-shelter paintings (e.g. Bueno Ramirez and Balbin Behrmann 1992; Gómes Barrera 1993). In north-west Iberia, recent research has also tended to include in this heterogeneous and multifaceted tradition a number of open-air sites displaying rock carvings with similar imagery. This similarity is usually remarked in terms of the analysis of individual motifs. There is, however, at least one site, Cueva Grande (Oteruelos, Soria), where Schematic Art imagery appears both carved and painted on the same surface, though on alternating panels (Gómes Barrera 1993, 218–20). One of the carvings is internally painted with red pigment.

Figure 4.2 The rock outcrop of El Pedroso (Trabazos, Zamora, Spain).

Given this evidence, Schematic Art ought primarily to be considered an assemblage of iconic concepts or an aesthetic device used in disparate contexts and fulfilling different roles during its long time-span. This can be illustrated by considering one typical iconic image from the figurative repertoire of Schematic Art which cuts across various physical settings. The example is the schematic animal figure, composed by a single horizontal line defining the top part of the animal, from the head to the tail, and four vertical grooves indicating the position of the limbs.

Schematic animal figures are frequently painted on the vertical panels of rock shelters or caves as, for example, at Peña Somera (Monte Valonsadero, Soria), and at the rock shelter of La Peña de los Plantíos (Fuentetoba, Soria) where one is inserted in a painted composition that represents a stela (Gómes Barrera 1991) (Figure 4.3). The same motif is also present on the slabs of megalithic tombs. The Cubillero de Lara passage grave (Lara de los Infantes, Burgos) is a long polygonal chambered tomb displaying, on one slab on the right-hand side of the passage, carvings of two schematic animal figures, associated with four other motifs which are typical of the Schematic Art figurative repertoire (Delibes de Castro and Rojo Guerra 1988, 9; Gómes Barrera 1993, 230–3) (Figure 4.4). The formal characteristics of schematic animal figures also recall the carvings of the same motif found on the vertical faces of the rock outcrop at Montedor, an open-air rock-art site in north-west Portugal (Lanhas 1969).

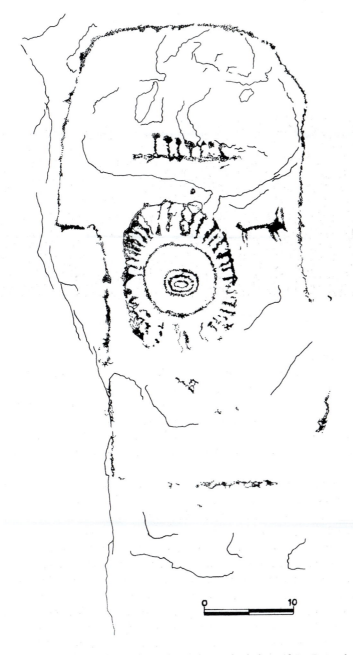

Figure 4.3 Representation of a stela at the rock shelter of La Peña de los Plantíos (Fuentetoba, Soria, Spain) (after Gómes Barrera 1991).

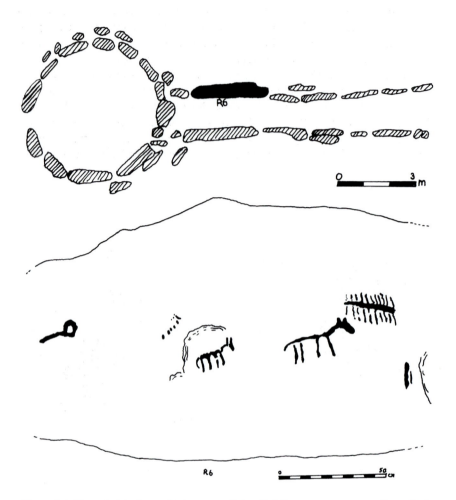

Figure 4.4 Carved slab from the passage of the Cubillero passage grave (Lara de los Infantes, Burgos, Spain) (after Urribarri Angulo 1975).

In modern archaeological reasoning, rock–art studies based exclusively on the formal analysis of individual motifs are insufficient to give a closer understanding of the stimulus behind the production of rock art both on natural features in the landscape and on stone-built monuments. It is nonetheless necessary to recognise the permeability of the contextual interface framing such analogies, notably as regards the use of similar visual motifs in different spatial, temporal and conceptual contexts. This calls for a conscious prudence in making inferences about the relationship between the Schematic Art found on natural rock formations and in megalithic monuments, even though the two are partly contemporary and spatially convergent. In addition, in-depth research on the archaeological contexts of art at Iberian megalithic monuments is virtually non-existent, with the exception of very recent studies carried out in south-west Spain (Bueno Ramirez and Balbín Behrmann 1992; Bueno Ramirez *et al.* 1999). This should not, however, impede the development of interpretational procedures intended to kindle discussion on the subject and to open new avenues for thinking about rock art.

Systematic fieldwork in the province of Badajoz, in south-west Spain, has provided new insights into the association of Schematic Art with funerary contexts. At the rock shelter of Charneca Chica, Collado Giraldo and his team (Collado Giraldo *et al.* 1997, 143–9) have identified five decorated panels, one of which displays paintings of decorated schist plaques which are typical of the burial paraphernalia found at megalithic monuments in southern Portugal. These motifs were found alongside classical Schematic Art imagery (Figure 4.5).

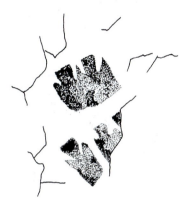
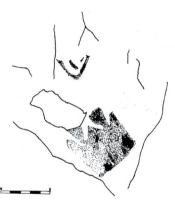

Figure 4.5 Paintings in Schematic Art style at the Charneca Chica rock shelter (Oliva de Mérida, Badajoz, Spain) (after Collado Giraldo *et al.* 1997).

Excavations of the sediments in the shelter produced no archaeological evidence, yet the cave situated just in front of the Charneca Chica rock shelter appears to have been used as a burial chamber. The study of material recovered from the cave suggests two phases of activity, dated respectively to the Late Neolithic and the Copper Age.

Notwithstanding the fact that Schematic Art was used in disparate contexts, Schematic Art sites appear to share certain conceptual features in their relationship to topological space. Although complementary to this analysis, analogies which draw exclusively upon iconography lack context, and overlook the cultural and natural backdrop that constitutes the essence of rock art. It may be more productive to focus on the setting of the imagery in the landscape, following the idea that 'local physiographic features are recognised increasingly as the source and subject of the symbols' (Morphy 1995, 186). These arguments will be grounded on the analysis of Schematic Art in relation, first, to the physical attributes of the surrounding landscape; secondly, to the experience of space; thirdly, to the orchestration of internal spaces; and finally, to the interaction between the imagery and the morphology of the rock surface.

From the landscape to the rock face

Field surveys at a regional scale have demonstrated that Schematic Art sites are rarely found in isolation but rather are grouped at particular places in the landscape (e.g. Sanches 1996, 222; Martínez Perelló and Collado Giraldo 1997) and must be approached as an articulated whole. Schematic Art is located on distinctive geomorphological units within conspicuous landforms, usually mountain ranges which dominate the wider landscape or the edges of major river valleys.

In most of the regional assemblages in north-east Portugal, the main geomorphological feature may be seen from afar, though the views outwards from the sites themselves are restricted to the immediate topography as, for instance, at the painted rock shelters of Regato das Bouças, in Mirandela (Sanches 1996). Here, one of the rock shelters commands wider views but it differs from the remainder for it is the least accessible, the most dangerous to reach. It also presents the highest density of paintings. Elsewhere in northern Portugal, Schematic Art open-air carvings are frequently found at physically enclosed spaces such as natural amphitheatres, as in the case of Gião (Baptista 1981a). Coincidentally, a large number of painted megalithic monuments are also placed in enclosed landscapes. They frequently occupy the centre of highland plateaux, circular basins or the bottoms of minor river valleys. Regional variations should, however, be noted. In south-west Spain, the painted rock shelters in the province of Badajoz are located on the cliff edges of major mountain ranges where they dominate extensive vistas (Martínez Perelló and Collado Giraldo 1997).

Painted rock shelters are not generally found on the highest mountain peaks. Instead, they are positioned half-way up the slopes of prominent rock formations which stand out as a conspicuous feature in the line of the ridge. The river valleys and basins overlooked by an observer standing in one of the shelters comprise short stretches of important natural routes across the landscape. In northern Portugal, the views from Cachão da Rapa, Pala Pinta and Penas Roias command only particular sections of major rivers in the background.

To sum up, Schematic rock-art sites are usually concealed within a confined area of prominent and highly visible landscape features, although these are only visible at a short distance. Rock shelters and carved outcrops occupy enclosed spaces in the landscape, even though they are only a few metres away from specific locales that dominate extensive vistas.

Comparison between the distribution of painted rock shelters and that of rock shelters devoid of decoration reveals that the painted rock shelters appear to obey certain rules in their setting in the landscape. At Regato das Bouças, in the Passos Mountain, there are in addition to the painted rock shelters a number of other shelters and shallow caves that provide evidence of human occupation although, with only one exception, these were not decorated (Bradley and Fábregas 1998, 305). The great majority of painted rock shelters are actually devoid of deposits and, apart from the rock art, only exceptionally do they show evidence of human activities, as at Pinho Monteiro rock shelter in southern Portugal (Gomes 1989). Conversely, a large number of Schematic Art sites are located a short distance from late prehistoric hilltop settlements. Unfortunately, though the proximity is striking, there has been insufficient research into the relationship between rock-art sites and these settlements, which might have been at least partly contemporary.

As regards the immediate topography, some paintings are within easy reach, whilst others are concealed on cliff-faces. There are cases, however, where access to the space immediately in front of the rock shelter is unproblematic whilst access to the actual rock art involves a greater physical effort. Space within painted rock shelters is usually constraining as most have room for only two or three persons. The rock art is generally found near the entrance but it may also be placed in the deepest recesses. The experience of place implies movement into the rock, as they are concealed within the natural landform. This observation recalls the positioning of art in passage graves, where the approach to the art encompasses bodily movement through the passage, into the chamber and back out again.

Several authors have observed that the distribution of the imagery inside megaliths appears to conform to a stereotyped pattern (Jorge 1986). The composition becomes progressively more complex towards the rear of the chamber. Moreover, human figures are usually absent from the orthostats closer to the entrance, where the decoration is mainly abstract. The arrangement recalls the distribution of iconic and non-iconic motifs at El Pedroso. This is a cave site located half-way up the south-eastern slope of a prominent hill, on top of which is a fortified Copper Age settlement (Figure 4.6). The vertical walls of the outer and inner chambers display a large number of Schematic Art carvings. In terms both of the natural architecture of the place and the orchestration of internal spaces by the rock art, this cave resembles a natural megalith. Not only does

Figure 4.6 The rock outcrop of El Pedroso with the entrance to the cave at its foot.

the composition become more complex towards the back of the inner chamber (Figure 4.7), but also the decoration of the outer chamber is exclusively composed of non-iconic imagery, i.e. elongated cup-marks (Figure 4.8). Cup-marks are universal symbols used in disparate contexts and are difficult to interpret (Bradley 1997). The closest counterparts for cup-marked stones, however, are found in nature – shallow concavities made by the elements. The boundary between natural and humanly made cup-marks is sometimes faint. At El Pedroso, the visitor who enters the cave is confronted by a chamber decorated almost exclusively with cup-marks. While it can be argued that the rock-art motifs in the outer chamber may easily be mistaken for natural features, ultimately the cave

Figure 4.7 El Pedroso, showing motifs at the back of the inner chamber.

presents the symbiotic relationship between the natural and the humanly made, which is clearly expressed in the dichotomy between the decoration of the outer and inner chambers. The decoration of the inner chamber is dominated by the human figure, an explicitly anthropic and culturally generated iconography.

Figure 4.8 El Pedroso: elongated cup-marks in the outer chamber.

The orchestration of the internal spaces in Schematic Art sites encompasses an intimate dialogue between the morphological characteristics of the rock surfaces and the configuration of the space available. Several authors have pointed out that, as far as the paintings in rock shelters are concerned, semi-detached panels delimited by natural fissures appear to have been preferred (García Arranz 1990; Collado Giraldo and Fernández Algaba 1998). This is the case with the painted rock shelter of Casal dos Mouros (Freixo-de-Espada-à-Cinta, Bragança), where red ochre paintings are placed on a vertical schist panel that appears to be coming out of the main rock outcrop.

There is in fact a close relationship between rock paintings and natural features of the rock face, such as fissures, textures, colours and geological intrusions. The reasons underlying the selection of particular panels to receive decoration seem to go beyond the regularity of the surface or the availability of space, for the choice of semi-detached square-shaped panels predominates. The depictions are actually framed by the natural fissures. Martínez and Collado Giraldo have noticed that some paintings in the province of Badajoz were intentionally placed to interact with the morphology of the rock face. At Cueva del Bercialejo, schematic animal figures parade towards a fissure on the edge of the panel, and at Buitres IX the composition adapts ideally to the panel morphology (Figure 4.9). Moreover, Gómes Barrera has pointed out that at the painted rock shelters of El Mirador and Peña Somera, located in the natural park of Valonsadero (Soria), some paintings were placed at particularly lumpy locations of the rock-face to give the impression of volume and embossment (Gómes Barrera 1993, 174).

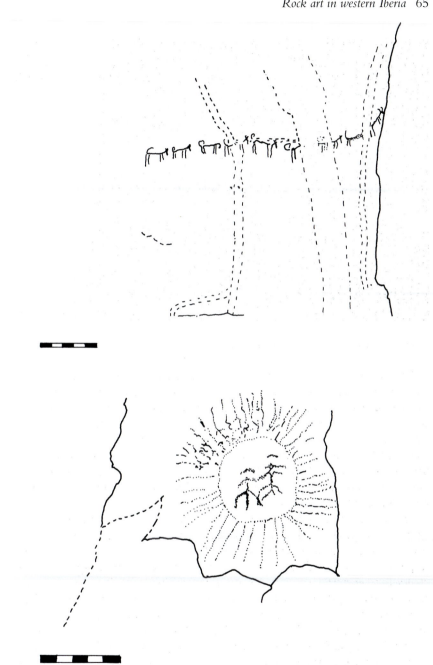

Figure 4.9 Relationship between positioning of Schematic Art paintings and physical characteristics of the rock-face: (above) Cueva del Bercialejo; (below) Buitres IX (Badajoz, Spain) (after Martínez Perelló and Collado Giraldo 1997).

It is also worth noting that Schematic Art sites seem to privilege specific geological environments. Ethnographic research on Australian and South African rock art has discussed the selection of particular geologies as significant backdrops for the rock art. Quartzite rock shelters and white quartz features, in particular, are given a special significance not only for their shimmering properties but also because they are imbued with cosmological symbolism. In his study on the symbolism of stone use in Arnhem Land, Taçon (1991) has remarked that some quartzite rock formations are believed to be charged with ancestral power, for they are ancestral beings who have been petrified at particular locations during the Dreamtime. Perhaps coincidentally, research across Iberia has demonstrated that painted rock shelters are frequently located on quartzite crests (García Arranz 1990; Martínez Perelló and Collado Giraldo 1997; Sanches and Santos 1989, 6; Collado Giraldo and Fernández Algaba 1998). It is very common to find a close association between white quartz rock formations and Schematic Art paintings. Even in geological areas where granite dominates, Schematic paintings are found on rock surfaces containing significant amounts of white quartz, as at Pala Pinta and Cachão da Rapa in north-east Portugal (Santos Júnior 1933, 35; 1934). At Serra dos Louções, in south-western Portugal, groups of painted rock shelters occupy rock formations which are entirely white in colour. The red mono-chrome paintings when applied directly on to a white quartz background create a spectacular effect.

In their positioning on rock panels, Schematic paintings often interact with natural incrustations or mineral intrusions present in the rock. The red ochre paintings found in group 7 of Peña de los Plantíos occupy a fraction of a rock panel incrusted with white quartz and black pebbles (Gómes Barrera 1993, 182). Furthermore, at the rock shelter of Pala Pinta the paintings are placed alongside, and even intermingle, with black tourmaline intrusions (Santos Júnior 1933) which themselves resemble black-painted wandering lines.

To sum up, antithetic principles appear to characterise the siting of Schematic Art in the landscape. Schematic paintings in rock shelters may be taken as an example. First, concentrations of such sites are found at enclosed locations on or within conspicuous landmarks that dominate the wider landscape. Second, even though the main geomorphological feature is visible from afar, the views outward from the rock shelters are restricted to the immediate topography. Third, the valleys and basins overlooked by an observer standing in one of the painted rock shelters are relatively accessible and constitute parts of major routes of movement across the landscape, though the rock shelters themselves frequently occupy dramatic and dangerous locations. Finally, the confined space within the painted rock shelters – most of which have room for only two or three persons – contrasts with the placement of the rock art itself, which is rarely located in the deepest recesses but rather near the entrance. It provides a feeling of open space since it leads us to look outwards.

Schematic Art appears to be a complex phenomenon which intersects a multiplicity of sociocultural and symbolic contexts, and more specifically those concerning funerary and ritual activities. In burial contexts, Schematic Art imagery is not limited exclusively to megalithic monuments but is also closely associated with Late Neolithic cave burials, as for example at Escoural in southern Portugal (Gomes *et al.* 1983) and Charneca Chica. In terms of landscape setting, Schematic Art predominantly decorates the interstices of mountain ranges and the rock outcrops on river banks, the rock art of the Tagus Valley being an excellent example (Baptista 1981b).

Concluding remarks

Ethnohistorical studies of rock art show that, regardless of the variability of forms and techniques, the use of natural rock formations as a means of establishing contact with a transcendental world beyond the rock-face is widespread through time and space (e.g. Whitley 1998, 16). Prehistoric rock-art sites in western Europe have been separated from their original meaning – the stories, songs, or names with which they were associated – and sit passively, quietly, demanding interpretation from passers-by. The original significance of Iberian prehistoric rock art is enclosed in a perhaps intangible sociocultural and religious sphere. It is nonetheless the case that a mythical-symbolic meaning assigned to ancient markings in the landscape has persisted in the memory of the people who presently inhabit the same territory (Alves 2001). Contemporary readings of prehistoric art reinforce the idea that a fundamental relationship between people and the natural world has to some extent been maintained, and is apparent in common attitudes and feelings towards particular features in the landscape. While it is not possible to use reliable ethnographic records in this study area, this may provide added justification for supposing that there was some symbolic intention behind the selection of particular natural formations for the placement of rock art. In essence, rock art is a medium by which symbolic meaning is materialised at a natural place, as the act of carving or painting adds a visual, and therefore cultural, layer of meaning to a previously significant natural feature. Rock art seems to have been one means of materialising cosmological beliefs, encoded in the physical world.

References

Acosta, P., 1968. *La pintura rupestre esquemática en España*. Salamanca: Universidad de Salamanca.

Alves, L., 2001. Rock art and enchanted moors: the significance of rock carvings in the folklore of north-west Iberia, in R.J. Wallis and K. Lymer (eds), *A Permeability of Boundaries? New Approaches to the Archaeology of Art, Religion and Folklore*. Oxford: British Archaeological Reports, 71–8.

Baptista, A.M., 1981a. A arte do Gião, *Arqueologia*. 3. 56–66.

Baptista, A.M., 1981b. *A Rocha F-155 e a origem da arte do vale do Tejo*. Porto: Grupo de Estudos Arqueológicos do Porto, Monografias Arqueológicas 1.

Bradley, R., 1997. *Rock Art and the Prehistory of Atlantic Europe*. London: Routledge.

Bradley, R., 1999. *An Archaeology of Natural Places*. London: Routledge.

Bradley, R., and Fábregas, R., 1998. Crossing the border: contrasting styles of rock art in the prehistory of north-west Iberia. *Oxford Journal of Archaeology* 17, 287–308.

Bradley, R., Criado, F., and Fábregas, R., 1995. Rock art and the prehistoric landscape of Galicia. *Proceedings of the Prehistoric Society* 61, 142–53.

Breuil, H., 1917. La roche peinte de Valdejunco à la Esperança, près Arronches (Portalegre). *Terra Portuguesa* 2 (13–14), 17–27.

Breuil, H., 1932–33. *Les peintures rupestres schématiques de la Péninsule Ibérique*. Paris: Lagny.

Bueno Ramirez, P., and Balbín Behrmann, R., 1992. L'art mégalithique dans la Péninsule Ibérique. Une vue d'ensemble. *L'Anthropologie*, 96, 499–572.

Bueno Ramirez, P., Balbin-Behrmann, R., Barroso Bermejo, R., Aldecoa Quintana, M.A., and Casado Mateos, A. B., 1999. Arte megalítico en Extremadura: los dolmenes de Alcantara, Cáceres, España. *Estudos Pré-históricos* 7, 85–110.

Chippindale, C., and Taçon, P., 1998. An archaeology of rock art through informed methods and formal methods, in C. Chippindale and P. Taçon (eds), *The Archaeology of Rock Art*. Cambridge: Cambridge University Press, 1–10.

Collado Giraldo, H., and Fernández Algaba, M., 1998. Arte rupestre en Extremadura: últimas investigaciones. *A Pré-história na Beira Interior. Actas do Colóquio*. Viseu: Centros de Estudos Pré-históricos da Beira Alta, 207–19.

Collado Giraldo, H., Fernández Algaba, M., Pozuelo Lorenzo, D., and Girón Abumalham, M., 1997. Pinturas rupestres esquemáticas en la transición del IV as III milenio a.C. El abrigo de la Charneca Chica (Oliva de Mérida, Badajoz). *Trabajos de Prehistoria* 54, 143–9.

Delibes de Castro, G., and Rojo Guerra, M., 1988. En torno al origen del foco megalitico del oriente de la Meseta: de nuevo el sepulcro de Cubillero de Lara. *Boletin del Seminario de Estudios de Arte y Arqueologia* 54, 5–21.

Esparza Arroyo, A., 1977. El castro Zamorano del Pedroso y sus insculturas. *Boletin del Seminario de Estudios de Arte y Arqueologia* 43, 27–39.

García Arranz, J.J., 1990. *La pintura rupestre esquemática en la comarca de Villuercas (Cáceres)*. Cáceres: Diputacion Provincial de Cáceres, Institucion Cultural 'El Brocense'.

Gomes, M.V., 1989. Arte rupestre e contexto arqueológico. *Almansor* 7, 225–69.

Gomes, R.V., Gomes, M.V., and Farinha dos Santos, M., 1983. O santuário exterior do Escoural. Sector NE (Montemor-o-Novo, Évora). *Zephyrus* 36, 287–307.

Gómes Barrera, J.A., 1991. El motivo estela de "Peña de los Plantíos" (Fuentetoba, Soria). *Soria Arqueológica* 1, 87–102.

Gómes Barrera, J.A., 1993. *Arte rupestre prehistórico en la Meseta Castellano-Leonesa*. Valladolid: Junta de Castilla y León.

Ingold, T., 1986. *The Appropriation of Nature. Essays on Human Ecology and Social Relations*. Manchester: Manchester University Press.

Jorge, V.O., 1986. Arte rupestre em Portugal. *Trabalhos de Antropologia e Etnologia* 26, 143–58.

Lanhas, F., 1969. As gravuras rupestres de Montedor. *Revista de Etnografia* 13, 367–86.

Martínez Perelló, M.I., and Collado Giraldo, H., 1997. Arte rupestre esquemático en la provincia de Badajoz. *Extremadura Arqueológica* 7, 151–73.

Morphy, H., 1995. Landscape and the reproduction of the ancestral past, in E. Hirsh and M. O'Hanlon (eds), *The Anthropology of Landscape: Perspectives on Place and Space*. Oxford: Clarendon Press, 184–209.

Sanches, M.J., 1996. Passos/Santa Comba mountain in the context of the late prehistory of northern Portugal. *World Archaeology* 28, 220–30.

Sanches, M. J., and Santos, B.C.T.O., 1989. *Levantamento Arqueológico de Mirandela*. Mirandela: Câmara Municipal de Mirandela.

Santos Júnior, J.R., 1933. O abrigo pré-histórico da 'Pala Pinta'. *Trabalhos de Antropologia e Etnologia* 6, 33–43.

Santos Júnior, J.R., 1934. As pinturas pré-históricas do Cachão da Rapa. *Trabalhos de Antropologia e Etnologia* 6, 185–222.

Taçon, P., 1991. The power of stone: symbolic aspects of stone use and tool development in western Arnhem Land, Australia. *Antiquity* 65, 192–207.

Taçon, P., 1999. Identifying ancient sacred landscapes in Australia: from physical to social, in W. Ashmore and A.B. Knapp (eds), *Archaeologies of Landscape. Contemporary Perspectives*. Oxford: Blackwell, 33–57.

Whitley, D., 1998. Finding rain in the desert: landscape, gender and far western North American rock art, in C. Chippindale and P. Taçon (eds), *The Archaeology of Rock Art*. Cambridge: Cambridge University Press, 11–29.

Urribarri Angulo, J.L., 1975. *El fenómeno megalítico burgalés*. Burgos: Instituición Fernán González.

Part II

Atlantic France

Introduction

North-west France contains some of the most famous Neolithic monuments in Atlantic Europe: the Carnac stone rows, the Grand Menhir Brisé, the Barnenez passage graves. It is also, like central Portugal, an area with Late Mesolithic sites that pose the question of continuity with the earliest Neolithic. In southern Brittany, the offshore islands of Téviec and Hoëdic have Mesolithic shell middens with burials within them which show features that may be antecedent to Neolithic tombs: the use of slab-lined cists, the practice of collective inhumation, and an incipient monumentalism in the form of small tumuli and stone stelae. The alternative view relates the emergence of monumentalism very closely to the Neolithic transition, and places particular emphasis not on local continuity from the Late Mesolithic, but on influences from the east. Since the 1930s, it has been recognised that long mounds belong early in the Breton monument sequence, and the idea that these derive in some way from the longhouse tradition continues to be widely discussed (e.g. Sherratt 1990; Boujot and Cassen 1992).

This quest for the origins of monumentalism operates at the level of general ideas rather than the specificity of the material evidence; thus it was the idea of the longhouse that was translated into the long mound, but the form of the mound and the burial chamber, the associated tradition of standing stones, and the concept of monumentality itself are not explicitly addressed. Nor is the issue of broader-scale patterns, where north-western France takes its place as one of several regions within western Europe where monumentalism with strong funerary connections arose during the 5th millennium BC. Calado, in the previous section, has already emphasised the parallels between Brittany and Alentejo, and has posited direct maritime links between the two regions. Maritime connections may also have been instrumental in the development of related Neolithic monument traditions in Britain and northern Europe (Clark 1977). Thus the genesis of monumentalism must be sought in processes operating across a range of communities throughout the Atlantic façade, whatever the specific nature of the developments in each individual area.

This suggests once again that we should look at monument origins in terms of the Atlantic landscape, for what these monuments share in common is the use of landscape features in their conceptualisation and construction. This includes both the use of local materials and the placement in the landscape with respect to geology and topography, coastlines and rivers. The two papers in this section consider monuments as the transformation or extension of the landscape, straddling or accentuating the junction between culture and nature. In the first, Luc Laporte and his co-authors discuss the ways in which megalithic monuments may represent the modification of natural features. Yet, while the distinction between natural and constructed may be partially concealed, structures such as the Prissé-la-Charrière long mound also employ design effects, such as perspective, which are intended to enhance their monumentality. This tension between the desire to blend with local landforms and to stand prominently apart appears characteristic of Neolithic monumentalism along the Atlantic façade (Scarre 2000).

The second paper focuses on coastline as a locus of special significance for Neolithic communities. Most of the passage graves of northern Brittany were located overlooking the sea, and ethnography from northern Europe and North America suggests how this liminal zone, marking the junction of land, sea and sky, may have held a particular importance in terms of prehistoric cosmology. Thus it may be in the qualities of the landscapes themselves, and their mytho-logical and cosmological associations, that we should seek to understand Neolithic monumentalism.

References

Boujot, C., and Cassen, S., 1992. Le développement des premières architectures funéraires monumentales en France occidentale, in *Paysans et Batisseurs. Actes du 17e Colloque Interrégional sur le Néolithique* (ed. C-T. Le Roux). Revue Archéologique de l'Ouest, Supplément 5, 195–211.

Clark, J.G.D., 1977. The economic context of dolmens and passage-graves in Sweden, in V. Markotic (ed.), *Ancient Europe and the Mediterranean*. Warminster: Aris & Phillips, 35–49.

Scarre, C., 2000. Forms and landforms. The design and setting of Neolithic monuments in western France, in *Neolithic Orkney in its European Context* (ed. Anna Ritchie). Cambridge: McDonald Institute for Archaeological Research, 309–20.

Sherratt, A., 1990. The genesis of megaliths: monumentality, ethnicity and social complexity in Neolithic north-west Europe. *World Archaeology* 22, 147–67.

5 The perception of space and geometry

Megalithic monuments of west-central France in their relationship to the landscape

Luc Laporte, Roger Joussaume and Chris Scarre

Our perception of megalithic monuments is closely tied to a number of fundamental principles, which go without question: they are created spaces, achieved by human labour at the cost of a considerable effort, sometimes on a scale which stimulates our admiration. Should we be called upon here to distinguish between the works of nature and culture, we would not hesitate for an instant. We know, however, that the world-views developed by traditional societies are often much less compartmentalised than our own. Was the nature/culture distinction as clearly perceived by those who oversaw the construction of monuments during the Neolithic?

The investigations recently undertaken at Prissé-la-Charrière (Deux-Sèvres) in west-central France (Figure 5.1), have demonstrated a striking continuity between the external architectural features of the cairn and the natural bedrock on which it stands, and which has itself been shaped by human action. The monument in question is a trapezoidal long mound, 100 metres in length. Such Neolithic long mounds are characteristic of Atlantic France, those of Brittany, such as Saint-Michel, Er-Grah and Barnenez, being among the best-known monuments of this type, though each of them is very different from the others. What is less well known is that numerous long mounds also exist in west-central France, south of the Loire, where over forty examples are currently recorded (Joussaume 1997). Several of these long mounds south of the Loire are of impressive dimensions and in that sense they are certainly no less striking than massive Breton long mounds such as the Tumulus de Saint Michel. To cite just one example, at Tusson in Charente, three long mounds are aligned 100 metres apart from each other on the crest overlooking the small valley of the Bief. The central mound measures 120 metres long by 40 metres wide and some 10 metres high. Even the smallest of the three reaches a length of 60 metres. Along the same north–south crest, within a two-kilometre radius, at least five other monuments are located, some of them well preserved, some less so. On the far side of the Bief valley are five more megalithic monuments, situated opposite those just mentioned and distributed along a length of one kilometre. One of these five,

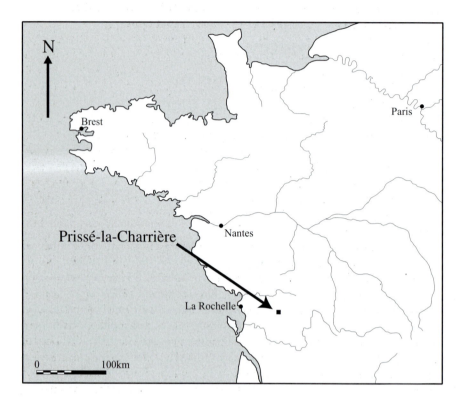

Figure 5.1 Location of Prissé-la-Charrière.

La Motte de la Garde, has a mound measuring approximately 50 metres long by 25 metres wide, although only the burial chamber has been excavated, and that somewhat cursorily. This complex of monuments is visible from a distance of more than five kilometres around and still forms an impressive marker in the landscape (Joussaume *et al.* 1998). Very few long mounds south of the Loire have been excavated, however, and none of them in a systematic manner. It was for this reason that the decision was taken to mount a major excavation of one such monument, and for that purpose to select one of the best preserved examples: tumulus C at Prissé-la-Charrière.

The cemetery of Prissé-la-Charrière in fact comprises two long mounds. Tumulus A measures 6 to 8 metres high and some 50 metres in length. Tumulus C, which is likewise oriented east–west, measures 19 metres wide at its eastern end by 3 metres high, this being both the broader and the taller end. The mound is trapezoidal in plan, and is edged along the whole of its perimeter by a pair of parallel kerbs running some 2 metres apart. The outer kerb formed the edging of a low bench which can never have exceeded 0.5–0.7 metres in height. This bench is placed up against the inner kerb which at the eastern end of the mound stands to a height of some 1.3 metres. A paved platform occupied the crest of the mound, extending probably along its entire length; owing to the excellent state of preservation, part of this platform still survives. Within the body of the mound there are two passage graves, one opening from the northern flank some two-thirds of the distance from the eastern end. The passage leads to a small rectangular burial chamber, though unfortunately both passage and chamber are heavily disturbed.

Such was the character of the monument in its final form, the phase that interests us here, leaving aside for present purposes the complex history of its earlier development. The quarry pits of this final phase monument were located along each of its long sides at a distance of 10 metres or so from the outer kerb. Between the edge of the quarries and the foot of the monument, however, the limestone bedrock had not been left untouched but had been cut into a series of steps or ledges so forming a kind of pedestal some 30 metres wide on which the monument was built.

The entire surface of this low limestone eminence had thus been shaped and modified. The principal objective may have been to accentuate the monumentality of the structure, and in this respect a similar phenomenon had already been noted during the study of the megalithic cemetery of Champ-Châlon at Benon (Charente-Maritime) especially in the case of Champ-Châlon A and C. At Prissé, however, the succession of rock-cut steps, each around 20 centimetres high, finds an architectural prolongation in the two outer kerbs which delimit the edges of the trapezoidal mound (Figure 5.2). This modelling of the bedrock thus creates a continuity between the built monument properly speaking and the natural bedrock on which its rests. There can be no doubt that the effect is intentional: the concavity of the excavated bedrock blends smoothly into the convexity of the built monument. It is from the built façade, cutting across the two kerbs and the low bench between them, that the passages open that give access to the burial chambers. The passages thus emerge on to a façade which was certainly constructed but which was evidently conceived as the continuation of the steps cut in the bedrock. The arrangement may have been fashioned in this manner specifically as a way of marking out the passage entrances as the access to a subterranean world.

The reverse of this pattern is represented at a number of natural caves used for funerary purposes, where the cavity has to some degree been intentionally reworked and structured. One example is grave 39 at Los Millares in Spain (Figure 5.3) (Siret 1893). Some Neolithic burial caves employ elements characteristic of megalithic architecture, and this is particularly striking in the case of the Aven de la Boucle at Corconne in the south of France. This cave has been the subject of investigations by Cours, Duday and Jallet for more than ten years. One of the chambers contains Late Neolithic burials (Néolithique récent and Néolithique final), and access to the burial cave is by a shaft communicating with a network of crevices. After following a twisting passageway for some 10 metres the crevices lead out into an area open to the sky, but excavation has shown that this open-air section was originally covered by horizontally laid capstones (Duday 1993;

Figure 5.2 Prissé-la-Charrière from the north-east, showing the rock-cut steps revealed along the northern side of the long mound.

Figure 5.3 Grave 39 in the cemetery of Los Millares (Spain). One side of the chamber is constructed of slabs placed on edge, the other cut into the bedrock of the hillside. (After Siret 1893.)

1997). The passage giving access from here to the burial chamber had also been modified and made less uneven: steps and ledges were cut to facilitate the descent, the sides were straightened in places by building sections of walling, and these walls sometimes continued upwards as corbelled vaulting. Finally, at the bottom of the access shaft, a platform had been carved out in the burial chamber itself. The system giving access to the burial cave thus possessed several architectural characteristics common to the passage of a passage grave, such as the placing of capstones over the open-air section near to the entrance and the construction of lengths of corbelled walling.

The Aven de la Boucle is certainly the most spectacular example of its kind, but in recent years other Late Neolithic caves in southern France have been found to have modifications which are comparable in at least some degree. Such is the case at the burial cave of Rec d'Aigues Rouges at Saint-Pons de Thomières (Hérault) where the system of access – a single natural entryway carefully modified – leads to a small artificial platform on which rests part of the funerary deposit (Courtaud and Janin 1994). These therefore are examples where the shape of natural spaces has been extensively transformed, notably by the deployment of architectural techniques that are widely used elsewhere in megalithic constructions. But over and above the question of specific techniques, it is the conception of the funerary area as a whole which is significant. In these examples we see how a complex and multi-branched karstic void has been transformed to create a single access passage ending at a burial chamber which in a sense here takes the place of the burial chamber within the core of a megalithic monument. In the earlier example at Prissé-la-Charrière, the burial chambers constructed within an enormous megalithic monument opened on to a façade that had been conceived as a continuation of a natural landscape extensively refashioned by human intervention. Conversely, in these cave sites an underground space to be used for burial activities has been modified using architectural techniques and a design principle widely encountered in the context of megalithic constructions. The examples cited above are perhaps too diverse in form and too few in number, but they nonetheless appear to belong strangely together in the sense that they share the same conception of an access and a funerary space which descend progressively below the ground. For us, however, the greatest contrast is the presence in the former case, and the absence in the latter, of a monumental structure designed to signal to the eyes of the living the location of the burials.

It is clear that these monuments are the product of an architectural design project that was conceived in advance of its implementation in the field. That much is now beyond question, and for the largest of the monuments, the observation would apply to each stage of their development. To take a single west French example, the ground plan of the monument of Pey de Fontaine (Vendée) was laid out first, using a basal course of white stones which contrast in colour with the other courses of the outer kerb of the cairn (Joussaume 1999). Furthermore, the architecture of these monuments is frequently governed by certain elementary structuring principles based on symmetry. For most of these monuments the overall intention can readily be identified from the ground plan, setting aside minor irregularities which might be attributed to uncertainties or errors in the execution of the construction project. It is clear that when they judged it necessary, Neolithic societies were perfectly capable of employing strict symmetry in the design of these early funerary architectures, and implementing it in the field with rigour and precision. This can equally well take the form either of a radial symmetry, as seen in circular monuments such as that at Ernes in Normandy, or an axial symmetry in the case of quadrangular monuments like La Joselière (Loire-Atlantique) or Sainte-Radegonde (Charente-Maritime) (L'Helgouach *et al.* 1989; Gachina 1998; San Juan and Dron 1997). This symmetrical principle sometimes extends also to the plan of the internal walls of the cairn, even though these would have been hidden within the interior of the structure. Thus tumulus C in the Champ-Châlon cemetery at Benon displays a cellular internal structure which is laid out exactly symmetrically in relation to the central axis of the monument (Cadot and Joussaume 1986).

The concept of symmetry is closely associated with asymmetry. Symmetry in mound design comes perhaps as no surprise. What has hitherto been much less remarked is the recurrence of certain asymmetrical features, particularly in the long mounds of west and west-central France. Are these a chance result, or do they indicate intentionality on the part of those who conceived what are among the most monumental of all prehistoric constructional projects?

Asymmetry is especially evident in certain mounds in the Carnac region, such as Mané Pochat, Mané Ty Ec and Le Manio II (Figure 5.4). These measure some 40 metres in length and are trapezoidal in plan. The three mounds were excavated by Scottish antiquary James Miln in the 1870s, and the ground plans were surveyed with a good degree of accuracy. From this we may deduce that in the case of these three monuments, and perhaps others, the broadest end of the mound is not symmetrically placed in relation to its long axis. While one of the long sides is straight, the other displays a kink or change of direction some half-way along its length, widening out towards the broader end of the mound. As an isolated instance, such an architectural detail has every chance of being accidental, but when it recurs in several monuments it is necessary to consider its significance more seriously. It is furthermore intriguing to remark, without rushing to hasty conclusions, that a similar asymmetry is found in the ground plan of the Early Neolithic house (attributed to the Villeneuve-Saint-Germain group) at Le Haut Mée on the eastern fringes of Brittany (Cassen *et al.* 1998). In the context of that domestic structure, the asymmetry may be explained by the Y-shaped plan of the central truss; this is a specific feature of what is the most westerly known Bandkeramik house. It is more curious to find a slight asymmetry of the same type in the majority of those long mounds of northwest France where the plan is established in sufficient detail: for example at Guennoc III, Barnenez, Benon A, Colombiers-sur-Seulles, Er Grah, Availles-sur-Chizé and Prissé-la-Charrière (Giot 1987; Cadot and Joussaume 1986; Chancerel *et al.* 1992; Le Roux *et al.* 1996; Bouin and Joussaume 1998). In all these instances, the broader terminal of the monument is slightly offset and oblique relative to the central axis of symmetry (Figure 5.5). At Prissé and

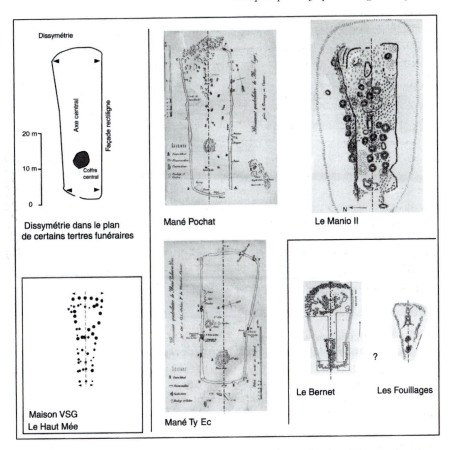

Figure 5.4 Neolithic funerary monuments on the Atlantic façade of France showing asymmetry in their plans. (After Miln 1883; Le Rouzic 1933; Joussaume 1987.)

Barnenez, where the volume of the built monument is known with sufficient accuracy, this asymmetry is represented also in an asymmetry in the angle of slope of the opposing flanks of the cairn, one side being significantly steeper than the other.

The recurrence of this architectural detail is too systematic to be considered the result of simple coincidence. In every case, regardless of the arrangement of funerary chambers within the monument, the slight asymmetry leads to the differentiation of the two longitudinal flanks of the mound. It is also true in each case, however, that it is the broader, more steeply sloping flank that provides the façade on to which open the passages leading to the burial chambers. Thus this slight differentiation in the trapezoidal plan of the cairn is directly linked to the asymmetry which necessarily results from the presence of a passage, opening from one side of the mound and leading to a burial chamber. The repeated

In introducing a slight asymmetry in the trapezoidal plan of a long mound, they took account of the asymmetry that was imposed at a more fundamental level by the positioning of the burial chambers. This more fundamental asymmetry was essentially hidden within the body of the cairn since it was caused by the positioning of the burial chambers and the passages that gave access to them. The builders also played on the perception of distances by using effects of perspective. For those who conceived these architectural projects, was this not a way of appropriating a given space that was both funerary and ceremonial? It may also have been a way of demonstrating control over nature, on the one hand, and control, on the other, over those who were accustomed to visit these locations. Why cheat about reality in this way if not to demonstrate the degree to which individuals had the power to transform it?

This is the crucial point. A new relationship with space is established in these monuments. It was doubtless by no means accidental that this new outlook was expressed among agricultural or pastoralist societies that were among the first in western Europe to adopt the domestication of plants and animals. Leaving aside the technologies needed to build such structures, it is far from certain that the basic principles which underlie these architectural projects could have originated or developed to such a level in the context of the cognitive systems and world-views associated with hunter–gatherer societies. Above all, it is striking to observe how, almost from the very beginning, these monumental constructions carried within themselves the germs of devices which came subsequently to be developed and elaborated extensively. It is almost as if they were an integral part of their very essence.

References

Bouin, F., and Joussaume, R., 1998. Le tumulus du Planti à Availles-sur-Chizé (Deux-Sèvres), in X. Gutherz and R. Joussaume (eds), *Le Néolithique du Centre-Ouest de la France. Actes du XXIe Colloque Interrégional sur le Néolithique*. Chauvigny: Association des Publications Chauvinoises, 169–82.

Cadot, R., and Joussaume, R., 1986. Les tumulus néolithiques de Champ Châlon à Benon, Charente-Maritime, France: présentation préliminaire. *Arqueologia* 14, 44–57.

Cassen, S., Audren, C., Hinguant, S., Lannuzel, G., and Marchand, G., 1998. L'habitat Villeneuve-Saint-Germain du Haut-Mée (Saint-Etienne-en-Coglès, Ille-et-Vilaine). *Bulletin de la Société Préhistorique Française* 95, 41–76.

Chancerel, A., Kinnes, I., Lagnel, E., and Kirk, T., 1992. Le tumulus néolithique de la Commune Sèche à Colombiers-sur-Seulles (Calvados), in C.-T. Le Roux (ed.), *Paysans et Bâtisseurs. Actes du 17e Colloque Interrégional sur le Néolithique. Revue Archéologique de l'Ouest, Supplément n°5*, 17–29.

Courtaud, P., and Janin, T., 1994. La grotte sépulcrale du Rec d'Aigues Rouges à Saint-Pons-de-Thomières (Hérault). *Gallia Préhistoire* 36, 329–356.

Duday, H., 1993. Corconne, Aven de la Boucle. *Bilan scientifique de la région Languedoc-Roussillon*, 64–6.

Duday, H., 1997. Corconne, Aven de la Boucle. *Bilan scientifique de la région Languedoc-Roussillon*, 54.

Gachina, J., 1998. Le dolmen de la Grosse Pierre à Sainte-Radegonde (Charente-Maritime), in X. Gutherz and R. Joussaume (eds), *Le Néolithique du Centre-Ouest de la France. Actes du XXIe Colloque Interrégional sur le Néolithique.* Chauvigny: Association des Publications Chauvinoises, 193–202.

Giot, P.-R., 1987. *Barnenez, Carn, Guennoc.* Rennes: Travaux du Laboratoire d'Anthropologie, Préhistoire, Protohistoire et Quaternaire Armoricains.

Joussaume, R., (ed.), 1987. *Mégalithisme et société.* La Roche-sur-Yon: Groupe Vendéen d'Etudes Préhistoriques.

Joussaume, R., 1997. Les longs tumulus du Centre-Ouest de la France, in A. Rodríguez Casal (ed.), *O Neolitico Atlantico e as Orixes do Megalitismo.* Santiago de Compostela: Consello da Cultura Gallega, 279–97.

Joussaume, R., 1999. Le tumulus du Pey de Fontaine au Bernard (Vendée). *Gallia Préhistoire* 41, 167–222.

Joussaume, R., Laporte, L., and Scarre, C., 1998. Longs tumulus néolithiques et organisation de l'espace dans l'ouest de la France, in N. Cauwe and P.-L. van Berg (eds), *Organisation Néolithique de l'Éspace en Europe du Nord-Ouest. Actes du XXIIIe Colloque Interrégional sur le Néolithique. Anthropologie et Préhistoire* 109, 259–75.

Le Roux, C.-T., 1997. Aspects non-funéraires du mégalithisme armoricain, in A. Rodríguez Casal (ed.), *O Neolitico Atlantico e as Orixes do Megalitismo.* Santiago de Compostela: Consello da Cultura Gallega, 233–44.

Le Roux, C.-T., L'Helgouach, J., Cassen, S., Gaumé, E., Lecerf, Y., Tinevez, J.-Y., Leroy, D., and Le Potier, C., 1996. Reprises des fouilles à Locmariaquer (Morbihan), in J.-P. Mohen (ed.), *La Vie Préhistorique.* Dijon: Faton, 440–43.

Le Rouzic, Z., 1933. Morphologie et chronologie des sépultures préhistoriques du Morbihan. *L'Anthropologie* 63, 225–57.

L'Helgouach, J., Le Gouestre, D., and Poulain, H., 1989. Le monument mégalithique transepté de la Joselière au Clion-sur-Mer (Loire-Atlantique). *Revue Archéologique de l'Ouest* 6, 31–50.

Miln, J., 1883. Exploration de trois monuments quadrilatères. *Bulletin de la Société Polymathique du Morbihan 1883*, 30–49.

San Juan, G., and Dron, J.-L., 1997. Le site néolithique moyen de Derrières-les-Près à Ernes (Calvados). *Gallia Préhistoire* 39, 151–238.

Sellier, D., 1991. Analyse morphologique des marques de la météorisation des granites à partir de mégalithes morbihannais. L'exemple de l'alignement de Kerlescan à Carnac. *Revue Archéologique de l'Ouest* 8, 83–97.

Siret, L., 1893. L'Espagne préhistorique. *Revue des Questions Scientifiques.* October 1893, 1–78.

6   Coast and cosmos

The Neolithic monuments of northern Brittany

Chris Scarre

The Neolithic monuments of western Europe, in their use of natural materials such as earth, stone and timber, appear consciously to have explored and exploited the interplay between human constructions and features of the landscape. Large stones were typically left unshaped, to resemble rock outcrops. Timber uprights may have stood for trees or, grouped in clusters, for the edges of forest clearings in which the monuments were located. At the same time, other aspects of landscape were evoked as much by the placement and setting of these sites. Among the most dramatic locations of all were coasts and islands, where the boundary between land and sea – or land, sea and sky, when looking towards the distant horizon – will have had especial relevance. Recorded ethnographies of the peoples of the north-west coast of North America, and of the Saami of northern Europe, emphasise the significance attached to the land–sea boundary in traditional cosmological understandings (Suttles 1990; Bradley 2000; Scarre 2001).

Distributional patterns strongly suggest that the special significance of shorelines was a key consideration in the locations chosen for ritual monuments by some Atlantic Neolithic societies. A coastal emphasis is apparent in the chambered tombs of the Orkney islands (Fraser 1983; Davidson and Henshall 1989) and is equally striking in the case of Brittany (Figure 6.1). The coastal emphasis of Neolithic chambered tombs in Brittany was remarked by Daryll Forde as long ago as 1930. He interpreted it as a result of a sea-borne colonisation by the Neolithic population, but also as evidence for the importance of maritime traffic in the spread of ideas and cultural innovations. He also noted that the many islands of the southern and far western coast of Brittany were occupied 'without exception' and that on some, megalithic remains were 'very numerous' (Forde 1930, 69). Forde's maritime settlers may be considered the close cousins of (if not identical with) Childe's 'megalithic missionaries' (Childe 1957), bringing new systems of belief and new architectural forms from the Mediterranean via the western seaways.

Subsequent writers have interpreted the maritime emphasis of megalithic distribution in terms of marine economies based on fishing (Clark 1977; Kaelas 1990). Kaelas has argued for Brittany that 'it is the Atlantic and the estuaries which have been the enormous protein source that made the mysterious

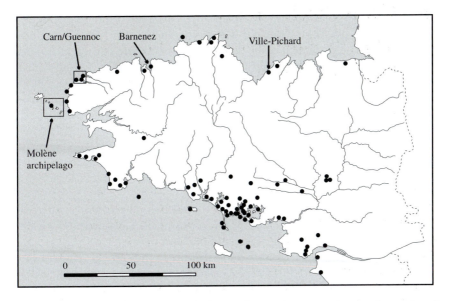

Figure 6.1 Distribution of early passage graves in Brittany, indicating locations of individual sites and groups of sites referred to in the text.

explosion . . . of the high culture of megalith builders' society possible in Brittany' (Kaelas 1990, 100). Leaving aside the questionable term 'high culture', it must be noted that stable isotope evidence throws doubt on the role of a diet high in marine fish. Marine foods do appear to have been a major resource for the Mesolithic populations buried at Téviec and Hoëdic (Richards and Hedges 1999a). If the Breton evidence proves analogous to that from Denmark, Portugal and southern Britain, however, there was very likely an abrupt switch away from marine resources at the beginning of the Neolithic (Tauber 1981; Lubell *et al.* 1994; Richards and Hedges 1999b). This would imply that the coastal distribution of megalithic tombs in Brittany does not result from an overwhelming economic emphasis on the use of marine resources.

Considerations of good arable land are still less likely to have played a major role in the coastal emphasis of the passage graves. The distribution of fertile loess soils (Giot *et al.* 1998, 74) is suggestive for the north coast but these soils are restricted to small pockets and do not extend to the southern coast where the distribution of tombs is most dense. There is nothing here to support the idea that tombs were located close to patches of arable land, in the model made famous by Renfrew in his work on the Scottish islands of Arran and Rousay (Renfrew 1973, 146–51). Subsequent research on Arran has indeed shown that the chambered tombs were not located close to patches of arable land (Hughes 1988). Furthermore, the pollen evidence from the north coast of Brittany suggests that while clearances occurred during the Neolithic, systematic cultivation did not begin until the 2nd millennium BC (Marguerie 1992).

The importance of coastal locations is hence not readily understood within traditional models of economy or territoriality. Given the nature of the monuments, and the practices associated with them, such a conclusion is perhaps unsurprising. The placement of the dead at the very margins of the land is more likely an evocation of the symbolic nature of the shoreline. Here we must recall that the coast is not merely a geographical line separating land from sea but a world with its own special qualities of sound and spectacle: the crashing or soughing of the waves, the drawing together of sea and sky at the far horizon, the beaches or cliffs which fringe the edge of the land, and the dramatic transformation wrought twice daily by the tides. There can be few more dramatic settings for major ritual monuments, and it is probable that the innate liminality of the coastal zone and its special qualities lay behind the frequent location of ritual monuments on headlands or islands.

Approached from the land, the vista of the sea beyond provides an effective backdrop to many of these tombs. Yet in terms of their orientation, it is the direction of sunrise rather than features of the landscape which appear to have been most significant. L'Helgouach notes that the Breton passage graves have a prevailing orientation such that passages or entrances face towards the east, which he considers standard practice among the passage graves of Atlantic Europe: 'Overall, the classic passage graves of Brittany correspond well as concerns orientation with the passage graves of the Atlantic façade' (L'Helgouach 1965, 79). At a detailed level, however, it is possible to suggest that variations within the easterly orientation, or deviations from it, can be understood in the context of the landscape settings of individual monuments and, more particularly, in their relationship to the shoreline. The quest, then, is for an understanding or appreciation of these tombs in terms of Neolithic cosmologies, involving not only the landscapes of shoreline and island, but also the sky above, and in particular the rising and setting sun.

The numerous passage graves recorded on the low-lying islands of the Molène archipelago off the north-west corner of Brittany provide the basis for a study of one group of sites (Scarre 2002). These passage graves are known to us principally through the inventory compiled by Paul Du Châtellier following a brief visit to the islands in 1901 (Du Châtellier 1902). He reported a large number of chambered tombs, along with several 'cromlechs' and standing stones. Though caution is required in interpreting his report, there seems little doubt that the small low-lying islands of the Molène archipelago contained an unusually high number of what were probably Neolithic passage graves, especially when their small size and relatively remote location are considered.

The size and topography of the islands must however be assessed against the changes wrought by sea-level rise since the Neolithic. Morzadec-Kerfourn has argued that the level of the highest tides 7,000 years ago was equivalent to that of the lowest tides at the present day (Morzadec-Kerfourn in Giot *et al.* 1998, 437–40). On this basis we may conclude that the islands of the Molène archipelago were at that time joined into a single larger island, though this would have been separated by deep channels from the mainland to the east and Ouessant to the west. How many Neolithic monuments have been lost through this process of marine encroachment it is difficult to estimate, though while passage graves are found in low-lying coastal locations, most follow what Giot has called 'La loi des sommets relatifs' and were placed at locally high positions within the landscape (Giot 1987, 191). These would correspond to the islands of the present day.

Thus the Neolithic monuments of the Molène archipelago stood probably in clusters on small patches of higher ground within a larger low-lying island itself fringed by an extensive inter-tidal zone. The broken and indented coastline of the island meant that the sea was never very far way and this must have been very much a maritime setting. The effect was enhanced by the huge inter-tidal zone, which was transformed from land to sea on a regular cycle twice every day. The operation of the tides may have had a key bearing on the cosmology of these coastal landscapes, enhancing their liminal character and making them especially appropriate as settings for the disposal of the dead.

The mainland passage graves

The study of the Molène archipelago passage graves confirms the special importance of liminal locations. It is limited, however, by the absence of excavational information for any of these sites. For that we must turn to the adjacent mainland.

The published literature (notably L'Helgouach 1965 and Giot 1987) lists some twenty-five burial mounds along the north coast of Brittany containing fifty separate passage graves. Most of them today stand close to the sea edge, though the lower sea level of *c.*5000 BC will have placed them further away. Those which today are on coastal headlands or tidal islands will originally have stood on low hills looking out over a coastal plain. The importance of a relatively prominent location is thus a key element in the siting of the tombs, though exceptions are found in lower-lying situations, as at Roc'h Avel (Giot *et al.* 1979) or indeed at Ezer on the southern coast of Brittany (Giot and Morzadec 1992). In almost all cases the proximity of the sea would have been apparent.

The coastal context of passage-grave locations gains added significance if it is considered alongside the evidence of tomb orientations. The majority of Breton passage graves cluster in the south-east quadrant, with a particular concentration around 135° (L'Helgouach 1965, 76), but the examples from the north coast stand out by reason of their diversity (Figure 6.2). These range from 45° (Guennoc cairn III chamber D) to Brétouaré (262°). Only the north-west quadrant (270° to 360°), and the half quadrant east of North (0° to 45°) appear entirely to be avoided. Within the multi-chambered mounds, the passage graves usually have closely similar orientations. This is perhaps only to be expected, fitting as they do within constrained architectural ensembles. At the same time, different cairns adopt different orientations: of the six multi-chambered cairns for which good information is available, the range of orientations varies between around 50° (Guennoc III) to 220° (Ville-Pichard). This indicates that in each

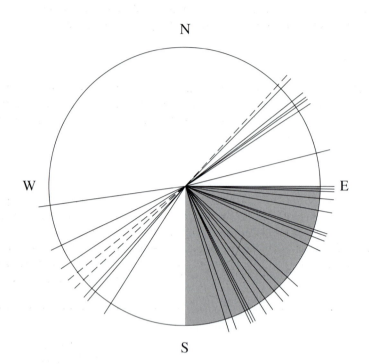

Figure 6.2 Neolithic passage-grave orientations in northern and southern Brittany. Southern passage graves lie between 90° and 180° (shaded area), save for three outliers (indicated by dashed lines). Orientations of northern passage graves (indicated by continuous lines) demonstrate a much broader spread of alignments, with as many as one-third of cases falling outside the south-east quadrant. Data on southern passage graves (*c.*50 sites) provided by L'Helgouach 1965; data on 35 northern passage graves taken from L'Helgouach 1965 with additions from Giot 1987. Note that these incorporate a measure of inaccuracy, and orientations calculated from plans in Giot 1987 give slightly different results from the figures provided in L'Helgouach 1965. Where such differences occur, the present diagram shows the average of the two readings. It should be recognised, however, that the concept of alignment in a passage grave is itself open to question. Few are so regular as to possess a clear major axis, and passages are frequently curved, sometimes to the extent that it is not possible to see directly from the passage entrance into the chamber. In the present study, where orientation has been calculated from published plans, the axis has been determined by drawing a line from the mid-point of the outer passage entrance to the mid-point of the passage/chamber entrance.

location, a particular orientation was preferred, and thus the orientations of the north-coast cairns appear to be related to local topographic concerns.

Three studies

The interplay between coastline, topography and monument design may be illustrated by three detailed studies. The first two of these consider individual multi-chambered cairns at Ville-Pichard and Barnenez; the third, the group of passage graves on Île Guennoc.

Ville-Pichard

The long mound of Ville-Pichard (Côtes-d'Armor) containing three passage graves is located on a low hill immediately overlooking the present shoreline, 20 kilometres east of St-Brieuc (Figure 6.3). Some 800 metres to the west stands the rocky headland of the Pointe de Pléneuf, forming one end of a concave coast which ends 7 kilometres to the east at the Cap d'Erquy. Six thousand years ago the coastline would have been more sharply concave since the tidal island of

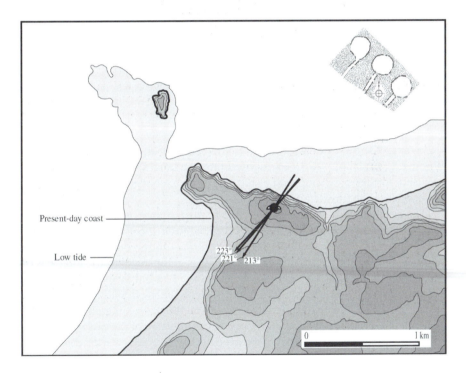

Figure 6.3 Location of Ville-Pichard showng orientation of the passage graves. Contours at 10-metre intervals. Limit of low tides corresponds to approximate location of shoreline *c.*5000 BC. Inset: plan of monument (from Fornier 1887).

Le Verdelet would have been joined to the Pointe de Pléneuf. The former configuration of the coastline between the two headlands is more difficult to establish. The present wide beach is gently shelving and is punctuated by rocky outcrops, and the submarine contours indicate shallow water extending for some distance offshore. There may have been a low-lying coastal plain with hills, or an indented shore with rocky headlands. For most of its length, however, the beach is backed by a steep rise to a line of hills and headlands standing some 60–70 metres above sea level. These are broken in places by streams running down to the sea through narrow, steep-sided valleys, but the line of hills would always have formed a prominent linear feature, a ridge or crest marking the limit between the upland to the south and the coastal lowland beyond.

The cairn of Ville-Pichard stands on the crest of this ridge, at an altitude of 71 metres. The ground falls away on all sides: to the north, a steep slope down to the rocky shoreline and the beach; to the east and west, towards narrow valleys with stream channels; to the south, to a shallow hollow separating the coastal ridge from the hinterland. The cairn is elongated in form, oriented SE–NW, its long axis parallel to the shore. The three chambers are of circular form, with megalithic slabs placed against the lower part of the dry-stone walls. They were covered by corbelled vaults. The 19th-century plan shows single stones at either end of the passage of the central and eastern tombs, suggesting blocking walls similar to that excavated by Giot in the central chamber of Île Carn (Giot 1987). The western chamber lacks these features, and is of slightly different plan with an offset rather than an axial passage. Furthermore the side slabs of the western passage appear not to continue to the outer edge of the cairn, and it is possible that the tombs were built in a series of stages, the short passage of Ville-Pichard west being extended when it was incorporated in a larger cairn, perhaps at the same time that the central and eastern passage graves were built. In the absence of better evidence, however, this must remain uncertain. The plan provided by Fornier does not indicate the outer edge of the tumulus. This is a site which badly demands further excavation, and which may prove to contain other passage graves additional to the three excavated in the 1880s.

The orientations of the three Ville-Pichard passage graves lie towards the south-west (respectively 223°, 213° and 221° (L'Helgouach 1965, 78), and as such are unusual among Breton passage graves as a whole. On the other hand, they are entirely as expected in running approximately at right angles to the long axis of the cairn (Figure 6.3). The cairn itself follows the line and form of the ridge on which it stands. Furthermore, climbing up towards the site from the lower ground to the south, the cairn stands facing the visitor on the skyline. Reaching the cairn (engulfed today in scrub vegetation), one becomes aware of the seascape behind. Thus topography and shoreline appear to be the key determinants: the topography of the ridge, and the panorama of the sea beyond. Viewed from the land, the cairn of Ville-Pichard is effectively backed against the sea, and this would be essentially the same even were there an extensive coastal plain.

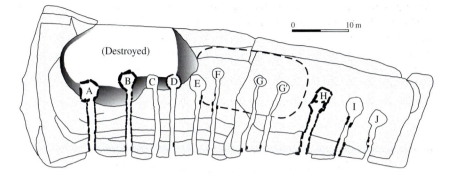

Figure 6.4 The Neolithic cairn of Barnenez; broken line indicates the possible early phase core containing passage graves F, G and G'. (After Giot 1987.)

Barnenez

The long mound of Barnenez (Finistère) with its eleven passage graves is among the best-known Neolithic monuments of Brittany (Figure 6.4). Excavated by Giot between 1955 and 1968, it is the sole survivor of a group of two straddling the headland of Kernéléhen. The greater part of what remained of Barnenez North, containing at least one passage grave (of dry-stone construction with capstone), was finally destroyed by quarrying in 1954. It was only when quarrying switched to the much larger southern mound in 1955 that official action was taken to stop the destruction and allow archaeological excavation (Giot 1987, 20ff).

A series of radiocarbon dates indicate that the cairn was built in the middle centuries of the 5th millennium BC. Giot's excavations led him to conclude that construction had been achieved in two distinct phases: a 'cairn primaire' containing passage graves G to J; and a 'cairn secondaire' with passage graves A to F. Yet it is clear from Giot's own account that the pattern of construction was more complex than this, and in the final report, he suggested that J (situated on the highest point of the site) was the earliest tomb, followed by I (and perhaps H), and by G and G' (Giot 1987, 52). Subsequently, L'Helgouach proposed that passage graves G and G' were the earliest structures, beginning as short passage graves centrally located between the original northern and southern faces of the cairn. Only subsequently were H, I and J added, and it was later again that the passages of all five tombs were lengthened (L'Helgouach in Giot et al., 1998, 243–8).

Rather than a unified product of two or so phases of construction, therefore, it is more realistic to interpret Barnenez South as the end-result of multiple small phases. It is possible that a series of separate small cairns lies beneath the current mound, each with one or more short-passage passage graves. Equally possible is that the monument grew step by step from an original core around chambers F, G and G', to which further chambers were successively added; a sequence like that seen at Île Carn. Whichever reconstruction is correct, the appearance of

Barnenez today is clearly the result of a series of final additions in which short passages were lengthened and outer kerbs straightened and aggrandised. At one point in this sequence, the western end of the mound was faced with a row of large vertical granite slabs to create a particularly fine façade, though afterwards this was hidden behind a low outer kerb of dry-stone construction. Thus we may envisage an early phase with several passage graves, or a small multi-chambered cairn, growing gradually over a period of a few centuries into the enormous cairn whose eleven chambers could be reached by extended, exceptionally long passages. The final emphasis on scale and external appearance may well be totally at odds with the modest size of the original passage graves.

The passage graves of Barnenez South vary in orientation from 139° to 163° (Figure 6.5). There is a very slight change in axis between the eastern (*cairn primaire*: 153° to 163°) and western (*cairn secondaire*: 139° to 152°) sections of the monument. If we assume that passage graves F, G and G' form an early nucleus, these range in orientation from 139° to 154°. There is little to be drawn from these slight differences in orientation, save to remark that, taken together, the passages show a tendency to fan outwards towards the north, as if converging from a point some 100 metres in front of the southern façade. In a general sense, however, the eleven passages share the same orientation to SSE. This indicates that, insofar as orientation may have related to local topography, such a relationship was established as soon as the first of the Barnenez passage graves was laid out. At the same time, it is clear that the extended cairn of the final phase makes a particularly powerful statement, lying across the southern slope of the headland – as if to emphasise in its greater size and scale what the modest original passage graves had already begun to express.

The headland on which the cairn stands is flanked today by marine inlets: on the east, the shallow Anse de Térénez, which is entirely exposed at low tide; on the west, the deeper and wider Rade de Morlaix, which is the ria or estuary of the Morlaix river (Figure 6.5). The promontory itself is steep-sided and is connected to the mainland by a narrow and lower neck of land. Changes in sea level have made substantial changes to this landscape. If we follow Morzadec-Kerfourn in assuming that the highest tides 7,000 years ago were equivalent to the lowest tides of the present day, the Neolithic shoreline at its nearest point would have passed a kilometre north of the Barnenez cairn, approximately twice as far distant as the present coastline. L'Helgouach argues that the Anse de Térénez was certainly dry in the 5th millennium, and that the broad ria of the Morlaix river, 7,000 years ago, was only a small stream, and the steep cliffs which mark its edges today must have been covered by alluvial deposits (L'Helgouach in Giot *et al.* 1998, 243). Whether the shoreline of an estuary such as the Rade de Morlaix is to be read in such a straightforward manner, however, may be called into question. Analogy with the Marais de Dol to the east indicates the role that may have been played by alluviation and sedimentation in the development of the Rade de Morlaix (Lautridou *et al.* 1995).

Whatever the precise configuration of the shoreline, it is reasonable to suppose that the small rocky Île Stérec immediately to the north of the Kernéléhen

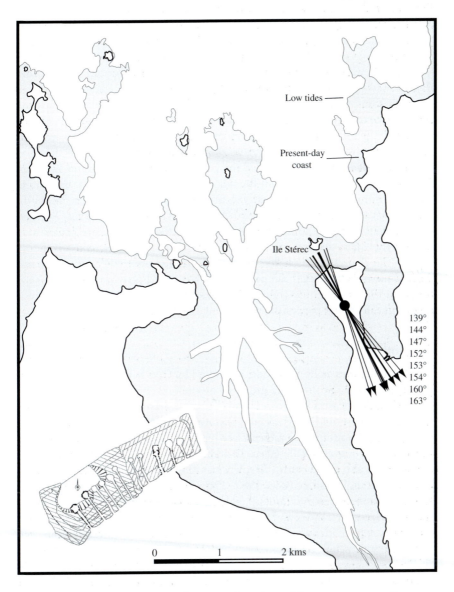

Low tides

Present-day coast

Ile Stérec

139°
144°
147°
152°
153°
154°
160°
163°

0   1   2 kms

Figure 6.5 Location of Barnenez showing orientation of the passage graves. Contours at 10-metre intervals. Limit of low tides corresponds to approximate location of shoreline *c*.5000 BC. Inset: plan of monument (from Giot 1987).

peninsula was joined to it at the time Barnenez was built. Stérec was the source of the granite that was used extensively in the cairn, notably for larger elements such as capstones, and for the series of slabs which formed the impressive western façade.

Whatever the precise nature of the lower-lying land around its foot, the Barnenez headland formed a prominent landscape feature, essentially isolated to either side by steep slopes, and affording only a narrow access across the connecting ridge to the south. The headland may indeed have been considered a place set apart. The passage graves of Barnenez South faced towards this approach, confronting the visitor from the dry land to the south. But they also backed against the open sea. Indeed the passage alignments, between 139° and 162°, fall almost centrally within the window of seascape framed by the Pointe Saint-Samson to the north-east (at 5°/185°) and the Penn ar Waremm promontory to the north-west (at 305°/125°). This is not to suggest that a precise orientation was in question; but it may be argued that the cairn was placed so as to have the open sea behind. Thus in entering the passages, and advancing towards the chambers where the dead were interred, one was moving towards the open sea; even though the position of Barnenez below the summit of the headland meant that only the edges of the seascape vista were visible from the cairn, the greater part of the view being blocked by rising ground.

Île Guennoc

The passage graves of Île Guennoc, excavated by Giot between 1960 and 1972 (Giot *et al.* 1987), are among a group of monuments lying within the angle of sea framed on the west by the peninsula of Sainte-Marguerite and to the south by the north coast of Léon (Finistère), beyond which the Breton shoreline swings sharply south. In addition to those of Île Guennoc, there are well-known passage graves at Roc'h Avel and Île Carn. In addition, Giot cites Devoir to the effect that Île Garo also had a cairn (Devoir 1913 in Giot 1987, 137), and suspects a further cairn on Île Tariec (Giot 1987, 176) (Figure 6.6).

The location of these monuments on headlands and islands is striking. Île Carn, Roc'h Avel, and Îles Tariec and Garo are separated from the mainland at high tide twice a day, while Guennoc is a permanent island. They constitute an archipelago of small islands which includes others between Garo and Carn, notably the Île du Rosservo and Île du Bec, along with smaller rock massifs to the west of Île Carn. The visitor sensitive to landforms cannot fail to be struck by the forms of the outcrops which form the core of several of these islands, and serve to anchor the dunes. The similarity in profile between the cairn of Île Carn and the Karreg Cros outcrop is especially close, suggesting an intention to mimic or reference the local landforms in the shape of the built monument (Scarre 2000).

This stretch of coast has however undergone a considerable transformation over the past 6,000 years. Assuming highest tides *c.*5000 BC reached the same level as present-day lowest tides (Morzadec-Kerfourn in Giot *et al.* 1998, 437) the rise in sea level must have been equivalent to the present-day tidal range of 8.2–8.5 metres

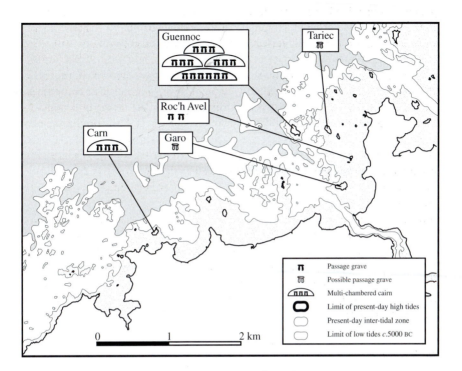

Figure 6.6 Neolithic island monuments of the Île Guennoc area (following Giot 1987). Limit of low tides corresponds to approximate location of shoreline *c.*5000 BC.

(855cm at Aber Benoît, 820cm at Portsall: figures provided by Service Hydrographique et Océanographique de la Marine). With a sea over 8 metres below its present level, Garo, Carn, Roc'h Avel and Tariec would all have been hills or headlands within a low-lying coastal plain. Guennoc alone would have been an island, though Giot argues that this was not in fact the case but that soils and sand-dunes once covered the shallow intervening channel, providing continuous dry-land access from Tariec to Guennoc (Giot 1987, 135–6). Alternatively, Île Guennoc may have been a tidal island, similar to Île Carn or Roc'h Avel today.

The transformation of the landscape by the tides is an impressive feature of this low-lying coast. As Giot remarks: 'On this coast, the landscape takes on an extraordinary character at very low tide with all the rocks that emerge and the vast expanses of rocky shelves which are revealed. It is in these circumstances that the surface area of Guennoc increases by a factor of four' (Giot 1987, 135). The effect would have been equally impressive during the 5th millennium, albeit sea level was lower and the shoreline further out. This much is indicated by the many islets and rocks, some today permanently submerged, extending out to sea. We may conclude that while the shoreline has shifted by up to 1,000 metres, its essential character has not changed. Once again, the coastal setting of the

Neolithic funerary monuments, in a landscape continuously transformed by the changing tides, provides an emphatically liminal setting.

The Carn and Guennoc passage graves open mostly towards the east. The three Carn passages range between 109° (Carn North) and 136° (Carn South). In the four separate cairns of Île Guennoc, a more varied series of alignments is represented. Each of the four presents its own distinctive range of alignments, reflecting the fact that the passages are arranged approximately at right angles to the long axis of the cairns in which they stand (Figure 6.7). If the predominantly eastward focus of the Breton passage graves indicates an interest in the sunrise, then the orientation of five of the Guennoc III passage graves around 50° corresponds closely with the northernmost sunrise position at this latitude

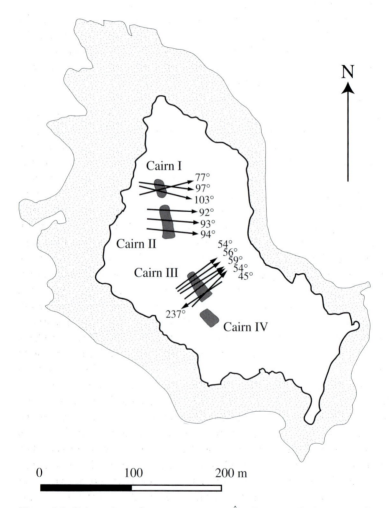

Figure 6.7 Orientation of passage graves on Île Guennoc (information from Giot 1987).

(midsummer sunrise at 50° 50'). Midwinter sunset falls at 230°, which would correspond approximately to the orientation of passage grave E (237°) in the same cairn. We cannot rule out the possibility that these directions were significant to the builders of Guennoc III.

More plausible, however, is an interpretation which links the precise orientation of the passages with the immediate topographic setting of the cairn. L'Helgouach attributed this unusual orientation of the Guennoc III passage graves to the impact of the topography of the island on the alignment of the cairn (L'Helgouach 1965, 79). All four Guennoc cairns lie along a low central ridge which begins at the north on an approximately north–south alignment, then swings steadily towards the east as one proceeds southwards across the island. It is the practice of following this ridge, and spacing the cairns in a certain way – cairns I and II adjacent to each other to the north of the island; cairns III and IV to the south; one is left to wonder whether an additional cairn once stood in the suitably sized gap between II and III – that has dictated the pattern of orientations represented in these cairns. It is possible that island topography and solar directions were jointly responsible for the sometimes aberrant alignment of the Guennoc passage graves.

The Guennoc cairns are all backed against the sea, in exactly the manner seen at Ville-Pichard and Barnenez. The passage graves of cairn III, with the most northerly orientation, align in the opposite direction with the northern limit of the mainland at Île Carn. The other Guennoc cairns are backed by vistas of the open sea to the north of this promontory. Thus here again, a concern with seascape may have been incorporated in the location and design of these tombs. Open-sea vistas also lie behind the passage graves of Île Carn and Roc'h Avel.

The relationship between the Guennoc cairns and their coastal setting is represented also in the use of materials. Giot observed how the cairn-builders obtained most of their materials from rocky outcrops projecting above the surface of the island, and from the higher parts of the cliffs where the migmatic granite was generally already broken into small slabs. In a recent study, Gouletquer has identified two specific quarry-locations on the foreshore, where large granite blocks were extracted from the coastal cliffs and hauled up onto the island, in one case by means of an artificial ramp (Gouletquer 2000). This use of locally available materials is only to be expected, and will have tended to blend the cairns with their immediate surroundings. But for the visible façades of the cairns, Giot notes the specific use of beach pebbles: for the infilling and the cairn façades, they also used pebbles, more or less rounded, which they collected from the foreshore and which were mostly redeposited material from former beaches or coastal cordons (Giot 1987, 136). This use of shoreline materials extends in the case of Guennoc III C to the deposit in which the human remains were placed. The paved floor of the chamber was covered by a sandy deposit some 20 centimetres thick consisting of *arène dioritique* with pockets of beach sand and pebbles. This extended into the passage, where the 'ghosts' of skeletal remains (notably the proximal end of a left femur) were detected in the *arène dioritique*, indicating that the latter was an intentional Neolithic deposit (Figure 6.8). As for the origin of

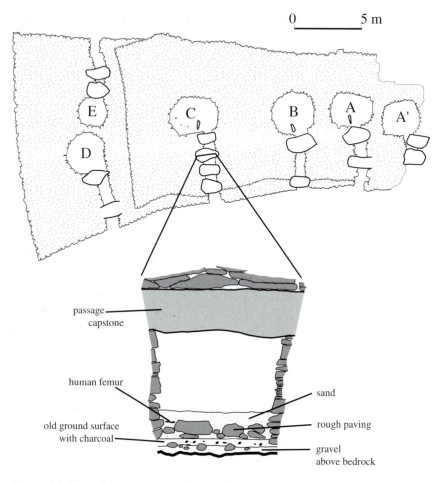

0 _____ 5 m

E
D
C
B
A
A'

passage — capstone

human femur

old ground surface with charcoal —

sand

rough paving

gravel
above bedrock

Figure 6.8 Plan of Guennoc mound III and section across passage of passage grave C
indicating deposit of beach sand. (After Giot 1987.)

this material, several pockets of beach sand were found mixed with the dioritic
sand showing that the latter was taken from weathered rocks accessible at the base
of the cliff on the south-west of the island (Giot 1987, 162). Giot argues that it
was either something in which to bury the bodies, or acted as a 'deodorant' (Giot
1987, 164). The use of sand, including beach sand, as a special burial layer may
perhaps be considered another instance of the link between death and the
shoreline: monuments built of beach pebbles, bodies buried in sand from the cliff
base, chambers located hard up against the liminal inter-tidal zone.

Conclusion

These studies suggest that a number of different factors may have influenced or dictated the setting and orientation of the North Breton passage graves. First, we have the immediate topographic setting: on headland or tidal island, fixed with regard to local terrain (in the case of Guennoc, following the curving ridge along the centre of the island). In second place, we have the general preference for the passages to open to the east, perhaps in response to beliefs associated with the symbolic attraction of sunrise: though Guennoc III is at the extreme northern limit of annual sunrise positions, while the Barnenez passages face south rather than east, and Ville-Pichard disregards this preference in adopting a south-westerly orientation. Third, and finally, we have the relationship to the sea, marked both by the liminal, sea-edge positions chosen for these tombs, and the apparent preference for a marine backdrop in the alignment of the cairns: a relationship which might explain the south-westerly orientation of the Ville-Pichard passages, is especially persuasive in the Barnenez case, and would also apply at Guennoc and Carn, though at these latter sites it must be borne in mind that any eastward-facing structure automatically will have the sea behind.

In terms of orientation, as we have seen, the passage graves of northern Brittany open mainly towards the east. This preference may be paralleled in many other regions of Atlantic Europe and could be connected with ideas of solar symbolism and rebirth. In southern Britain, unchambered long mounds and Severn–Cotswold tombs generally face east (Ashbee 1970, 28–30; Daniel 1950, 80). It is well known that the passage grave of Newgrange in Ireland faces towards the midwinter sunrise, at which time of year a shaft of light penetrates down the passage from the roof box (O'Kelly 1982; Patrick 1974). A similar phenomenon has been claimed for Maeshowe (Mackie 1997). The Camster cairns of north-east Scotland also face east. But there are many exceptions to this eastward-facing rule. The Belas Knap Severn–Cotswold tomb faces NNE (19°: Burl 1981). On Scilly, the entrance-graves show an easterly preference but spread all the way round the compass (Ashbee 1974). The same is true for tombs on Arran (Burl 1981). The passage graves of the Carrowkeel cemetery in western Ireland face north-north-west (possibly pointing towards Maeve's Cairn on Knocknarea: Patrick 1975; Burl 1981; Bergh, this volume, ch. 9); while the Clava cairns face almost universally SSW (Burl 1981). The wedge graves of western Ireland also face mainly westwards (De Valera and O'Nualláin 1961).

The orientational data from the Breton passage graves are indeed difficult to interpret with confidence. Both Burl (1981) and Ruggles (1999) place much emphasis on the patterning of alignments, and Burl provides a very clear example in his discussion of Neolithic chambered tombs on the island of Arran. The alignment of one of these tombs, Carn Ban, agrees closely with the direction of midsummer sunrise. Are we then justified in believing that this was a consideration on the part of the builders of the tomb? As Burl proceeds to indicate, such a conclusion would be premature given that none of the other nineteen chambered tombs on Arran faces in this direction. Indeed, they face almost every direction of the compass. From such cases comes the argument that alignments must only be taken as well founded if they are repeated across a whole category of sites: 'only the detailed study of a whole group would show whether such orientations were accidental or intended' (Burl 1981, 256).

This may, methodologically, appear the only safe way to proceed. Yet we cannot assume that every tomb in a particular category or in a particular area was positioned in accordance with the same combination of factors. There is no reason why sites and their symbolisms – especially in their landscape settings – might not have been unique. The case for the midsummer sunrise orientation at Stonehenge surely does not depend crucially on its replication at other sites. Thus, while the passage graves of northern Brittany display the predominantly eastern orientation of all Breton passage graves, it is possible at a more detailed level to argue that variations within the easterly orientation, or deviations from it, can be understood in the context of the landscape settings of individual monuments and, more particularly, in their relationship to the shoreline.

The transformative power of the land–sea boundary is an important theme in the cosmology of north-west coast peoples of North America, such as the Nootka and Kwakiutl (Drucker 1951; Walens 1981). These peoples commonly held the belief that the underwater world ran parallel in some way to the terrestrial world, with wolves and killer-whales, for example, being the terrestrial and marine manifestations of the same beings. Among the Saami peoples of northern Europe, the cosmos was conceived as divided into sky, earth and underworld, these three divisions corresponding to air, land and water, or forest, tundra and sea. The underworld was associated with the dead and with fish, and places where rivers meet the sea were among the locations that provided access to the underworld. Islands or rapids were especially significant, and were visited by shamans (Bradley 2000, 12).

None of these schemes can be taken to indicate in detail the systems of cosmology and belief that prevailed among the Middle Holocene communities of Atlantic Europe. The similarity in beliefs about the shoreline, shared between traditional peoples of both northern Europe and North America, do however support the argument that the shoreline may have been imbued with particular significance. Deposition of human remains in the earth may have been one way of returning them to the realm of the ancestors; if the sea itself was regarded as the world of the dead, then burial close to the sea edge will have been a symbolic practice of particular power. Yet in seeking symbolic associations we should not forget the importance of the shoreline as a sensory experience, a world of sound and movement which sets it apart from the rest of the landscape. This will have further enhanced the significance of this liminal zone, a liminality which would be all the more pronounced as the twice-daily tidal regime successively exposed and engulfed vast areas of lowland. There can hardly have been a more evocative physical metaphor for the transition between life and death.

References

Ashbee, P., 1970. *The Earthen Long Barrow in Britain*. London: Dent.

Ashbee, P., 1974. *Ancient Scilly from the First Farmers to the Early Christians: An Introduction and Survey*. Newton Abbot: David & Charles.

Bradley, R., 2000. *An Archaeology of Natural Places*. London: Routledge.

Burl, A., 1981. 'By the light of the cinerary moon': chambered tombs and the astronomy of death, in *Astronomy and Society in Britain during the period 4000–1500 B.C.* (ed. C.L.N. Ruggles and A.W.R. Whittle). Oxford: British Archaeological Reports (British Series 88), 243–74.

Childe, V.G., 1957. *The Dawn of European Civilization*. 6th edn. London: Routledge & Kegan Paul.

Clark, J.G.D., 1977. The economic context of dolmens and passage-graves in Sweden, in V. Markotic (ed.), *Ancient Europe and the Mediterranean*. Warminster: Aris & Phillips, 35–49.

Daniel, G., 1950. *Prehistoric Chamber Tombs of England and Wales*. Cambridge: Cambridge University Press.

Davidson, J.L., and Henshall, A.S., 1989. *The Chambered Cairns of Orkney*. Edinburgh: Edinburgh University Press.

De Valera, R., and O'Nualláin, S.P., 1961. *Survey of the Megalithic Tombs of Ireland, I: County Clare*. Dublin: Stationery Office.

Drucker, P., 1951. *The Northern and Central Nootkan Tribes. Smithsonian Institution Bureau of American Ethnology Bulletin 144*. Washington: US Government Printing Office.

Du Châtellier, P., 1902. Les monuments mégalithiques des îles du Finistère de Béniguet à Ouessant. *Bulletin Archéologique du Comité des Travaux Historiques et Scientifiques* (1902), 202–13.

Forde, C.D., 1930. Early cultures of Atlantic Europe. *American Anthropologist* 32, 19–100.

Fornier, M., 1887. Enceintes gauloises de la Ville-Pichard en Pléneuf. *Bulletins et Mémoires de la Société d'Emulation des Côtes-du-Nord* 25, 250–60.

Fraser, D., 1983. *Land and Society in Neolithic Orkney*. Oxford: British Archaeological Reports.

Giot, P.-R., 1987. *Barnenez, Carn, Guennoc*. Rennes: Travaux du Laboratoire d'Anthropologie, Préhistoire, Protohistoire et Quaternaire Armoricains.

Giot, P.-R., and Morzadec, H., 1992. Des dolmens à couloir au péril des mers actuelles. *Revue Archéologique de l'Ouest* 9, 57–66.

Giot, P.-R., Hallegouet, B., and Monnier, J.-L., 1979. Le cairn au péril de la mer de l'îlot de Roc'h Avel en Landéda (Finistère). *Bulletin de la Société Archéologique du Finistère* 57, 23–31.

Giot, P.-R., Monnier, J.-L., and L'Helgouach, J., 1998. *Préhistoire de la Bretagne*. 2nd edn. Rennes: Ouest-France.

Gouletquer, P., 2000. Fins de carrières à l'île Guennoc (Landéda, Finistère) in S. Cassen, C. Boujot and J. Vaquero, *Eléments d'architecture. Exploration d'un tertre funéraire à Lannec er Gadouer (Erdeven, Morbihan). Constructions et reconstructions dans le Néolithique morbihannais. Propositions pour une lecture symbolique*. Chauvigny: Association des Publications Chauvinoises, 555–61.

Hughes, I., 1988. Megaliths: space, time and the landscape – a view from the Clyde. *Scottish Archaeological Review* 5, 41–56.

Kaelas, L., 1990. Which was the economic basis of the megalith builders in Brittany? in *La Bretagne et l'Europe Préhistoriques (Revue Archéologique de l'Ouest, Supplément No. 2)*, 97–100.

L'Helgouach, J., 1965. *Les Sépultures Mégalithiques en Armorique*. Rennes: Travaux du Laboratoire d'Anthropologie Préhistorique de la Faculté des Sciences.

Lautridou, J.-P., Clet-Pellerin, M., and Morzadec-Kerfourn, M.-T., 1995. Evolution de la baie du Mont-Saint-Michel: Pléistocène et Holocène, in L. Langouet and M.T. Morzadec-Kerfourn (eds), *Baie du Mont-Saint-Michel et Marais de Dol. Milieux naturels et peuplements dans le passé*. Saint-Malo: Centre Régional d'Archéologie d'Alet, 27–31.

Lubell, D., Jackes, M., Schwarcz, H., Knyf, M. and Meiklejohn, C., 1994. The Mesolithic–Neolithic transition in Portugal: isotopic and dental evidence of diet. *Journal of Archaeological Science* 21, 201–16.

Mackie, E.W., 1997. Maeshowe and the winter solstice: ceremonial aspects of the Orkney Grooved Ware culture. *Antiquity* 71, 338–59.

Marguerie, D., 1992. *Evolution de la végétation sous l'impact humain en Armorique du Néolithique aux périodes historiques*. Rennes: Travaux du Laboratoire d'Anthropologie, Préhistoire, Protohistoire et Quaternaire Armoricains.

O'Kelly, M.J., 1982. *Newgrange: Archaeology, Art and Legend*. London: Thames & Hudson.

Patrick, J.D., 1974. Midwinter sunrise at Newgrange. *Nature* 249, 517–19.

Patrick, J.D., 1975. Megalithic exegesis: a comment. *Irish Archaeological Research Forum* 2, 9–14.

Renfrew, C., 1973. *Before Civilization*. London: Cape.

Richards, M.P. and Hedges, R.E.M., 1999a. Stable isotope evidence for similarities in the types of marine foods used by Late Mesolithic humans at sites along the Atlantic coast of Europe. *Journal of Archaeological Science* 26, 717–22.

Richards, M.P. and Hedges, R.E.M., 1999b. A Neolithic revolution? New evidence of diet in the British Neolithic. *Antiquity* 73, 891–7.

Ruggles, C., 1999. *Astronomy in Prehistoric Britain and Ireland*. New Haven and London: Yale University Press.

Scarre, C., 2000. Forms and landforms: the design and setting of Neolithic monuments in western France, in *Neolithic Orkney in its European Context* (ed. A. Ritchie). Cambridge: McDonald Institute for Archaeological Research, 309–20.

Scarre, C., 2002. A pattern of islands: the Neolithic monuments of north-west Brittany. *Journal of European Archaeology* 5.

Suttles, W. (ed.), 1990. *Handbook of North American Indians, 7: Northwest Coast* Washington: Smithsonian Institution.

Tauber, H., 1981. 13C evidence for dietary habits of prehistoric man in Denmark. *Nature* 292, 332–3.

Walens, S., 1981. *Feasting with Cannibals. An Essay on Kwakiutl Cosmology*. Princeton, NJ: Princeton University Press.

Part III

Britain and Ireland

Introduction

The maritime character of Atlantic Europe gains increased prominence in the case of Britain and Ireland. These are not only islands themselves but Britain in particular is fringed by smaller islands, notably to the north and north-west, which contain some of the best-known Neolithic monuments. The postglacial colonisation of these island groups demonstrates the importance of maritime contact in the Early Holocene, and polished stone axe distributions reveal particularly close Neolithic contacts across the Irish Sea, with numerous British finds of Irish porcellanite axes balanced by Great Langdale axes in Ireland (Cooney 2000, 204). Cultural contacts beyond artefact exchange are illustrated by the Irish-style passage-grave art at Bryn Celli Ddu and Barclodiad y Gawres on Anglesey, at Calderstones near Liverpool, and at Pierowall Quarry on Orkney (Shee Twohig 1981). Connections across the Channel with northern France, on the other hand, appear less pronounced. Only a handful of dolerite axes from Plussulien in Brittany have been found in southern Britain, in contrast to the thousands of examples in north-west France. Parallels between the megalithic art of Ireland and Brittany have been proposed but are difficult to evaluate (Le Roux 1992; O'Sullivan 1997). The apparently late colonisation of the Isles of Scilly may also suggest that direct sailing across the western end of the Channel was too hazardous with the seacraft available to have been regularly undertaken.

It is western Ireland and highland Britain, with their igneous geology and coastal cliffs and promontories, that in landscape terms have most in common with Brittany and western Iberia. These regions have standing stones, stone settings and passage graves reminiscent of those of Atlantic France and Iberia, albeit with specific regional variations. In lowland Britain, related categories of Neolithic monument (including cursuses, long mounds and henges) form part of the same broad tradition but differ signficantly both in landscape setting and local materials. Such differences went far beyond the materials of construction, and must also imply divergent attitudes to openness and topography (Bradley 1998a).

The papers in this section focus on the highland zone of Britain and western Ireland, where the dramatic nature of landscape makes resonance between the cultural and the natural particularly clear. Vicki Cummings observes that in south-west Wales, many Early Neolithic monuments appear to have been deliberately placed so that distinctive natural rock outcrops are visible on the horizon. Studies in the south-western peninsula of Devon and Cornwall have drawn similar conclusions, highlighting the close relationship of Neolithic chambered tombs to natural outcrops, and suggesting that to Neolithic communities, natural tors on Dartmoor and other uplands may have been confused with ruined portal dolmens (Tilley 1996; Bradley 1998b). In Wales, the location and nature of the monuments changed during the course of the Neolithic, suggesting significant shifts in the understanding of and engagement with the landscape. Change is also the key theme of the second paper in this section, where Richard Bradley shows how both the Clava cairns at Balnuaran of Clava and the recumbent stone circle of Tomnaverie underwent modification as part of the ritual practices, involving treatment of the dead, that were enacted at them. These practices connected the monuments both to the landscape and to the sky, and regular cycles of the sun and moon may have provided the prompts which set the time-frame of these actions.

The second pair of papers consider landscape and monuments in north-west and south-west Ireland respectively. The isolated mountain of Knocknarea in Co. Sligo must by its unusual form and striking setting, backed against the Atlantic, have inspired mythical understandings among the very earliest settlers in the region. During the Neolithic period, as Stefan Bergh shows, it was the focus for a succession of cultural constructions, including notably the massive Maeve's Cairn on the summit, and the systems of banks defining the ritual area. Maeve herself was a figure of early Irish legend, and the name illustrates how monuments were reinterpreted as traditions changed and new understandings emerged. This temporality is the subject of O'Brien's study of south-west Ireland, where the sequence of monuments suggests how, in a process of continuity and change, a core religious belief associated with Neolithic portal cairns and wedge tombs may have endured to be reinterpreted by later generations in the Bronze and Iron Ages. Monuments are about memory, and their visibility and prominence may well have served to anchor beliefs across both space and time.

References

Bradley, R., 1998a. *The Significance of Monuments. On the Shaping of Experience in Neolithic and Bronze Age Europe.* London: Routledge.

Bradley, R., 1998b. Ruined buildings, ruined stones: enclosures, tombs and natural places in the Neolithic of south-west England. *World Archaeology* 30, 13–22.

Cooney, G., 2000. *Landscapes of Neolithic Ireland.* London: Routledge.

Le Roux, C.-T., 1992. The art of Gavrinis presented in its Armorican context and in comparison with Ireland. *Journal of the Royal Society of Antiquaries of Ireland* 122, 79–108.

O'Sullivan, M., 1997. Megalithic art in Ireland and Brittany: divergence or convergence?, in *Art et Symboles du Mégalithisme Européen. Actes du 2ème Colloque International sur l'Art Mégalithique* (ed. J. L'Helgouach, C.-T. Le Roux and J. Lecornec). Revue Archéologique de l'Ouest, Supplément 8, 81–96.

Shee Twohig, E., 1981. *The Megalithic Art of Western Europe*. Oxford: Clarendon Press.

Tilley, C., 1996. The power of rocks: topography and monument construction on Bodmin Moor. *World Archaeology* 28, 161–76.

Studying Materiality can reveal change

7 All cultural things

Actual and conceptual monuments in the Neolithic of western Britain

Vicki Cummings

In Britain, stone-built monuments were first constructed in the landscape during the Early Neolithic. These monuments have frequently been understood as representing the first stages of the domestication of the natural world. In recent years, however, the conceptual dichotomy between nature and culture has increasingly been called into question as it seems likely that Neolithic people may not have understood the environment in the same way that we do. They are likely to have had a quite different conception of what we call the natural world. Furthermore, it can be argued that the conceptual origins of monumentality may lie within the Mesolithic, a possibility which has implications for the ways in which we interpret the earliest monuments. Using examples primarily from south-west Wales, and also south-west Scotland, I will discuss how the first monuments were carefully fitted into a landscape already filled with potent and symbolic places. I will suggest that it was the presence of monuments in the landscape which began to transform peoples' understanding of the world. We might understand this as the beginnings of the dualism between nature and culture. In prehistory, however, it might have been understood as part of a broader process of negotiation between people and ancestral places.

The construction of monuments in Early Neolithic Britain has been understood as a fundamental shift in the way people understood their place in the world. For many years the beginnings of monument construction were equated with the onset of agriculture (e.g. Clark 1966; Daniel 1962; Piggott 1954; Sherratt 1990; 1995). It now seems clear, however, that monuments may not be a consequence of economic change (Bradley 1993, 9–18; Thomas 1999, 16; Tilley 1994; 1996; Whittle 1996). Hodder, for example, conceptualised the beginning of the Neolithic as the 'domestication of society' (Hodder 1990, 30). This view of the Neolithic was directly concerned with oppositions between wild and domestic and culture and nature. The transformation of the wild into the cultural was seen to manifest itself in different ways throughout Europe; in Britain, monuments expressed the domestication of the wild, society and nature (Hodder 1990, 154). More recently, this approach has been criticised as it is evident that the dichotomy of culture and nature is a modern conception of the world (Bender 2000, 25; Sharples 2000, 108; Tilley *et al.* 2000). Prior to the advent of geology as an academic discipline, the difference between natural and constructed features may have been rather ambiguous (Bradley 2000, 34). Archaeologists are trained to look at the world in a certain way and to distinguish between natural rock outcrops and artificial architecture, but this may not always have been the case. This ambiguity has been discussed by Richard Bradley (1998a) in relation to the portal dolmens of south-west England. Bradley suggests that these monuments were not simply imitating local tors, since portal dolmens occur in other parts of the landscape where such features are absent. They may, however, reflect an understanding of natural formations which was rather different to our own. He argues that people may have thought that these places were built, and the construction of Neolithic tombs was, in many respects, the continuation or recreation of an ancestral tradition (Bradley 1998a, 20).

It is against this background that I have attempted to address three issues in my own research. First, what was the relationship between monuments and natural features, in particular rocky outcrops? Second, did natural topographic features influence the appearance of monuments? And third, did the construction of monuments entail a new understanding of the world, perhaps related to distinctions between culture and nature?

The Early Neolithic

In south-west Wales the earliest stone-built monuments were structures with large raised capstones supported by stout uprights (Figure 7.1). Three of these sites have been excavated and pottery and radiocarbon dates support an Early Neolithic date (Grimes 1960; Lynch 1969; 1975; Rees 1992). It has been suggested that these sites were part of the broader Irish Sea portal-dolmen tradition which was established at an early date in south-west Wales (Lynch 1976, 65). These Early Neolithic monuments are large and impressive structures and they seem to have been located in the landscape in relation to a wide range of quite distinctive natural places. The landscape settings of these monuments have already been discussed by Tilley (1994) and re-examined by myself as part of a broader study (Cummings 2001).

At the outset, it is clear that monuments were carefully positioned in the landscape in relation to certain features. Many of the early sites seem to have been carefully positioned so as to have views of specific mountains (cf. Bergh this volume, ch. 9), which are repeatedly referenced from several monuments. Tilley (1994, 105) has already discussed the importance of Carn Ingli which is visible from sites like Llech y Dribedd and Pentre Ifan (Figure 7.1). Tilley (1994, 105) has even suggested that the slope of the capstone at sites such as Pentre Ifan may reflect the shape of the mountain (although see Fleming 1999, 121 for a critique). Carn Ingli is certainly one of the most spectacular landforms in the area and may have had an enclosure on its summit (Drewett 1987). The distinctive outcrops of Carn Meini in the Preseli Mountains also seem to have been important in the Early Neolithic. This hill was one of the local sources of Group VIII stone axes

Figure 7.1 Pentre Ifan with Carn Ingli visible in the distance.

(David and Williams 1995, 435). Several monuments seem to have carefully contrived views of this mountain, such as Carreg Samson located over twenty-two kilometres away. At Carreg Samson, the view to the west looks towards a distinctive outcrop one kilometre away, with Carn Meini visible on the horizon directly beyond the outcrop.

Other Early Neolithic sites are located to have clear views of the sea and this may relate to the symbolic importance of water (Richards 1996) or the coast more generally (Scarre this volume, ch. 6). A view of the sea may also be concerned with origins, perhaps ultimately referencing the means by which the new ideas and material culture of the Neolithic arrived (Case 1969). Several early sites seem to have been carefully positioned so that the sea is visible. For example, at the site of White Horse only a very small portion of the sea is visible. Had the site been positioned a few metres downslope the view of the sea would have been totally obscured. Likewise, if the site had been positioned any further up the hill on which it stands, the outcrop located a few hundred metres away would not have been skylined (see below). Other Early Neolithic sites seem to have been located near to watercourses, in particular at points of transition. Tilley (1994, 109) has already noted that Gwal y Filiast is located within the sound of waterfalls on the River Taf. The monument of Mountain is positioned at the source of the Eastern Cleddau river, while Colston is set at the point where the Afon Anghof and the Afon Glan-Rhyd meet to form the main Western Cleddau watercourse (Figure 7.2). Carreg Coetan is located just above the point where the Afon Nyfer meets the sea.

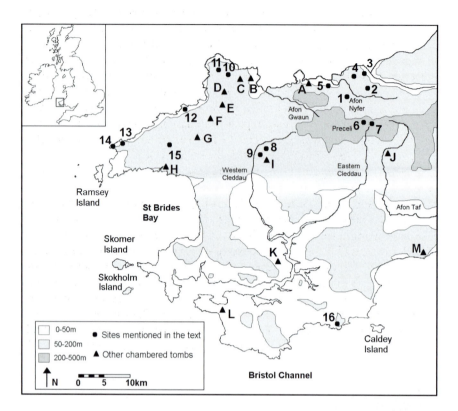

Figure 7.2 South-west Wales. Numbered sites are mentioned in the text. 1. Pentre Ifan. 2. Trefael. 3. Llech y Dribedd. 4. Trellyffaint. 5. Carreg Coetan. 6. Carn Meini. 7. Mountain. 8. Colston. 9. Garn Turne. 10. Carn Wnda. 11. Garn Gilfach. 12. Carreg Samson. 13. Carn Llidi. 14. Coetan Arthur. 15. White Horse. 16. King's Quoit. Lettered sites are other chambered tombs. A. Cerrig y Gof. B. Garn Wen. C. Parc y Cromlech. D. Ffynnon Druidion. E. Ffyst Samson. F. Trewalter Llywd. G. Treffynnon. H. St Elvies. I. Parc y Llyn. J. Gwal y Filiast. K. Hanging Stone. L. Devil's Quoit. M. Morfa Bycham

Many of the early sites are also located in relation to outcrops. This relationship has already been discussed by Tilley who notes that many monuments were positioned near to outcrops which he describes as 'natural or non-cultural megaliths' (1994, 99). For example, the site of Pentre Ifan seems to have been carefully positioned so that four prominent outcrops are visible on the skyline (Tilley 1994, fig. 3.18). Many Early Neolithic monuments in south-west Wales appear to have been deliberately placed so that distinctive outcrops are visible on the horizon (Cummings 2001). I have already discussed how White Horse was located to have a view of the sea in one direction and an outcrop visible on the horizon in the other direction. A similar phenomenon occurs elsewhere. The

Great Treffgarne rocks are one of the most impressive inland outcrops and the site of Garn Turne seems to have been positioned in the landscape in relation to them. As one approaches the façade and chamber at Garn Turne, the Great Treffgarne rocks are visible on the skyline (Figure 7.3). This is a pattern repeated at many sites. It appears, then, that many Early Neolithic monuments in south-west Wales were carefully positioned in relation to prominent outcrops. It seems, however, to have been considered inappropriate to build monuments right up against these outcrops. This may explain why no Early Neolithic sites are built next to outcrops, in direct contrast to the later sites (see below), even though it may have been more efficient to exploit the stones in this way.

So, how might the people who built and used these monuments have understood these outcrops? It is possible that people thought that rocks like these were significant and symbolic (Kahn 1990; Taçon 1991). Certainly, the Early Neolithic chambered tombs in south-west Wales seem to have been very carefully positioned in the landscape so that the outcrops were skylined. In addition, many of the Early Neolithic monuments bear a physical resemblance to these outcrops although they are not direct replicas of them (Figure 7.4). Thus although the monuments appear to share some characteristics with natural forms found in the surrounding area, they predominantly represent part of a broader architectural tradition which can be found along the Irish Sea zone (Lynch 1969). Indeed, it has already been suggested that the monuments in south-west Wales have their origins in the portal-dolmen tradition in Ireland (Lynch 1976). The Early

Figure 7.3 The façade and chamber at Garn Turne with the Great Treffgarne rocks visible on the horizon. The insert is a close-up of the Great Treffgarne rocks.

Figure 7.4 A natural rock formation on the summit of Carn Meini, Preseli.

Neolithic sites seem therefore to have been built as part of a broader mode of monument construction while taking into account the form of local geological features.

Although the built architecture of the region bears a resemblance to local geological formations, I would like to reiterate that this is a distinction that relates to our modern conception of the world. If people in the Neolithic did not recognise natural outcrops as geological features, it is possible that they understood them as ancient buildings, perhaps built by supernatural or ancestral forces (Bradley 1998a, 20). This would have implications for the ways in which we understand the origins of monumentality in this region. It could be suggested that people in the Mesolithic thought these outcrops were constructed. In most readings of the Mesolithic, the act of building monuments and thereby permanently altering the landscape was unthinkable and inconceivable (Bradley 1998b, 34). This is because it is envisaged that Mesolithic people had a very close relationship with the natural world (Ingold 1994; 1996; Kent 1989). Hunter-gatherers are seen to exist as part of nature in what has been described as a 'cosmic economy of sharing' (Bird-David 1988). There is evidence from the Mesolithic, however, which casts doubt on this interpretation. First, people in the Mesolithic were capable of creating large, permanent places in the landscape. For example, on the small island of Oronsay in the Inner Hebrides, enormous shell middens were created which were quite monumental in size (Mellars 1987). Elsewhere, sites such as Portland (Palmer 1990) and Eskmeals (Bonsall *et al.* 1990) suggest that sizeable buildings were constructed. There is also evidence for Mesolithic people transforming the landscape by burning or woodland management (Edwards 1990). At the future site of Stonehenge a series of enormous timbers were set upright in the ground (Cleal *et al.* 1995). Ethnography also supports the suggestion that people understood the landscape as filled with mythical beings and symbolic places (Kahn 1990; Tilley 1994; Carmichael *et al.* 1994).

It seems plausible, then, that people in the Mesolithic may also have thought features such as outcrops were constructed. If people believed that the landscape was already filled with symbolic and constructed places, to begin building monuments may not have taken a great conceptual leap. Thus the change that occurs in the Early Neolithic need not have entailed a sudden conceptual division of culture and nature. Instead, people were now prepared to build their own monuments in the landscape, similar but not identical to those which already existed. This does represent an important shift in the way people understood the world, representing 'new ways of initiating memorability' (Thomas 2000, 79). It may also be part of a broader acculturation of the mythical past by the living population. If this were the case, however, instead of the first monuments being the result of a change in world-view, they may actually have perpetuated a shift in the way that people understood their place in the world (Bradley 1993, ch. 1; Barrett 1994, 28). I would like to suggest that monuments can be seen as one of the early stages in a longer process of the acculturation of a mythical past by the living. Over time, the relationship between people and their ancestral past seems to have been transformed, so that in the later Neolithic, people began to build monuments in quite different parts of the landscape.

The later Neolithic

As increasing numbers of monuments were constructed in the landscape, people may have begun to understand their world rather differently. In south-west Wales, the form and setting of the later 'earth-fast' Neolithic monuments are rather different from the earlier sites and seem to suggest that people had begun to engage more directly with natural places. Again, however, this need not indicate that they conceptualised these places as natural. The earth-fast sites are quite small and usually hidden away in the landscape. These monuments have modest capstones which are raised up at one end to create a small internal space (Figure 7.5). The interiors created are confined and would only permit the deposition of small quantities of material culture, but at present there is little artefactual evidence which supports a later Neolithic date for these sites. Only Carn Wnda has been excavated, and that in the 19th century (Barker 1992, 32); excavations produced an urn and burnt bones (Fenton 1848). Rather, it is the size and landscape setting of these monuments which suggests that they are of later Neolithic date. The earth-fast sites are positioned right up against rock formations which seem to be an integral part of these monuments. This is in complete contrast to the earlier sites, as we have seen above. Furthermore, the earth-fast sites are considerably smaller than the earlier sites, a phenomenon which is paralleled elsewhere in the country (for example in south-west Scotland – see below). Morphologically, the earth-fast sites are quite different to the monuments of portal-dolmen type, with no direct parallels in the Irish Sea zone, suggesting an indigenous development after the initial introduction of monuments from elsewhere.

One of the most distinguishing features of these later monuments is that they more closely resemble natural places, and can even incorporate natural features

Figure 7.5 The site of Carn Wnda, with prominent rocky outcrops directly behind the chamber.

Figure 7.6 The King's Quoit chamber, with natural upright slabs to the left which appear to be part of the monument itself.

in their structures. For this reason it may be suggested that these sites had a rather ambiguous status, one which has extended into recent times. The King's Quoit, for example, is placed against a series of large natural slabs that appear to be part of the monument (Figure 7.6). Antiquaries were unsure whether 'this particular object were a cromlech at all, and not simply an accidental formation' (Anon.

1851 quoted in Barker 1992, 38). At Garn Gilfach, the capstone is virtually indistinguishable from the surrounding outcrops and this led to the suggestion that the entire hillside was covered with 'many cromlechs' (Fenton 1810, 22). Likewise, Carn Wnda (Figure 7.5) is positioned right up against rocks and is surrounded by formations which resemble monuments. Indeed, all of the later Neolithic monuments in south–west Wales are located in areas that are covered with rocky outcrops.

These monuments also seem to be carefully positioned in the landscape so that certain visual effects are possible. The distinctive propped capstone of Coetan Arthur can clearly be seen when approached from inland, but from the north and the east the site blends in with the other rocks in the vicinity (Figure 7.7). Just one kilometre to the east, the double-chambered tomb of Carn Llidi is so inconspicuous that it appears to be part of the outcrop it stands against, or even just a natural boulder. This effect is perhaps most pronounced at Carn Wnda where the impressive lifted capstone appears to be a natural slab when approached from behind.

The ambiguity between artificial and natural is further exemplified in south–west Wales at the site of Trefael (Figure 7.8). This slab of stone has been interpreted as the remains of a chambered tomb (Lynch 1972, 79), but may equally be a natural slab. Whatever its status, it is covered by depressions and at least twenty-eight of these are cup-marks (Barker 1992, 52). An additional seventeen may be natural. This juxtaposition of natural and artificial hints at a mind-set exploring differences and similarities between what we call cultural and natural. Just over three kilometres to the north-west of Trefael, the Early

Figure 7.7 To the left, the distinctive lifted capstone of Coetan Arthur. To the right, the capstone of the same monument appears to blend into the surrounding outcrops when viewed from a different direction.

Figure 7.8 The slab of Trefael, with Carn Ingli in the distance. The cup-marks can be seen at the left and centre of the slab.

Neolithic monument of Trellyffaint has a series of cup-marks on its capstone (Barker 1992, 18–19). Some of these cup-marks may be natural, but again it seems likely that some are artificial. Since rock art is primarily Late Neolithic or Early Bronze Age in date (Bradley 1997), these cup-marks may have been added many centuries after the monument was first constructed. Here people were literally inscribing a monument with a new understanding of the world which emphasised the ambiguity between natural and artificial.

It is possible to argue that south-west Wales has a rather unique monumental record and a distinctive landscape which may not be representative of other areas of Britain. The juxtaposition of natural and artificial does, however, occur elsewhere (see Alves this volume, ch. 4), and it may be helpful briefly to examine the evidence from south-west Scotland as a comparison. The later Neolithic monuments in this region consist of small box-like chambers predominately covered by round cairns (Henshall 1972, 2–14; see Murray 1992 for discussion of typology). They are set in the uplands of south-west Scotland mostly on the lower slopes of the Merrick mountain range. These sites are in complete contrast to the Early Neolithic sites, which are located in much lower-lying areas around the coast. Again, the precise dating of the later sites is not confirmed, although White Cairn, Bargrennan, produced later Neolithic pottery (Piggott and Powell 1949). Many of the later Neolithic sites are set among distinctive knolls which often make the monuments hard to distinguish from natural features. Kenny's

Cairn is positioned in a landscape filled with hummocks and is quite difficult to spot at a distance. This effect is most pronounced at the Caves of Kilhern which is surrounded by mounds that have rocky protuberances which look similar to the stone-built structures of the monument (Figure 7.9). Many of these later Neolithic sites are positioned close to outcrops. These outcrops are not as sizeable as those in south-west Wales, but are often quite distinctive, frequently with striking features such as natural cup-marks or laminations. Indeed, some of the monuments in south-west Scotland also incorporate natural features into their structures. One side of the chamber at Auld Wife's Grave is formed by a natural boulder (Henshall 1972, 537). At Cairnderry, a whole series of natural cup-marks can be found on the capstone of one of the chambers. Even the rock art in the area seems to be playing out contrasting ideas of natural and artificial. At the site of Lamford near Loch Doon (Morris 1979, 137), there are several panels where rings have been engraved around natural cup-marks.

Returning to south-west Wales, it was already suggested above that Carn Meini in the Preseli Mountains may have been important in the Early Neolithic as both a source of stone axes and as a reference point for monuments. By the later Neolithic it may have become one of the most potent places in the region. This is because it is a rather ambiguous place, where natural outcrops share qualities with the monumental architecture of both early and late chambered tombs (Figure 7.4; see also Bradley 2000, fig. 27). Indeed, the hilltop was described by one antiquary as 'masses of rock starting out of the ground, in fantastick shapes and uncommon groupes, easily mistaken at a little distance, for

Figure 7.9 The Caves of Kilhern in south-west Scotland. The chambers and mound are the first large lump behind the wall, but they blend into the landscape which is covered with natural mounds and outcrops.

the immense remains of architectural prodigies' (Warner 1799, quoted in Barker 1992, 49). Without our modern ability to distinguish geological and archaeological formations, people in the Neolithic may have believed that this mountain was literally covered in monuments. For this very reason, I would suggest that in the later Neolithic this place became a primary focus for negotiations between the living and their mythical past. Two features were constructed near to the summit of Carn Meini, and although they have not been securely dated, comparisons with sites elsewhere suggest they are later Neolithic. The first is a chambered cairn (Barker 1992, 49–50) which appears to be set at the top of a distinctive river of boulders that runs down the hillside. The cairn blends into the flow of boulders so that it is impossible to tell where the cairn stops and the natural boulders start. Secondly, a small construction (Figure 7.10) has been located by a survey on the summit of Carn Meini (Drewett 1987). It remains difficult to tell whether this feature is built or natural, but a whole series of similar structures have been found on Bodmin Moor (Tony Blackman personal communication), where it has been confirmed that some, at least, were built by people (Tilley *et al.* 2000).

Conclusion

In the past it has been suggested that the construction of monuments required people to have a new understanding of the world, but I have proposed that the

Figure 7.10 A view of the summit of Carn Meini, Preseli. In the foreground to left of centre is the unclassified monument.

conceptions of the world which allowed monuments to be constructed were already present in the Mesolithic. Instead, the beginnings of monumentality in Britain may have had more to do with the appropriation of a mythical past by the living. This process began in the Early Neolithic when structures were built close to, but not right up against, symbolic and important outcrops. The presence of these monuments in the landscape may have resulted in a change in people's world-views and, by the later Neolithic, the first tentative encroachments had been made upon potent ground. Ambiguity seems to have been key in rene-gotiating relationships between living populations and the relics of a mythical past, possibly because it increasingly challenged and undermined the sense of a timeless and unchangeable past. These places now became locales where people could come to negotiate their own understanding of the world, and their place within it. As such, certain places may have become particularly potent in the later Neolithic. Carn Meini was perhaps the most ambiguous place of all, and this may help explain why it was chosen as the source of the Stonehenge bluestones. The circular arrangement and carefully dressed stones of Stonehenge are not directly replicated in nature. By taking stones from an ambiguous place like Carn Meini and incorporating them into a henge, people were making a statement about a new understanding of the world. This statement was not that they had conquered nature, but rather that they had begun to appropriate the most potent ancestral places. Ultimately this may have been one of a number of fundamental turning points on the way to the appropriation of the entire landscape, the adoption of agriculture wholesale, and a whole new set of ideas about the world.

Acknowledgements

A version of this paper was first presented at the 'Society in Nature' session at TAG in Cardiff, and I would like to thank the organisers of that session, Josh Pollard, Stephanie Koerner and Robert Johnson, for accepting my paper. Many thanks also to Chris Scarre for inviting me to participate at the EAA meeting in Lisbon and for the invitation to contribute to this volume. Richard Bradley, John Evans, Niall Sharples and Alasdair Whittle have all been kind enough to comment on various drafts of this paper.

References

Barker, C., 1992. *The Chambered Tombs of South-West Wales: A Reassessment of the Neolithic Burial Monuments of Carmarthenshire and Pembrokeshire*. Oxford: Oxbow.

Barrett, J., 1994. *Fragments from Antiquity: An Archaeology of Social Life in Britain, 2900–1200 BC*. Oxford: Blackwell.

Bender, B., 2000. Investigating landscape and identity in the Neolithic, in A. Ritchie (ed.), *Neolithic Orkney in its European Context*. Cambridge: McDonald Institute for Archaeological Research, 23–30.

Bird-David, N., 1988. Hunter-gatherers and other people: a re-examination, in T. Ingold, D. Riches and J. Woodburn (eds), *Hunters and Gatherers: History, Evolution and Social Change*. Oxford: Berg, 4–14.

Bonsall, C., Sutherland, D., Tipping, R., and Cherry, J., 1990. The Eskmeals project: late Mesolithic settlement and environment in north-west England, in C. Bonsall (ed.), *The Mesolithic in Europe*. Edinburgh: John Donald, 175–205.

Bradley, R., 1993. *Altering the Earth*. Edinburgh: Society of Antiquaries of Scotland.

Bradley, R., 1997. *Rock Art and the Prehistory of Atlantic Europe: Signing the Land*. London: Routledge.

Bradley, R., 1998a. Ruined buildings, ruined stones: enclosures, tombs and natural places in the Neolithic of south-west England. *World Archaeology* 30, 13–22.

Bradley, R., 1998b. *The Significance of Monuments: On the Shaping of Human Experience in Neolithic and Bronze Age Europe*. London: Routledge.

Bradley, R., 2000. *The Archaeology of Natural Places*. London: Routledge.

Carmichael, D., Hubert, J., Reeves, B., and Schande, A. (eds), 1994. *Sacred Sites, Sacred Places*. London: Routledge.

Case, H., 1969. Neolithic explanations. *Antiquity* 43, 176–86.

Clark, G., 1966. The invasion hypothesis in British archaeology. *Antiquity* 159, 172–86.

Cleal, R., Walker, K., and Montague, R., 1995. *Stonehenge in its Landscape: Twentieth Century Excavations*. London: English Heritage.

Cummings, V., 2001. Landscapes in transition? Exploring the origins of monumentality in south-west Wales and south-west Scotland. PhD thesis, Cardiff University.

Daniel, G. E. 1962. The megalith builders, in S. Piggott (ed.), *The Prehistoric Peoples of Scotland*. London: Routledge, 39–70.

David, A., and Williams, G., 1995. Stone axe-head manufacture in the Preseli Hills, Wales. *Proceedings of the Prehistoric Society* 61, 433–60.

Drewett, P., 1987. An archaeological survey of Mynydd Preseli, Dyfed. *Archaeology in Wales* 27, 14–16.

Edwards, K., 1990. Fire and the Scottish Mesolithic: evidence from microscopic charcoal, in P. Vermeersch and P. van Peer (eds), *Contributions to the Mesolithic in Europe*. Leuven: Leuven University Press, 71–80.

Fenton, J., 1848. Cromlech at Llanwnda, Pembrokeshire. *Archaeologia Cambrensis* 3, 283–4.

Fenton, R., 1810. *A Historic Tour through Pembrokeshire*. London.

Fleming, A., 1999. Phenomenology and the megaliths of Wales: a dreaming too far? *Oxford Journal of Archaeology* 18, 119–25.

Grimes, W., 1960. *Pentre-Ifan Burial Chamber*. Ministry of Works.

Henshall, A., 1972. *The Chambered Tombs of Scotland*, 2. Edinburgh: Edinburgh University Press.

Hodder, I., 1990. *The Domestication of Europe*. Oxford: Basil Blackwell.

Ingold, T., 1994. From trust to domination: an alternative history of human–animal relations, in A. Manning and J. Serpell (eds), *Animals and Human Society: Changing Perspectives*. London: Routledge, 1–22.

Ingold, T., 1996. Hunting and gathering as ways of perceiving the environment, in R. Ellen and K. Fúkui (eds), *Redefining Nature*, Oxford: Berg, 117–55.

Kahn, M., 1990. Stone-faced ancestors: the spatial anchoring of myth in Wamira, Papua New Guinea. *Ethnology* 29, 51–66.

Kent, S., 1989. Cross-cultural perceptions of farmers as hunters and the value of meat, in S. Kent (ed.), *The Implications of Sedentism*. Cambridge: Cambridge University Press, 3–32.

Lynch, F., 1969. The megalithic tombs of north Wales, in T. Powell, J. Corcoran,

F. Lynch and J. Scott (eds), *Megalithic Enquiries in the West of Britain*. Liverpool: Liverpool University Press, 107–48.

Lynch, F., 1972. Portal dolmens in the Nevern Valley, Pembrokeshire, in F. Lynch and C. Burgess (eds), *Prehistoric Man in Wales and the West*. Bath: Adams and Dart, 67–84.

Lynch, F. 1975. Excavations at Carreg Samson megalithic tomb, Mathry, Pembrokeshire. *Archaeologia Cambrensis* 124, 15–35.

Lynch, F., 1976. Towards a chronology of megalithic tombs in Wales, in G. Boon and J. Lewis (eds), *Welsh Antiquity: Essays Mainly on Prehistoric Topics Presented to H. Savory*. Cardiff: National Museum of Wales, 63–79.

Mellars, P., 1987. *Excavations on Oronsay*. Edinburgh: Edinburgh University Press.

Morris, R., 1979. *The Prehistoric Rock Art of Galloway and the Isle of Man*. Poole: Blandford Press.

Murray, J., 1992. The Bargrennan group of chambered cairns: circumstance and context, in N. Sharples and A. Sheridan (eds), *Vessels for the Ancestors*. Edinburgh: Edinburgh University Press, 33–48.

Palmer, S., 1990. Mesolithic sites of Portland and their significance, in C. Bonsall (ed.), *The Mesolithic in Europe*. Edinburgh: John Donald, 254–8.

Piggott, S., 1954. *The Neolithic Cultures of the British Isles*. Cambridge: Cambridge University Press.

Piggott, S., and Powell, T., 1949. The excavation of three Neolithic chambered tombs in Galloway. *Proceedings of the Society of Antiquaries of Scotland* 83, 103–61.

Rees, S. 1992., *A Guide to Ancient and Historic Wales: Dyfed*. London: HMSO.

Richards, C., 1996. Henges and water: towards an elemental understanding of monumentality and landscape in late Neolithic Britain. *Journal of Material Culture* 2, 313–36.

Sharples, N., 2000. Antlers and Orcadian rituals: an ambiguous role for red deer in the Neolithic, in A. Ritchie (ed.), *Neolithic Orkney in its European Context*. Cambridge: McDonald Institute for Archaeological Research, 107–16.

Sherratt, A., 1990. The genesis of megaliths: ethnicity and social complexity in Neolithic northwest Europe. *World Archaeology* 22, 147–67.

Sherratt, A., 1995. Instruments of conversion? The role of megaliths in the Mesolithic/Neolithic transition in north-west Europe. *Oxford Journal of Archaeology* 14, 245–60.

Taçon, P., 1991. The power of stone: symbolic aspects of stone use and tool development in western Arnhem Land, Australia. *Antiquity* 65, 192–207.

Thomas, J., 1999. *Understanding the Neolithic*. London: Routledge.

Thomas, J., 2000. The identity of place in Neolithic Britain: examples from southwest Scotland, in A. Ritchie (ed.), *Neolithic Orkney in its European Context*. Cambridge: McDonald Institute for Archaeological Research, 79–87.

Tilley, C., 1994. *A Phenomenology of Landscape*. Oxford: Berg.

Tilley, C., 1996. *An Ethnography of the Neolithic*. Cambridge: Cambridge University Press.

Tilley, C., Hamilton, S., Harrison, S., and Anderson, E., 2000. Nature, culture, clitter. *Journal of Material Culture* 5, 197–224.

Whittle, A., 1996. *Europe in the Neolithic: the Creation of New Worlds*. Cambridge: Cambridge University Press.

8 The land, the sky and the Scottish stone circle

Richard Bradley

This book is about the archaeology of 'monuments', and that is a term which can give rise to problems. The word comes from the Latin verb *monere*, to remind, and at once it suggests that monuments were memorials: they were a vital part of the material culture of memory (Holtorf 1997). Because those places had resisted natural decay, they recalled the past in the lives of later generations. It is why they can be studied now.

But that simple definition, which informs much recent writing, conceals a number of traps. If the people who built these monuments enshrined the past in architectural form, how would they have thought about the future? And would later interpretations of these buildings have been consistent with the intentions of the people who had designed them? Like archaeologists, their descendants would have been forced to interpret what they saw, and they might have codified those interpretations by reconstructing the monuments or by building others of their own (Bradley 1993, ch. 6).

The paradox is that monuments refer to a past but they are often directed to a future. Yet the very process of interpreting them is retrospective. Archaeologists tease out the changing forms of these constructions until they can isolate the original core. Then they seek to explain the evolution of particular places in terms of their changing significance. The phasing of individual monuments provides the backbone of their field studies, but their interpretations refer to the ways in which the basic design was modified. In many cases it means that they are studying how the evolution of a monument or group of monuments reflected changing ideas about the world. Archaeologists accept that many monuments were built to last, but all too rarely do they consider whether those who built them might also have planned how those structures were to develop over time. There are many cases in which that might have been true.

One example is extremely familiar. This is the blocking of megalithic tombs that is found widely in Atlantic Europe. All too often it remains unexplained, as if it happened at a time when these sites had lost their significance. The process might be seen as one of ideological change (Masset 1993, chs 8 and 9). But what if the people who had built these tombs actually meant them to have a limited life-span? In that case, the closure of individual monuments might have been part of the original design. Indeed, it could have represented the completion of that scheme. The life history of any one tomb could have played out a narrative – a ritual – whose course was determined from the start.

Another instance comes from a paper by Parker Pearson and Ramilisonina (1998). They suggest that many of the stone enclosures of the British Neolithic period went through the same cycle of construction. The original monument was a timber circle and this might have been associated with extensive deposits of artefacts and with the debris of feasting. In time, the circle of posts was rebuilt in stone, and this kind of monument is associated with the remains of the dead. Stonehenge provides the best-known example of this sequence. They suggest that the first structure was connected with the living and for that reason it was made out of an organic material: wood. It was formed from a living substance and would eventually decay. When the site was recreated in stone, it was associated with the dead and that is why it was now formed from a material which would last for ever. Although part of their argument depends on analogy with recent practice in Madagascar, its greatest strength is the way in which it characterises a sequence that is found very widely in the British Isles. Timber monuments were often rebuilt in stone and, after that, they remained largely unaltered. The relationship between their successive plans is so close that the sequence may well have been envisaged from the outset. If so, the stone circle was the culmination of a plan that brought the sequence of construction to an end.

Sequences of this kind are sometimes found at monuments which incorporate celestial alignments; Stonehenge is perhaps the most famous instance. Many structures may be directed towards striking elements of the natural landscape and draw some of their power from the fact that features like mountains and rock outcrops remain unchanged (Tilley 1996). The positions of the sun and moon, on the other hand, change in predictable ways and this allows people to anticipate particular events and even to build them into the operation of their monuments (Ruggles 1999). The motions of the heavenly bodies can be used to create a series of effects that extend far into the future.

That contrast between the unchanging features of the land and those seen in the sky raises another issue. There have been a number of studies that interpret the changing forms of prehistoric monuments in relation to the natural topography, yet monuments that were directed towards the sky are studied in a rather different way – in terms of observation, prediction and exact measurement. Although some scholars talk about cosmology (for instance Ruggles 1999, ch. 8), their studies are still described as 'archaeoastronomy'. To some extent that is because they must employ precise observation if they are to establish the credentials of particular alignments in the past. But all too often the procedures required in modern fieldwork become confused with the original functions of these monuments. That was the error made by Alexander Thom (1971).

In fact, one of the important results of such fieldwork has been to suggest the spacing of particular events at particular sites: annual cycles in the movements of the sun or the more complex cycle associated with the moon. All these could be related to the ways in which the use of monuments was expected to develop over time.

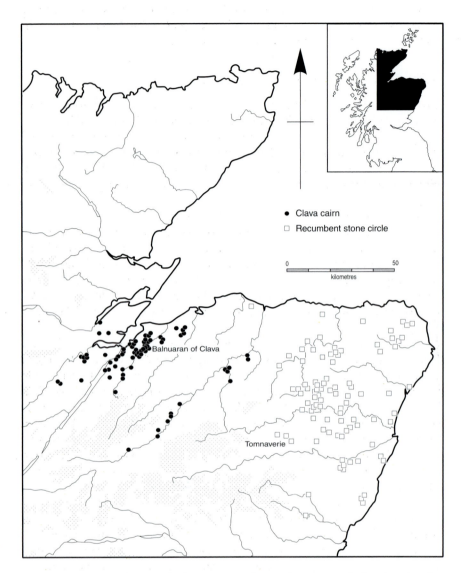

Figure 8.1 The distribution of Clava cairns and recumbent stone circles, showing the locations of the excavated monuments at Balnuaran of Clava and Tomnaverie.

I would like to explore these problems using two groups of monuments in the north of Scotland which have played a part in discussions of this kind. These are Clava cairns and recumbent stone circles (Figure 8.1). There are structural similarities between the two and they may have been of similar dates to one another. Recent excavations suggest that Clava cairns were in use between approximately 2300 and 1750 BC (Bradley 2000), whilst the recumbent stone circles may be associated with the use of Beaker pottery (Burl 2000, 215–33). In each case this account is based on recent fieldwork.

Balnuaran of Clava, Inverness-shire

Clava cairns take two distinct forms and consist either of circular rubble enclosures (ring cairns) or of passage graves. In each case the stones of their outer kerb are graded in height, so that the shortest are towards the north-east and the tallest to the south-west. They are sometimes held in place by an external platform built against the main structure of the cairn. The other feature that unites these groups of monuments is that each is enclosed by a ring of monoliths which are graded in height according to exactly the same principle (Figures 8.2–8.4; Henshall 1963, 12–39; Burl 2000, 233–42).

There are approximately fifty Clava cairns. For the most part they were built in inconspicuous positions in the landscape and they seldom command long-distance views. Their locations were only rarely influenced by striking features of the topography and field survey has established that many of them were constructed at the heart of the domestic landscape (Bradley 2000, chs 8 and 9). One of these monuments was actually built over the remains of a house (Simpson 1996).

The entrances of the Clava passage graves are directed towards the south-west, and this alignment is reflected by the grading of the kerbstones and the ring of monoliths. That feature is shared with the Clava ring cairns, which do not have any entrances and for that reason could not adhere to a precise alignment. That south-western axis can be related to the position of the summer moon, for the orientations of these sites cover too wide an arc for all the sites to have been directed towards the sun (Ruggles 1999, 130). On the other hand, the two passage graves in the cemetery at Balnuaran of Clava, the most substantial group of monuments of this kind, are aligned exactly on the midwinter solstice: a phenomenon that can still be observed today (Scott and Phillips 1999).

Because the celestial alignments of the Clava cairns are so clearly demonstrated, it is all too easy to suppose that the primary function of these monuments was for observing the sky. That is why these sites feature in accounts of prehistoric astronomy. Recent excavation at the type site, Balnuaran of Clava, suggests a completely different approach (Bradley 2000). The structural sequence here may document the course of a ritual played out over time. It was a process that involved both the land and the sky and one whose distinctive character seems to have been laid down from the start.

There has been controversy over the structural development of Clava cairns. This has concerned two main elements: the rubble platforms that seem to have been built against the external kerbs of both kinds of cairn, and the outer rings of monoliths (Henshall 1963, 21–8; MacCarthy 1996). This problem seems to have been resolved by excavation at Balnuaran of Clava, but one effect of determining the building sequence at that site is to raise a broader question of interpretation.

Figure 8.2 The north-east cairn at Balnuaran of Clava, showing the passage grave and part of the stone circle.

Figure 8.3 The south-west cairn at Balnuaran of Clava, showing the back of the passage grave, the external platform under excavation and the position of a monolith in the stone circle.

The sequence is most obvious at the two passage graves at Balnuaran of Clava. The earliest activity on the site may be represented by a lithic scatter, by reused building material incorporated into the cairns, and by environmental evidence that suggests that the cemetery was built within an established clearing with evidence of cultivation (Bradley 2000, ch. 4).

The north–east passage grave was erected on the edge of that clearing and was exactly aligned on the midwinter sunset. It was a circular cairn with a narrow passage and a corbelled chamber at its centre. The lower part of that chamber was built of orthostats which were graded in height from north-east to south-west in the same manner as the kerb that defined the outer edge of the monument. Little is known about any burial associated with this cairn, although a small quantity of bones were found there in the 19th century. The ground surface in front of the entrance had been slightly lowered by erosion during the initial use of this monument (Figure 8.5A).

The original cairn was structurally unstable because the external kerb was not bedded into the subsoil. That feature was also graded in height, with the result that the kerbstones flanking the entrance were capable of retaining the mass of the cairn whilst those at the rear of the monument would soon have been pushed out of position. During a second phase of construction, these were buttressed by the addition of an external platform of rubble. This platform continued across the mouth of the passage and would have made access to the interior much more difficult (Figures 8.4 and 8.5B).

The outer limit of that platform was marked by the ring of monoliths which again lacked substantial sockets of their own. They were simply bedded into this

Figure 8.4 Excavation outside the north-east cairn at Balnuaran of Clava, showing the kerb of the passage grave, a segment of the external platform and the positions of two monoliths in the stone circle.

deposit of rubble, so that it seems as if the two features were built simultaneously. But there is a complication. A similar sequence was found at all three of the excavated sites at Balnuaran of Clava and in each case the newly erected monoliths appear to be 'paired' with individual kerbstones in the already-existing cairns. These links were constituted in a number of different ways and concern the colour, shape or raw material of the individual stones. In most cases these pairings are apparent because individual monoliths were erected directly opposite matching stones in the kerb, but in the excavated ring cairn at Balnuaran of Clava some of these connections were enhanced by building rubble banks linking these two elements together (Henshall 1963, 361–3).

Thus the sequence at this particular site combines three distinct elements: a clearing in the local woodland associated with domestic occupation; the

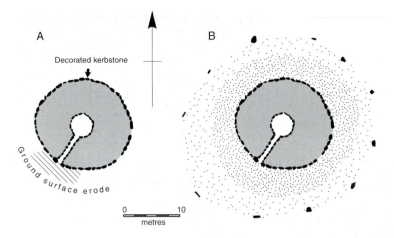

Figure 8.5A The original form of the north-east cairn at Balnuaran of Clava, showing the area of erosion around the entrance and the position of a decorated kerbstone towards the back of the monument. *Figure 8.5B* illustrates the subsequent development of the monument. Access to the entrance passage was impeded by the construction of an external platform of rubble, which also masked part of the decorated kerbstone. It was at this stage that the stone circle was built.

construction of two passage graves aligned on the position where the midwinter sun sets behind an area of raised ground; and the construction of rings of monoliths to enclose the individual cairns. When the latter took place, access to the interior of the passage graves became more difficult and the pecked decoration on the kerbstones was obscured.

At first sight, it might be possible to interpret this evidence in terms of a series of significance changes in the use of Balnuaran of Clava – a settlement associated with the living was replaced by a cemetery for the dead; a series of mortuary cairns were replaced by free-standing stone circles – but this does not do justice to the complexities of the excavated evidence. The basic alignment of the site depended on a prolonged period of observation of the sky, which was only possible because the original settlement had been located in a clearing. The orientation of the cemetery needed to be worked out before any of the cairns could be built. In the same way, the monuments that were constructed could only have had a limited life expectancy in their original form, for each of them was structurally unstable. As the mass of each cairn settled, the smaller kerbstones would have been forced out of position, for they did not have proper sockets. As all the fifty or so Clava cairns conform to the same design, it is highly unlikely that the builders would have been unaware of these structural problems. Rather, it seems as if the cairns were intended to be free-standing monuments only for a short period of time.

When the external platforms were built, the entrances to the passage graves were effectively blocked, although the rubble did not extend to the full height of the entrance, so that sunlight could still penetrate into the interior at mid-winter. It was at this stage that the stone circles were erected, but again their precise configuration seems to have been determined in advance for in many cases the newly erected monoliths were paired with individual components of the existing cairns. It is as if the full development of the monument had been envisaged from the start.

One way of viewing this sequence is to suppose that the separate cairns were indeed regarded as the houses of the dead. There is circumstantial evidence that some of their elements were built out of stone which had been quarried for another purpose, but, if so, no traces of older dwellings would remain on the site today. The passage tombs that took their place were in use for quite a brief period and were aligned on the setting sun at the shortest day of the year. Not long after they had been constructed their entrances were partially blocked and at this stage the tomb was encircled by a ring of monoliths whose separate components were selected to match those around the limits of the existing cairn. In that way an entirely open monument replaced the closed tomb of the dead, just as the tombs themselves could have replaced older houses. Every part of the sequence could be interpreted as a stage in a ritual that transformed the living into the ancestors and linked their burials to the movements of the sun. That is not unlike the interpretation of Stonehenge suggested by Parker Pearson and Ramilisonina (1998).

Tomnaverie, Aberdeenshire

Recumbent stone circles have three main elements (Burl 2000, 215–33). Again they consist of a ring of standing stones which may be graded in height, with the lowest towards the north-east and the tallest to the south-west. In this case the two highest pillars (known as 'flankers') frame a large flat block (the 'recumbent' stone). Inside the ring of monoliths there is generally a circular rubble wall supported on either side by a kerb. Such 'ring cairns' are sometimes associated with burnt material and enclose an open area in the centre of the monument. It seems to have been important that these sites were built on level ground and most examples were constructed by terracing them into a slope, although some of the sites were located on hilltops. In each case they command a view towards the south or south-west, framed by the recumbent stone and the flankers (Ruggles 1999, 91–9). In most instances that view excludes the immediate surroundings of the site and focuses on a more distant area of high ground. It also takes in a segment of the sky. Recent fieldwork suggests that, in contrast to the Clava cairns, these monuments had been built towards the edges of the settled landscape (Bradley *et al.* 2000).

There are roughly a hundred of these monuments, and they have been interpreted in several different ways. The chronological relationship between the stone circles and the cairns has been one point of interest, and until recently it seemed as if the cairns were a secondary addition to these sites (Shepherd 1987). This is certainly a common sequence at other kinds of prehistoric monument in Britain and it is sometimes considered to reflect a change in the significance of these places: enclosures that were originally used in public ceremonies were appropriated by a small section of society for the burial of their dead (Bradley 1998, ch. 9). At the same time, the orientation of recumbent stone circles suggests that they were directed towards the position of the summer moon (Ruggles 1999, 91–9).

Again there is a temptation to take this observation as evidence for prehistoric 'astronomy', but recent excavation at one of these monuments, Tomnaverie, suggests a quite different approach (Figures 8.6 and 8.7; Bradley *et al.* 2000). Like the cairns at Balnuaran of Clava, this site seems to have developed according to a prescribed sequence, so that the formation of the successive structures at Tomnaverie charts the course of a ritual that was played out over time. In this case the position of the sun did not influence the organisation of the monument, but the cycle that is suggested here may have begun and ended with observations of the moon. It also created a connection between the monument and a conspicuous mountain.

The structural sequence at Tomnaverie is based on a number of stratigraphic relationships (Figure 8.8). The first feature was an area of burnt material on the summit of a low hill commanding an extensive view over a glacial basin. Fires had been lit on the site and the ashes were associated with small fragments of bone, suggesting that the original core of the monument was a cremation pyre. This interpretation is supported by evidence that the burning had taken place *in situ* and resulted in changes to the magnetic susceptibility of the subsoil.

During a second phase, the summit of the hill was encapsulated within a massive cairn, although the pyre itself was left exposed and may have continued in operation. The outer edge of that cairn was supported by a kerb of slabs and boulders, buttressed on the exterior by a bank of rubble. This monument had been damaged by a modern quarry, but it was clear that the segment of its kerb directly opposite the recumbent stone was of particularly massive construction. Sherds of Beaker pottery had been placed against it.

During the final phase of construction a recumbent stone circle was con- structed around the existing cairn. One length of kerbstones was demolished so that the cairn could be enlarged, and then the kerb was realigned to join the monoliths on either side of the recumbent stone. That represents the last building phase at Tomnaverie, but, like Balnuaran of Clava, the monument was brought back into use for human burial many centuries later.

On one level that simple sequence undermines the basis on which recumbent stone circles have been discussed. The cairn was raised before the stone circle was erected and seems to have enclosed an even older pyre. At no stage was there a free-standing stone circle at Tomnaverie, and on those sites where the cairn had been significantly higher it would have been impossible to observe the moon between the flanking stones from anywhere inside the monument. In the same way, since the cairn at Tomnaverie was part of the original design it cannot have been built to appropriate the significance of an existing structure.

Figure 8.6 Excavation at Tomnaverie stone circle. This view shows the features of the monument when they were first exposed.

Figure 8.7 The excavated monument at Tomnaverie after the re-erection of the fallen stones. The recumbent stone and the two flankers are towards the top left of the photograph.

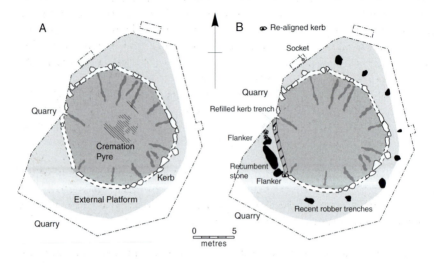

Figure 8.8A Outline plan of the pyre and primary cairn at Tomnaverie, showing the original course of the kerb and the positions of the radial divisions built into the structure of the monument. *Figure 8.8B* shows how the site was modified when the stone circle was erected in a later phase. Part of the original kerb was removed and the cairn was extended to link it to the recumbent stone and the flankers.

That is the usual way of regarding the archaeological sequence on such a site but it leaves out one vital observation, for once again each part of the monument was built in anticipation of those that came later. The cremation pyre at Tomnaverie was not located at random. It was placed on the end of a low ridge at a point which commanded a view in all directions. It was positioned at the edge of the slope so that there was no dead ground towards the south-west. Field survey has shown that it was also located on the limit of the settled landscape but in a position where it would have been seen on the skyline from all the occupation sites in the surrounding area. The smoke rising from the fires would have been visible to the local population. From the beginning, then, the transformation of the dead connected the land and the sky.

In time the pyre was encapsulated at the centre of a circular cairn, but that monument had a number of unusual features. Its surface was level with the summit of the hill so that it really consisted of a massive platform. That platform was not built symmetrically around the hilltop but was terraced out from the summit where the ground fell away steeply. Although the pyre may have continued in operation, the position of the monument already emphasised the view towards the south-west which is dominated by a prominent mountain, Lochnagar.

The construction of the cairn was unusual in other ways. At several points radial divisions linked the interior to the outer kerb. These were established as soon as construction began, but they were not distributed evenly around the perimeter of the site. They were mostly towards the north-east and south-east and only two examples were on the south-west side, which was the apparent focus of the monument. At the same time, the outer kerb was polygonal rather than strictly circular and the longest straight section was located to the south-west, where the slope of the hill was steepest.

These anomalies can be explained by what happened next, for the components of the stone circle seem to have been located in relation to these features. Put another way, the precise form taken by the cairn anticipated that of the stone setting which was built in the following phase. Thus the long straight section of kerb anticipates the position of the recumbent stone and the flankers; two of the radial divisions mark the section of kerb that was later extended; and five others point to the positions of monoliths erected during the subsequent phase. Still more important, the recumbent stone and the two flankers frame a view into the mountainous landscape that had already influenced the positioning of the cairn (Figure 8.9).

That view is the most dramatic feature of the monument, and it is no accident that it incorporates the most conspicuous mountain in the region, thirty kilometres away. Its distinctive form is echoed by the profile of the recumbent

Figure 8.9 The re-erected recumbent stone and flankers at Tomnaverie, framing a distant view of Lochnagar. Photo: Jim Henderson.

stone. Seen from Tomnaverie, Lochnagar is the only mountain that retains its snow cover for much of the year, and it may be no accident that the recumbent stone includes more quartz than the other parts of the monument. The southwest edge of the cairn contained several large boulders of quartz and this emphasis on the colour white may explain why the monument is also aligned on the moon as it passes over Lochnagar.

It would be easy to suggest that this sequence results from prehistoric quantity surveying – that it simply describes stages in a continuous process of construction – but that does not seem to be true. There is evidence that the cairn had originally been a free-standing monument, defined by a massive kerb around its entire perimeter. It was only when the circle was built that one section of that kerb was disrupted. The stones were removed from their original packing and a particularly massive kerbstone was chopped off at ground level. The resulting disturbance was filled in with large boulders. At this stage the surviving part of the kerb was redirected to link the cairn to the monoliths on either side of the recumbent. This would have involved so much effort that the process of building this monument should have extended over a significant period of time.

We do not know how long that interval was, but the circle at Tomnaverie is unusual because it is precisely aligned on the moon just once every eighteen and a half years. This is roughly a human generation and might provide a clue. Construction could not have started until the position of the moon had been observed over a lengthy period. Perhaps its building was completed when the moon returned to the same position in the night sky.

How should this sequence be understood? Here we must return to the three elements mentioned in the title of this paper: the land, the sky and the stone circle itself. The original cremation pyre was placed where the heavens met the earth and where the inhabitants of nearby settlements could observe smoke rising into the air. It was also located in the one place on the hilltop where the position of a distant mountain would correspond to that of the summer moon. The subsequent development of the site gave monumental expression to this relationship, gradually focusing that particular alignment until it was narrowed down to the space between the tallest stones. Now the monument was related explicitly to just one part of the sky and to the most dramatic feature on the horizon, Lochnagar.

Burl has compared the flankers to a monumental portal (2000, 218), and there are similar features in the entrances to other kinds of monuments, including Clava cairns. At Tomnaverie that portal communicated between two very different worlds. The stone doorway connected the cremation pyre and the sky; it joined a hill on the edge of the domestic landscape with a mountain remote from the daily world. Yet it is a door that was shut, for the focal point of the entire monument is the recumbent stone which weighs 6.5 tons and is difficult for anyone to cross (Figure 8.9). Once that doorway was blocked, activity at Tomnaverie seems to have come to an end. If the pyre had served to link the ancestors to the sky and the distant mountains, now a far more specific relationship was involved. The monument was closed to the living and only the light of the moon could cross the recumbent stone to illuminate the dead (cf. Burl 1980; 1981).

The building of this monument had followed an uneven path that may have extended over many years and its structural development formed an integral part of the rituals that were conducted there. But it seems as if those rituals were directed towards a single conclusion. Every generation, the moon returned to its original position in the night sky. Could this have been the time when the cycle was completed?

Conclusions

This paper has considered two kinds of monument in the north of Scotland, both of them the subject of recent fieldwork. There may have been close connections between the people who built and used these sites, and yet they display an interesting series of contrasts which go well beyond the problems of classification. Clava cairns were built in a domestic landscape. They were closely integrated into the settlement pattern, they occupied relatively inconspicuous positions in the natural topography and they were rarely orientated on prominent landmarks, although they could be aligned on the sun and moon. The recumbent stone circles, on the other hand, occupied more marginal positions in the landscape, some distance away from the settlements of the period. These sites began not as occupation sites but as cremation pyres, located in quite conspicuous positions in the terrain, in places where they commanded a considerable view of both the land and the sky. Like the Clava cairns they were directed towards the position of the summer moon but a number of examples were also aligned on prominent hills or mountains. These differences are just as important as the similarities between the two groups of monuments.

Instead of a purely formal analysis, which might highlight their ground plans, their orientations and the number and grading of the monoliths, it has been instructive to compare their histories, as represented by the excavated examples at Tomnaverie and Balnuaran of Clava. These comparisons are concerned less with purely formal attributes than with the rituals that took place there and the ways in which they were embodied in the changing structure of these buildings. More than that, the analysis extends to the relationship between those monuments and the natural topography and even to the movements of the sun and moon.

These monuments were not a passive backdrop to the ceremonies that were conducted there: their construction and modification formed an essential part of the rituals themselves and their course seems to have been established from the outset. In the same way, the landscape provided far more than the local 'environment' of such places, for its features were built into the very design of those structures. The monuments connected the earth to the sky as they linked the living to the dead.

These were buildings with an active life that may have been exceptionally short and yet the astronomical events that contributed so much of their symbolism can still be observed today. That is another paradox in the study of monumental architecture.

Acknowledgements

I am grateful to Margaret Mathews for the figure drawings, to Jim Henderson for his fine photograph of Tomnaverie, to Tim Phillips who undertook the field-walking survey around that site and to Historic Scotland for funding most of the work described in this paper.

References

Bradley, R., 1993. *Altering the Earth*. Edinburgh: Society of Antiquaries of Scotland.

Bradley, R., 1998. *The Significance of Monuments*. London: Routledge.

Bradley, R., 2000. *The Good Stones: A New Investigation of the Clava Cairns*. Edinburgh: Society of Antiquaries of Scotland.

Bradley, R., Ball, C., Campbell, M., Croft, S., Phillips, T., and Trevarthen, D., 2000. Tomnaverie stone circle, Aberdeenshire. *Antiquity* 74, 465–6.

Burl, A., 1980. Science or symbolism: problems of archaeo-astronomy. *Antiquity* 54, 191–200.

Burl, A., 1981. 'By the light of the cinerary moon': chambered tombs and the astronomy of death, in C. Ruggles and A. Whittle (eds), *Astronomy and Society in the Period 4000–1500 BC*. Oxford: British Archaeological Reports.

Burl, A., 2000. *The Stone Circles of Britain, Ireland and Brittany*. New Haven: Yale University Press.

Henshall, A., 1963. *The Chambered Tombs of Scotland, 1*. Edinburgh: Edinburgh University Press.

Holtorf, C., 1997. Megaliths, monumentality and memory. *Archaeological Review from Cambridge* 14.2, 45–66

MacCarthy, C., 1996. The disclosure of sacred ground: structural developments within megalithic monuments of the Clava group. *Proceedings of the Society of Antiquaries of Scotland* 126, 87–102

Masset, C., 1993. *Les dolmens. Les sépultures collectives d'Europe occidentale*. Paris: Editions Errance.

Parker Pearson, M., and Ramilisonina, 1998. Stonehenge for the ancestors: the stones pass on the message. *Antiquity* 72, 308–26.

Ruggles, C., 1999. *Astronomy in Prehistoric Britain and Ireland*. New Haven: Yale University Press.

Scott, R., and Phillips. T., 1999. Clava: light at the end of the tunnel. *Current Archaeology* 165, 332–5.

Shepherd, I., 1987. The early peoples, in D. Omand (ed.), *The Grampian Book*. Golspie: The Northern Times, 119–30.

Simpson, D., 1996. Excavation of a kerbed funerary monument at Stoneyfield, Raigmore, Inverness, Highland 1972–3. *Proceedings of the Society of Antiquaries of Scotland* 126, 53–86.

Thom, A., 1971. *Megalithic Lunar Observatories*. Oxford: Clarendon Press.

Tilley, C., 1996. The power of rocks: topography and monument construction on Bodmin Moor. *World Archaeology* 28, 161–76.

9 Knocknarea: the ultimate monument

Megaliths and mountains in Neolithic Cúil Irra, north–west Ireland

Stefan Bergh

A landscape is both the framework for human action and a creation of human action. People act in a landscape that already exists and thereby build on previous assumptions and ideas about that landscape. Some of these existing ideas are linked to large-scale geographical or topographical features, such as rivers, lakes and mountains. These are the ever-present features to which everyone in a region must relate, and which are part and parcel of the common knowledge and general experience of that landscape. Such features are usually given names and thereby included in the mental landscape of the people.

Apart from the major geographical and topographical features, a landscape also consists of an unlimited number of individual locations. Some of these acquire a meaning or importance from the context in which they are experienced. In a mobile hunter-gatherer context some of these locations could have been given meaning as reference points in a landscape of movement, where a cliff-face, an erratic, a tree or a certain view could have been places of identification and guidance. At other locations, similar features could have indicated places for worship or other ritual or communal activities. In a pre-Neolithic context these places of identification were related to natural features in the landscape. Individuals were hereby creating an identity by adapting themselves to the language of the natural landscape.

The perceived opposition between natural and cultural has been the focus for stimulating research in recent years, in particular with reference to the Neolithic (Keller 1994; Bradley 2000; Cummings this volume, ch. 7). In the present context I use the term natural landscape in its geographical and topographical sense.

One of the features that characterises the Neolithic is the changed attitude to place and landscape. The emergence of monuments indicates that individuals were no longer adapting themselves to the landscape but were making the landscape adapt to them. This process should not be seen as 'taming the wild' but as an adaptation of the language of the landscape, making it into a tool of influence.

The building of megalithic monuments in the Neolithic changed the landscape in a way never seen before. Places of significance could now be created independently of nature. The eternal stone-built monuments manipulated people's apprehension of the landscape, as places were created which from then on had to be related to. It is sometimes evident from the shape and material of the megalithic monuments that they were intended to be perceived as copies of natural features, but, and this is important, at locations chosen by people and not by nature (Tilley 1991; 1994, ch. 3; Bradley 1998).

The location of megalithic monuments has been extensively studied through a number of different approaches during the last thirty years. It is now evident that the modes of location of these monuments vary widely, and the factors directing the choice of location were directly linked to the local ideological context in which that choice was made. Sometimes the rules concerning location which appear to have been dominant in one region seem not to have had any role at all in another region. It is therefore of the utmost importance to concentrate on the regional level, as it was in the regional landscape that people lived and that their monuments were experienced and given meaning (Bergh 1995).

The different types of megalithic monuments of the Irish Neolithic vary widely in spatial pattern and ritual practice as well as in location. For the passage tombs, one feature among several that sets them apart from the other types is the preference for high ground. Even though the absolute height above sea level is not always particularly pronounced (Cooney 1983), the location of the monuments in the local landscape is always commanding. The monuments are sited on raised ground, ridges or mountain-tops.

The well-known Brú na Bóinne complex is a good example where moderately elevated ground, in this instance overlooking the River Boyne, has been used in an effective way. The Carrowkeel–Keshcorran complex of some twenty passage tombs in the dramatic landscape of the Bricklieve Mountains, Co. Sligo, illustrates the concern for a commanding location in a more mountainous landscape. The most spectacularly located passage tomb in Ireland is, however, the large cairn of Miosgán Meadhbha on the flat summit of the distinctive mountain of Knocknarea, Co. Sligo (Figure 9.1). This cairn can be regarded as the ultimate consequence of an ambition to achieve maximal visual impact for a burial monument. The cairn overlooks the large cluster of passage tombs within the Carrowmore complex, and is the focal point within the Neolithic ritual landscape of Cúil Irra (Figures 9.2 and 9.4).

Before discussing the significance of the mountain of Knocknarea and its burial monuments during the Neolithic, it might be worthwhile briefly to stress some general characteristics that set a place situated on a mountain apart from a place in a lowland setting.

First, a place on a mountain, in terms of its location, is easily recognised in the landscape. It is given an *identity* which is obvious and made present in the landscape by the sheer size and shape of the mountain. Even if the place itself, on the summit, only occupies a minimal area of the mountain, it comes to share the identity of the mountain. Secondly, a place on a mountain indicates *authority*. Its location is always present in the physical landscape though the place itself, and the activity carried out there, is out of sight. So while everyone knows where it

Figure 9.1 Knocknarea mountain, looking east from Carns Hill. Photo: Stefan Bergh.

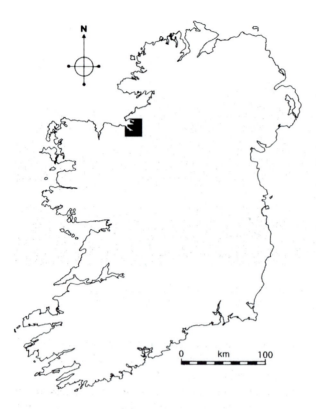

Figure 9.2 Location of the Cúil Irra region (for detail see Figure 9.4).

is, few know in detail what is actually happening up on the mountain. The creation of a relationship of power by concealment of knowledge is a common way of achieving authority, and it has been suggested that this is one of the factors at play in complex megalithic monuments (e.g. Whittle 1988, 165ff). Another kind of authority is exercised by the choice of high altitude in itself, as this imposes a certain degree of physical effort, and sometimes pain, in getting there. The place, or the mountain, can thus through this aspect be said to be 'in charge' during the approach to the site, until the summit is reached.

A third contrast between a place on a mountain and one in a lowland location is access. A lowland location can often be approached and departed from in a linear movement. It can be by-passed at relatively close range. Reaching a place on a mountain, on the other hand, entails often arduous ascent and subsequent descent (Figure 9.3). It cannot really be by-passed at close range, as an active decision has to be made whether to go there or not. In this respect the mountain can be seen as a vertical cul-de-sac.

These are some characteristics which distinguish a place on a mountain from lowland locations. But we are still left with questions as to the reasons for

Figure 9.3 Croaghaun in the Ox Mountains, south of Ballysadare Bay, looking east. A small passage tomb is located on the very restricted peak. Photo: Stefan Bergh.

choosing a place so far apart from everday activity as a mountain-top. Why is some ritual activity located at what we understand as the margins of the living world, and how are these margins to be understood?

In this context I can only briefly mention some of the possible reasons for choosing a place on a mountain (see Barnatt 1998 for other suggestions). Mountain-top locations may be an expression of the concept of liminality, as also are shorelines and islands (see Scarre this volume, ch. 6; Corlett 1998). In the case of any form of ritual activity linked to a religious context, proximity to the gods could of course have been a good reason, assuming of course that the gods were seen to be in the sky. But as there is an abundance of evidence for ritual activity on the lowlands, a perceived shorter distance to the gods cannot have been the sole reason for choosing a location at the physical edge of society. The degree of isolation that is achieved on a mountain-top could also have been important to the rituals performed there or the beliefs linked with them. Other frequently advanced reasons for location on high ground include the requirement for good conditions for astronomical observation, intervisibility with other sites or features, and perhaps even the dramatic view that a mountain-top affords. Mountains may also, by their sheer existence, have been held to embody a deity or an ancestral link, making them the natural place for any kind of ritual activity.

The Cúil Irra region

The mountain of Knocknarea is located at the western end of the Cúil Irra peninsula, on the north-west coast of Ireland (Figure 9.4). The region is

vertical sides, together with its isolated location against the Atlantic as backdrop. The only feasible access to the flat summit (at 320 metres above sea level) is up the steep slopes on the eastern side, as all other sides of the mountain consist of vertical precipices or very steep slopes. The most spectacular cliffs are found on the western side where vertical precipices up to 50 metres in height are exposed above the substantial scree. On the east side there is a ridge, some 800 metres long and 190 metres above sea level, jutting out towards the east (Figure 9.5).

The eastern half of the summit consists of a flat area measuring approximately 400 by 200 metres across. Within this area there are five passage tombs and at least two other sites, arranged along a north–south axis. The complex is totally dominated by the centrally placed cairn of Miosgán Meadhbha. Analysis of the visibility of the cairn has shown that it has been located on the summit in such a way as to give it maximum visibility when viewed from the east (Bergh 1995, 135). In contrast to Miosgán Meadhbha, the smaller monuments were not built to create a visual impact of any significance as they are not visible from the lowland.

Before the work of the Knocknarea Archaeological Project, the only pre-historic sites recorded on the mountain apart from the megalithic monuments were two hut sites on the eastern slopes (Bengtsson and Bergh 1984). Both sites were excavated and the finds were dominated by a large number of concave scrapers, made mainly of the locally available chert. The hut sites were dated to

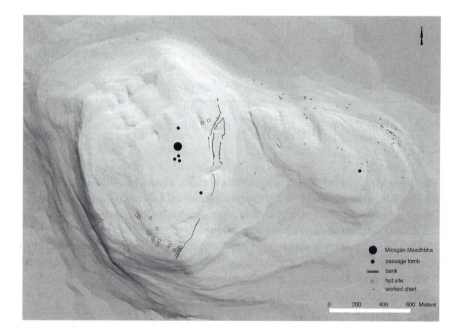

Figure 9.5 Knocknarea mountain showing location of passage tombs, banks, hut sites and stray finds of chert.

c.3000 BC. Recent surveys and excavations within the framework of the Knocknarea Archaeological Project have recorded extensive Neolithic activity on Knocknarea, the character of which opens up new approaches to the understanding of this mountain in the Neolithic.

Enclosure

Probably the most extraordinary discovery consists of a complex system of banks along the eastern side of the mountain (Figure 9.5). These are located along the 270-metre contour some 100–150 metres from the actual summit, and they cross the whole eastern side of the mountain (Bergh 2000). For the most part the bank is univallate, but at the northern end the layout is more complex. Here there are several parallel banks, some of which are segmented by gaps at irregular intervals. At this end and also at the southernmost end, the course of the banks does not follow the contour, but instead runs diagonally down the steep hillside. The total recorded length of banks comes to approximately 2.5 kilometres.

Limited trial excavations have revealed that the banks were constructed in two phases. The first phase consisted of a slab-built wall some 2 metres wide and 0.8 metres high, with a more or less rectangular cross section. In the second phase the wall was covered with smaller stones and gravel, giving it a smoother appearance with a total width of some 4 metres and a height of around 1 metre. The second phase of the bank is stratigraphically linked to extensive Neolithic activity, since large amounts of chert debris as well as flakes, cores and tools have been recorded in the gravel layer covering the bank. The finds are all confined to the uphill side of the banks, and in some areas more or less horizontal floors had been created where intensive production of chert implements took place. The all-dominating implement is the concave scraper which occurs in a wide variety of shapes and sizes. A few sherds of Neolithic decorated pottery have also been recorded, but these seem to be linked to the first phase of the bank.

Hut site

Another important discovery is the identification of approximately twenty hut sites, or hut-site features, on the southern part of the mountain (Figure 9.5). They measure 10–12 metres in diameter and consist of circular banks or stone-cleared areas. Several are attached to the southern end of the bank where it runs down the steep slope, and all of them are located on the uphill side of the bank. Limited trial excavation at two hut sites revealed that they contain identical finds to those made along the bank, that is to say, chert artefacts dominated by different types of concave scraper.

In addition to the large group of hut sites to the south, a few are located uphill from the northern end of the bank. The occurrence of hut sites on the mountain is hence restricted to the northern and southern terminals of the enclosure. The observation that the find assemblages from both the banks and the trial excavations at the hut sites are identical to those recorded from the previously excavated hut sites (Bengtsson and Bergh 1984) makes it reasonable to assume that they belong to the same cultural and chronological context, and that they should hence be dated to around 3000 BC.

Apart from the more evident banks and hut sites recorded during the survey, some thirty-five locations with worked chert have been recorded on the lower ridge to the east of the banks (Figure 9.5). Unfortunately this area is covered by a dense forest plantation which has left no surviving above-ground traces of constructed sites. The worked chert indicates, however, that there was Neolithic activity on this ridge.

Discussion

The general impression is that the large cairn of Miosgán Meadhbha is visible from everywhere round about, but this is not in fact the case. If the mountain is viewed from the north, west or south within a distance of 3–5 kilometres, the spectacular cairn is hardly visible at all. The exact location of the cairn seems to have been deliberately chosen to achieve the most striking visual impact when viewed from the centre of the Cúil Irra region, that is, from Carrowmore to the east. This easterly focus is also reflected in the general layout of the tombs on the mountain which form a north–south façade facing towards the east, turning their back to the sea. This linear layout resembles that found at Newgrange, where the monuments have been laid out like a façade facing the River Boyne below. The Carrowmore group of passage tombs, at the centre of the Cúil Irra peninsula, seems to have been the focus of the monuments on Knocknarea (Figure 9.6). The whole layout is reminiscent of a stage set, where there is a clear division between front and back. This is furthermore underlined by the probable

Figure 9.6 Looking east towards Knocknarea mountain, with Carrowmore monument 7 in the foreground. Photo: Stefan Bergh.

location of the quarry for the stones of the cairn, which is located 'backstage' some 100 metres west of the cairn, leaving the eastern slopes and the flat summit untouched.

The easterly aspect of the burial monuments on the summit is furthermore reinforced by the banks which occur only on that side of the mountain. These banks by their location and extent create an upper and lower zone, and thus distinguish the ritual area on the summit from the land below. It is interesting in this context to note that no parts of the banks, or any of the hut sites, are visible from the summit. This lack of intervisibility within the same area of the mountain could be deliberate, indicating different roles for huts and ritual monuments within a single ideological context.

As well as dividing the mountain into different zones, the banks could also have had a role in relation to the approach to the summit. The recorded Neolithic finds on the eastern ridge indicate that Neolithic activity on Knocknarea was not restricted to the higher and better-known part of the mountain, but extended to this lower ridge as well. The most convenient way of reaching the summit from the ridge is by a diagonal route up the hillside to the west. It is therefore interesting to note that the most complex part of the enclosure, where parallel banks run diagonally down the hillside, is located just at this point of the mountain. The banks here could have had a role in directing and controlling the approach to the upper zone on the summit.

The presence of large-scale tool production along some of the banks, and especially its very specialised character (the large quantity of concave scrapers) is intriguing. The chert, either as raw material or as finished products, seems however to have been critical to the activity along the enclosure and in the hut sites. As similar finds are associated with both the hut sites and the enclosure there is evidently a close link between the two, which are probably different aspects of a larger, coherent activity pattern.

At present two alternative hypotheses can be proposed to explain the worked chert. On the one hand, the production of implements might be linked to activities during the building and/or use of the ritual monuments on the summit. On the other, the extensive extraction of chert may have been carried out because the material had a special significance, originating as it does from this sacred and spectacular mountain. No proven chert quarry has yet been recorded, but there is an abundance of chert in the limestone beds of Knocknarea. Even though chert is in no way a rare material in Ireland, the parallel might be drawn with the stone-axe quarries at the Langdale Fells of Cumbria in north-west England or at Tievebulliagh in Co. Antrim, Ireland, as raw material from unusual locations could have had special value and meaning (Claris and Quartermaine 1989; Cooney 1998; Bradley 2000, 81). The conspicuous mountain of Knocknarea was an unusual location and the material extracted from it could well have had a special significance.

The role of the banks can be seen as defining the ritual space as well as directing the approach to it. As already mentioned, a characteristic of Irish passage tombs is their often commanding location in the local landscape. This aspiration for high visibility indicates a strong ambition to control the visual space of the landscape by erecting highly visible monuments, of which Miosgán Meadhbha is the most striking example. The presence of enclosed land in a passage tomb context represents another aspect of controlling space, as the banks make a physical as well as symbolic statement concerning the actual demarcation of space. These two aspects complement each other since the latter defines the former on the ground, creating a zone of special significance around the megalithic monuments.

Conclusion

It is now possible to suggest three different episodes in the Neolithic history of the spectacular mountain of Knocknarea.

- In a pre-cairn context, the isolated and eye-catching limestone mountain of Knocknarea was the focal point in the Cúil Irra region and beyond. Its presence influenced the location of the megalithic cemetery at Carrowmore at the foot of the mountain, a location directed by the language of the natural landscape.
- The active transformation of the skyline of Knocknarea by building the massive cairn of Miosgán Meadhbha on the flat summit erased the boundary between monument and landscape. The landscape was transformed into a monument, and became a tool of authority since the visual space was now controlled.
- By enclosing the mountainside with extensive banks, the ritual monuments on the summit were given a physical and symbolic definition. The ritual space of the mountain was defined on the ground.

I end with a question put to me by a local farmer last summer: 'Is Queen Maeve buried in the mountain?' he asked me. I hesitated in answering, as I realised that he saw the cairn on the summit as marking a tomb located in the mountain. For him the boundary between monument and landscape had been erased and the mountain had turned into a monument. I had to reply 'Yes, she is buried in the mountain'!

Acknowledgements

The Knocknarea Archaeological Project has mainly been financed by a Research Fellowship from The Swedish Foundation For International Co-operation in Research and Higher Education (STINT). The excavations were funded by Dúchas The Heritage Service, on the recommendation of the National Committee for Archaeology of the Royal Irish Academy, while the digital survey was funded by The Heritage Council. I wish to thank Eamon Cody for reading and commenting on a draft of this paper.

References

Barnatt, J., 1998. Monuments in the landscape: thoughts from the peak, in A. Gibson and D. Simpson (eds), *Prehistoric Ritual and Religion*. Stroud: Sutton, 92–105.

Bengtsson, H., and Bergh, S., 1984. The hut sites at Knocknarea North, Co. Sligo, in G. Burenhult (ed.), *The Archaeology of Carrowmore. Theses and Papers in North-European Archaeology* 14. Stockholm: University of Stockholm, 216–318.

Bergh, S., 1995. *Landscape of the Monuments.* Stockholm: Riksantikvarieämbetet Arkeologiska Undersökningar.

Bergh, S., 2000. Transforming Knocknarea – the archaeology of a mountain. *Archaeology Ireland* 52: 14–18.

Bradley, R., 1998. *The Significance of Monuments.* London: Routledge.

Bradley, R., 2000. *An Archaeology of Natural Places.* London: Routledge.

Claris, P., and Quartermaine, J. 1989. The Neolithic quarries and axe-factory sites of Great Langdale and Scafell Pike: a new field study. *Proceedings of the Prehistoric Society* 55, 1–25.

Cooney, G., 1983. Megalithic tombs and their environmental setting, a settlement perspective, in T. Reeves-Smyth and F. Hamond (eds), *Landscape Archaeology in Ireland*. Oxford: British Archaeological Reports, 179–94.

Cooney, G., 1998. Breaking stones, making places: the social landscape of the axe production site, in A. Gibson and D. Simpson (eds), *Prehistoric Ritual and Religion*. Stroud: Sutton, 108–18.

Cooney, G., 2000. *Landscapes of Neolithic Ireland.* London: Routledge.

Corlett, C., 1998. The prehistoric ritual landscape of the Great Sugar Loaf. *Wicklow Archaeology and History* 1, 1–8.

Keller, C., 1994. The theoretical aspects of landscape study, in T. Collins (ed.), *Decoding the Landscape*. Galway: University College Galway, 79–98.

Tilley, C., 1991. Constructing a ritual landscape, in K. Jennbert, L. Larsson, R. Petré and B. Wyszomirska-Werbart (eds), *Regions and Reflections. In Honour of Märta Strömberg.* (Acta Archaeologica Lundensia Series in 80, no. 20.) Lund: Almquist & Wiksell International, 67–79.

Tilley, C., 1994. *A Phenomenology of Landscape.* Oxford: Berg.

Whittle, A., 1988. *Problems in Neolithic Archaeology.* Cambridge: Cambridge University Press.

10 Megaliths in a mythologised landscape

South-west Ireland in the Iron Age

William O'Brien

From an archaeological perspective the 'sacred' component of landscape in prehistoric Ireland has largely been seen as spatially bounded: ritual 'sites' and monument 'complexes' that somehow stood apart from the world of everyday experience. An important temporal dimension to these sacred places is evident where there is an obvious developmental history. The Hill of Tara and the Boyne Valley 'necropolis' are prominent examples, where the past was appropriated in later times through the reuse of 'ancient' monuments. This study will consider how 'past' and 'sacred' were intertwined as deeply embedded elements in landscape perception in late prehistoric Ireland. Two themes will be examined. First, it is suggested that cults of sun worship were widespread in early religious belief in Ireland until the adoption of Christianity. An example here is the south-west region where such a religious orientation is evident in a succession of megalith 'traditions' from the Neolithic onwards. The second theme will be to consider how these 'ancient' megaliths played an active role in the creation of a mythologised landscape during the Iron Age, and how they manifest the enduring nature of religious belief through time.

The 'problem' of the Iron Age

The Iron Age in Ireland, from approximately 500 BC to the 5th century AD, has always been viewed by archaeologists as problematic, both in terms of archaeological visibility and in understanding the process of Celticisation. This is especially true for the south-west region where monuments and artefacts characteristic of this period are sparsely distributed (Figure 10.1). In particular, there is a general absence of material culture with obvious links to the Continental Celts, most notably the La Tène metalwork and art forms that appear elsewhere in Ireland from around 300 BC. The image of an 'empty landscape' at this time stands in marked contrast to a highly visible record of Bronze Age settlement in this region, and an equally rich archaeology for the Early Historic period.

Most commentators would agree that our understanding is undermined by a failure to appreciate the regionality of the Irish Iron Age, and by an approach that

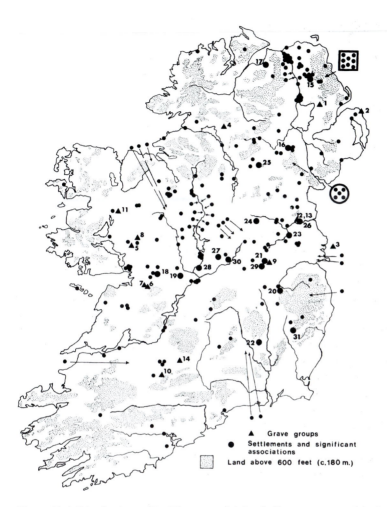

Figure 10.1 Distribution of La Tène material (excluding quernstones) in Ireland (after Raftery 1984).

gives primacy to the central place of the La Tène. The absence of a significant La Tène in south Munster has raised questions as to the precise nature of Iron Age settlement in this region. Recent discussion has focused on the possibility of a non-La Tène Iron Age, marked by significant continuity from the indigenous Late Bronze Age and a low archaeological visibility in material culture terms (Raftery 1998; Woodman 1998).

We can agree with Barrett (1999) when he says that our understanding of landscape organisation in prehistory has been limited by the approach that a particular period is characterised by reference to a range of monuments and other material residues created in that same period. The 'problem' of the Iron Age in south-west Ireland has generally been considered in these terms, with little reference to either its Bronze Age antecedents or subsequent transformation in Early Historic times. Yet this narrowness of approach can be redressed by focusing on the religious life of Iron Age communities in south-west Ireland and their use of the past. The contention is that the older prehistoric monuments of this region were an integral part of an Iron Age social landscape, which they helped to create.

Written in stone

The south-west region of Cork and Kerry is one of the best-known megalith landscapes in Ireland, marked by a dense proliferation of small stone monuments representing several Neolithic and Bronze Age ritual 'traditions'. Some 500 chambered tombs, stone circles and rows and related monuments still survive, to which many of the 600 or so single standing stones in this area could be added. A recent discussion (O'Brien 1999) has identified distinct cycles of stone monument construction during the prehistoric period.

Cycle 1

Cycle 1 is characterised by a sparse distribution of upland and coastal monuments, including simple portal tombs and cairns with passage-tomb affinities (O'Brien 1999, 5). While no secure chronology is available, these early megaliths are most likely mid 4th to early 3rd millennium BC in date. They probably represent a limited spread of agricultural settlement along the coastal region of Cork and Kerry from earlier Neolithic times.

Cycle 2

The mid 3rd millennium BC saw the emergence of a vigorous monument tradition in the form of the wedge tomb (De Valera and O Nualláin 1982; O'Brien 1999). Some 134 examples have been identified in counties Cork and Kerry, mostly distributed along the south-western peninsulas or in west-central Cork (Figure 10.2). These small gallery tombs represent the first significant agricultural settlement of this region, spanning a transition from the metal-using Neolithic (*c*.2400–2100 BC) to the beginning of Early Bronze Age society in around 2000 BC. Though used over many centuries, it is unlikely that wedge tombs continued to be built after 1700 BC.

Cycle 3

A new range of free-standing megaliths appeared in the Cork–Kerry landscape from around 1500 BC onwards, with some examples built as late as 800 BC (O'Brien 1993). These monuments include two variants of the axial stone circle, as well as stone rows, pairs of stones, single monoliths, boulder-burials, and radial stone cairns (Figure 10.2). Their spatial relationship has led to suggestions of a 'stone circle complex' (O Nualláin 1975; 1984), but it is equally possible that these monuments represent successive ritual traditions within the Middle to Late Bronze Age. It is likely from their close association in the landscape that they share common elements of religious belief.

Cycle 4

A further phase of megalith-building may have seen the continued erection of single standing stones after *c*.800 BC. The dating of this monument type is problematic, with a suggestion that at least some examples were erected in south-west Ireland during the Iron Age (O'Leary and Shee Twohig 1993). Also relevant here is the appearance of Ogham-inscribed stones, most probably in the 4th century AD (Moore 1998). The large number of Ogham stones that were carved in south-west Ireland over the next three centuries is evidence of significant settlement as the pagan Iron Age ended.

Cycle 5

The introduction of Christianity from the 5th century AD onwards had a profound influence on the sacred geographies of the south-west region. Echoes of the pagan world may be found in some monuments and rituals of the early Christian church. This period saw the appearance of a new 'megalith' tradition, in the form of pillar stones and cross-slabs with a distinctive Christian iconography (Okasha and Forsyth 2000), as well as an expanded use of Ogham stones, the use of slab shrines, and other features.

The ancient 'megalith' traditions of south-west Ireland map the spread of particular belief systems in time and space, as do other expressions of ritual in the landscape, from rock art to earthen barrows. These cycles have generally been seen in terms of ethnic or social discontinuity, with different monument traditions signifying different religious beliefs. While monuments may change in form, however, a core religious belief can endure to be reinterpreted by later generations, a rendering of the past that finds expression in new architectural 'traditions' or in patterns of activity at older monuments. These megalith distributions represent a palimpsest of contextualised landscapes through time, through which we can explore themes of continuity and transformation in the ritual sphere, and ultimately in society as a whole. The monuments went through different cycles of interpretation in a culturally inscribed landscape, from active ceremonial use as burial places and shrines to later perceptions of liminal and sacred space. Clearly we must distinguish between, on the one hand, the significance that these monuments held for the population groups who built and used them and their immediate descendants, and, on the other, their subsequent interpretation by later Bronze Age and Iron Age communities whose social and religious values were moulded by their own understanding of this past.

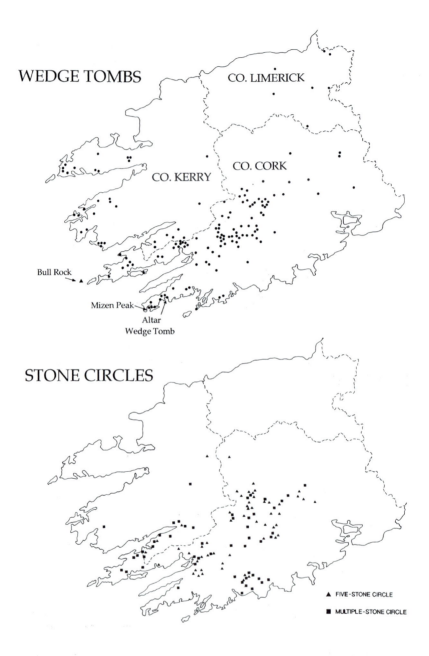

WEDGE TOMBS

CO. LIMERICK

CO. CORK

CO. KERRY

Bull Rock

Mizen Peak

Altar
Wedge Tomb

STONE CIRCLES

▲ FIVE-STONE CIRCLE

■ MULTIPLE-STONE CIRCLE

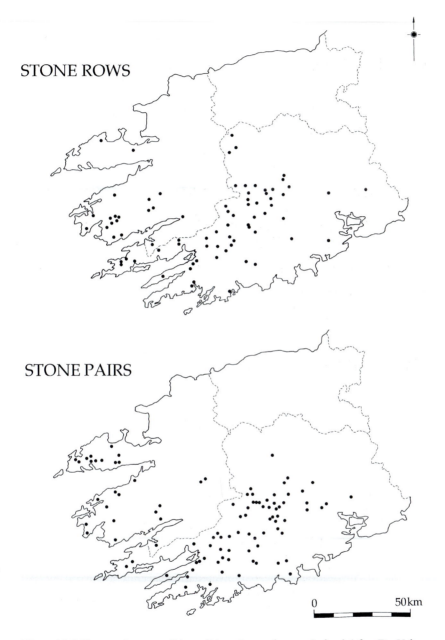

STONE ROWS

STONE PAIRS

0   50km

Figure 10.2 Bronze Age megalith traditions in south-west Ireland (after De Valera and O Nualláin 1982, O Nualláin 1984 and O Nualláin 1988; with additions).

Landscape, monuments and memory

People in Ireland in the late 1st millennium BC lived in landscapes that were imbued with meanings. These derived from a pre-existing world of the Bronze Age and were materialised through monuments and by association with elements of the natural landscape. The presence of a thousand or more Bronze Age mega-liths in the Cork–Kerry region will undoubtedly have affected how people in the Iron Age perceived, experienced and contextualised their landscape. For these communities, the 'ancient' megaliths were living reminders of the mythic past.

These Bronze Age monuments demarcate symbolic space in the landscape – sacred space that required an interpretation by Iron Age people of an older world. Barrett (1999, 256) makes the point that 'a pre-existing landscape offered an environment of potential experiences and signification', adding that 'the transformation of the landscape lay not so much in its physical modification as in its interpretation'. This is evidently true for south-west Ireland where social experience during the Iron Age was marked by an interpretation of the pre-existing Bronze Age landscape, just as the latter was conditioned by reference to an older Neolithic world.

Bradley (1993) reminds us that monuments are about memory and one of the main ways that societies remember is through ritual, when the past reaches into the present and is 'a source of timeless propositions about the world, of eternal verities whose authority is guarded by specialised methods of communication' (Bradley 1993, 2). While monuments endure as physical entities, the ideas and symbolism they embody are mutable as they are encountered by successive generations who see them from different perspectives. Bradley concludes that monuments 'epitomise a creative process by which the significance of the past was constantly rethought and reinterpreted. Monuments were adapted and altered to conform with changing circumstances. In this way, they provide a subtle index of deeper currents in society' (Bradley 1993, 93).

Bradley observes how monuments can dominate the landscape of later generations and so provide constant reminders of the past. People live their lives in relation to the past and they understand their world by reference to 'tradition'. He points out that tradition can be invented and the past can assume the status of a myth, while new developments are more secure when invested with the authority of the past (Bradley 1993, 119). Thomas (1991) observes that the reuse of monuments is a way of reintroducing the past into the present in a specific way. While this invocation can be manipulated to social ends, it will usually take the form of a contemporary cosmology, often expressed as a fervent religious belief.

The authority of the past

During the Iron Age, as in all periods of prehistory, ritual played an important role in shaping cultural identity. Ritual allows fundamental beliefs to pass down the generations, mediated through monuments that were central to the symbolic construction of community and identity. As Richards (1999, 84) observed, 'the past itself becomes a symbolic resource, and an essential component of the ritual impact of place, a dimension of meaning which can be manipulated to legitimise new political or social ideologies'.

Social conditions can be transformed not only by the construction of monuments but also by the changing patterns of their use. There are many instances where prehistoric ritual monuments were reinterpreted to legitimise a political elite. Tara and the Boyne Valley tombs are notable examples, but such acts of appropriation probably also extended to smaller monuments in local political contexts. The Bronze Age megaliths of south-west Ireland may have been viewed in a new light as the local communities entered the Iron Age, when their antiquity and mythological associations became a potent force in society. These 'ancient stones' were transformed as sacred places because the references by which they were known changed in a new social context. Their religious dimension endured to help create that new world as the monuments served to mythologise the wider cultural landscape.

This process may also be illustrated by the Iron Age of southern Britain where a new social order gained legitimacy by reference to a past represented by Neolithic and Bronze Age burial mounds (Barrett 1999, 262). The latter 'endured to become Iron Age monuments'; they received no further physical modification, but did however continue as a significant element in the Iron Age landscape and as such were presumably recognised and drawn into an understanding of that landscape. Even though these Bronze Age monuments do not appear on distribution maps of the Iron Age, 'they remained a crucial and integrated component of the Iron Age landscape, and . . . their lack of further modification holds a key to understanding how the inhabitation of that landscape accommodated them' (Barrett 1999, 258). Barrett concludes that the political relations of the Iron Age gained their validity in reference to these mythical origins.

Through the looking-glass

There are many difficulties in trying to understand human attitudes to the past during the Iron Age in south-west Ireland, not least of which is our poor understanding of almost every facet of human life here in this period! With ritual monuments we face the problem that their meaning was mutable through time, without necessarily involving physical change to these sacred sites. Even where archaeologists can identify Iron Age activity at these older monuments, understanding the deposition of artefacts and other material is highly ambiguous. While some advances have been made in dating (O'Brien 1993; 1999), the available chronologies still only provide a coarse index of the true continuum of ritual activity at these sites. We must also define what exactly is meant by 'continuity' and 'disuse' in the context of monument history. The continued use of a monument need not imply a background of social stability or a continuity of belief. Conversely, the absence of physical evidence for subsequent use does not shed much light on how a monument was regarded in later periods – it may have been so sacred as to be a taboo location.

There has been no attempt to examine the belief systems of Iron Age communities in south-west Ireland to date, largely because of our poor understanding of the contemporary settlement landscape and society. We can overcome this interpretative paralysis if we explore the Bronze Age heritage of these people, because to understand how they regarded the older monuments in their midst will provide an important insight into their cultural values and religious outlook. To attempt this, we must first examine what these megaliths meant to the Neolithic and Bronze Age societies who built them.

Bronze Age cosmologies

In our approach to Bronze Age 'religion' it is clear that wedge tombs, stone circles and related monuments gave physical expression to a sense of spirituality and a belief in an 'otherworld' existence. The rituals connected with these 'sacred sites' were part of a wider cosmological understanding of the world and the place of the people within it. Clearly, these stone monuments are inherently symbolic and so should reflect in some fundamental way the central beliefs of the religious practice concerned. These beliefs are materialised in the architecture and orientation of these monuments, and in their use-history. While the design of these monuments has functional possibilities (to receive offerings, to hold burials, to congregate people), the consistency of its execution over a wide geographical area suggests a deeper religious significance.

Portals to the otherworld

Among their many functions, megalithic tombs and stone circles offered a gateway to an otherworld in the consciousness of prehistoric people. These megaliths brought believers into direct contact with the supernatural and were central to their existential beliefs. The monument was a door between the living world and a higher plane of supernatural power and transcendent beings. To pass through was in effect to mediate with this otherworld. What mattered here was not only physical access to the sacred space, but rather the requisite knowledge to invoke the spirits of the monument. Each wedge tomb and stone circle played host to a community of believers, for whom the monument was a symbol of their collective belief in a supernatural power. This belief was expressed through their words and actions, in ritual ceremonies that celebrated the endurance of the community through reverence for the ancestors and appeasement of the tomb spirits.

The burial of human remains also played a part in this invocation of otherworld powers. Most of these Bronze Age megaliths in south-west Ireland were associated with mortuary practice, the form and significance of which varied across different monument traditions. Common elements include a desire to present human remains in a staged environment within the living landscape, thus placing the host community under the benign influence of supernatural powers. It is also apparent that only a small segment of these Bronze Age communities ever received burial in a wedge tomb or stone circle. The interments generally took place early in the history of these monuments, which were not considered appropriate for human burial after a certain passage of time. This is supported by the fact that no burials of a clearly 'secondary' character have been found in some twenty Bronze Age megalith sites excavated in the Cork–Kerry region.

These monuments may have been the focus for ancestral veneration, housing the remains of individuals who were important to the collective memory of the community. Ancestral figures are believed to have played an important role in wedge-tomb cosmology, where the monument served as a shrine to hold the relics of holy or important people (O'Brien 1999, 203–10). Ancestors may have been deified or served an important role as intermediaries between this world and the otherworld. Through the ancestral presence the wedge tomb may have been a place of oracle and divination where seers sought advice or offered prophecy. Ancestors were also important in the symbolic affirmation of group identity and in the control of resources (O'Brien 2000a). It is not clear whether the differences in mortuary practice between wedge tombs and stone-circle monuments signify an important change in the role of ancestors as the Bronze Age progressed. This does seem likely in the context of widespread social change in this period.

Children of the sun

A common element of religious belief across almost 4,000 years of megalith building in prehistoric south-west Ireland is the central place of the sun. The earliest suggestion of sun worship comes from the small number of passage tombs in the first cycle of megaliths in this region. Elsewhere in Ireland, passage-tomb cosmology is closely associated with sun worship, with solar symbolism apparent in monument art and design. This belief system penetrated into the south-west region to a limited extent, as indicated by the discovery of a ruined passage tomb on Clear Island, west Cork (O'Leary 1989). This monument has a possible summer solstice alignment, and can be linked to a local discovery of a stone decorated with spiral art of the Boyne Valley 'tradition'. It is interesting to speculate whether the prehistoric rock art of this region, with its cup-and-ring motifs and obvious affinities with passage-tomb art, is also connected with solar symbolism.

Crossing to the dark side

The appearance of wedge tombs from *c.*2400 BC saw a further expression of solar religion in Ireland. The sunset horizon was to become the dominant reference point for all ritual activity in the Cork–Kerry region over the next three millennia. A consistent feature of wedge-tomb design is an orientation of the chamber axis towards the west or south-west horizon (Figure 10.3). This is a

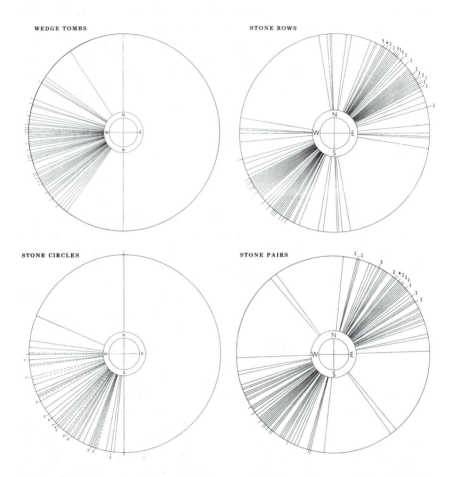

Figure 10.3 Orientation of Bronze Age megaliths in south-west Ireland (after De Valera and O Nualláin 1982, O Nualláin 1984 and O Nualláin 1988; with additions).

strong religious imperative with deliberate emphasis on the descending or setting sun in late autumn, winter or early spring. The spread of wedge-tomb orientations may relate to different solar or terrestrial alignments with respect to the distant horizon unique to each site. Alternatively, the orientation of each monument may reflect the position of the descending or setting sun on the day the monument was built or at the time of a human death.

It is common to find a belief among ancient peoples that the western horizon, where the sun 'died' each night, was perceived as the domain of the dead. This symbolism of the setting sun may have been central to how these Bronze Age people understood the passing of human life and the journey to the otherworld. In the case of wedge tombs these monuments served as funnel-shaped openings to the otherworld, facing the descending or setting sun to emphasise the symbolic dualism of light/life and darkness/death (Figure 10.4). We can envisage evening rituals when the descending or setting sun shone into the chamber, releasing the spirit of the deceased, already freed by cremation, as a final rite of passage. Various symbolic elements (solar energy, tomb design, material offerings, human remains) worked together in an expression of religious belief that embraced themes of transformation and renewal, death and rebirth. Gold 'sun-discs' may also have been part of the ritual paraphernalia in this cult of sun worship (O'Brien 1999, 284).

The orientation of wedge tombs has close similarities with the trend for many stone circles and rows in this region (Figure 10.3). This is broadly in harmony with the physical grain of this region, with its distinctive Hercynian folding of south-west trending ridges and valleys, peninsulas and bays. A study of the axial stone circles shows a general orientation between west and south (O Nualláin 1984). While there is no consistent astronomical or topographic alignment pattern (Ruggles 1999a, 99), a broad association with the sunset horizon is likely. This is emphasised by the specific solar alignment of individual monuments (Roberts 1996), one well-known example being the winter solstice alignment at Drombeg, Co. Cork (Figure 10.5). Similarly, the stone rows of Cork and Kerry have a consistent orientation along a north-east/south-west axis, which is seen as astronomically significant. Lunar alignments have been proposed (Lynch 1982; Ruggles 1999a, 103–7), but the general pattern also points to the significance of the rising and/or setting sun.

While previous research on these stone circles and rows has focused on specific astronomical alignment, which is indeed a feature of individual monuments, the overall picture is one of a general respect for the sunset horizon in the darker months of the year. There is an obvious connection between an emphasis on the setting sun in the season of death and the funerary use of these monuments. This was emphasised in other ways, most notably through the use of white quartz in wedge tombs and stone-circle monuments. Symbolic of light and the life-force, white quartz was used both as a structural element and as pebble scatters in these monuments (O'Brien 1999, 215–16). There is an obvious connection with solar power, and with the use of fire, in rituals that transposed continuity in the natural realm to the spirituality of the monument.

How did later Bronze Age people, who built stone circles, rows and related monuments, regard the older wedge tombs of the landscape? Although they frequently occur in the same landscape, stone-circle monuments generally avoid wedge tombs at a local level. There is no evidence that the stone-circle-builders deliberately damaged wedge tombs, nor did they actively embrace them within their own ritual architecture. Instead, we find evidence for occasional use in a manner that recognised the continued significance of these monuments. These include the pit deposits made at Altar and Toormore in west Cork, and the structural modification of Island wedge tomb, also in Cork. The discovery of 'secondary' Bronze Age artefacts in other wedge tombs in Ireland, from metal-casting moulds to coarse ware pottery, is relevant here (O'Brien 1999, 223–5). This evidence, though limited, points to continued veneration of some wedge

Figure 10.4 Altar wedge tomb, Co. Cork, with roofstones removed. A large pit used for Iron Age rituals is visible at rear of chamber (scale: 50cm divisions).

Figure 10.5 Drombeg, Co. Cork. This axial stone circle is aligned with a nearby hill notch where the sun sets at the winter solstice. Central pit cremation dated to 1124–794 BC.

tombs during the later Bronze Age. The wedge tomb was now regarded as an 'ancient' monument, a sacred place worthy of respect and fear, never ignored or desecrated.

The mythologised landscape

Several writers have referred to the pagan Celtic preoccupation with the supernatural, 'a people dominated by their religious belief, with deities and Underworld beings a continuous, lurking backdrop to their daily lives' (Raftery 1994, 178). The natural landscape is fully embedded in this mythologised understanding of the past, while older prehistoric monuments also came to be associated with this supernatural world. Early Irish mythology has a strong belief in a pre-Celtic race called the Tuatha Dé Danann, who retreated to the ancient tombs and cairns following their defeat by the Gaelic people (O hOgáin 1991, 408). We see a parallel existence of otherworld beings, a supernatural community living beside the human one in the ancient monuments, in caves, mountains, springs, rivers and lakes.

Tech Duinn

In early mythology Munster, the south-west province of Ireland, was conceptualised as the 'place of death' – the natural geographical connection to the outer province of the dead (Loffler 1983, 295–6). This otherworld was the realm of the death-god Donn ('the Dark One'), an ancestor deity of the Milesians, a mythical early Celtic race, who was drowned during an abortive invasion on the south-west coast. The eldest of the sons of Mil, his death is linked to a conflict with the Tuatha Dé Danann goddess Eriu, possibly symbolising the struggle between the pre-Celtic and Celtic worlds (Gwynn 1924, 311; Loffler 1983, 291). He inhabits Tech Duinn ('House of Donn'), identified as the Bull Rock, a small islet off the south-west coast of Co. Cork (Figure 10.6). In its most symbolic form the departure of the spirits of the dead was envisaged as following the course of the sun as it passed under the archway of Donn's dwelling into the sea and from thence to the otherworld (O hOgáin 1999, 59). In early mythology, Donn is a manifestation of the Daghdha, the great ancestor deity and Lord of the Otherworld, who also is the personification of the sun. The mythology of Donn was subsequently reinterpreted in folk tradition down to modern times (see Muller-Lisowski 1948)

The story of Donn, and its incorporation into an otherworld concept and Celtic origin myth, is open to various interpretations. This may be an allegory of how the south-west region resisted political transformation from the mid 1st millennium BC, only to be subsequently Celticised in the early centuries AD. Alternatively, it may relate to a Celtic otherworld belief that emerged in later mythology long after intrusive Iron Age populations appeared in this region. While various interpretations are possible, it is suggested here that embedded within the Tech Duinn myth are beliefs that owe their origin to an older Bronze

Figure 10.6 The Bull Rock, Co. Cork, is associated with the legendary otherworld
            portal Tech Duinn. The base is perforated by a natural sea tunnel, some
            150 metres long, 30 metres high and 12 metres wide, that faces the south-
            western horizon. Photo: John Eagle.

Age belief system. This was an interpretation of the south-west as a liminal zone,
the place of death/darkness, a perception reinforced by the dense concentration
of megaliths in this landscape. The Tech Duinn myth may mirror the religious
belief that underpinned the use of wedge tombs and stone circles in the Bronze
Age. Given that these monuments reveal an obvious belief in an otherworld
existence connected to a solar power, some such interpretation seems likely.

Messages from the past

It is well known that prehistoric burial mounds and other monuments were
important sacred places for many Iron Age communities in Ireland. Sites like
Newgrange and other passage tombs figure prominently in early Irish mythology
as places of otherworld power, while many have political significance as places
of inauguration and ceremony lasting into medieval times. There are numerous
other examples where Neolithic and Bronze Age mounds were reused for human
burial and other purposes during the Iron Age (see Raftery 1994, 180–99). In
Celtic mythology these mounds were considered to be inhabited by the spirits
of the noble dead and to contain passageways that led to the otherworld
(O hOgáin 1999, 104).

Turning to south-west Ireland, apart from ring-barrows and probably standing stones we cannot identify any other ritual sites that were built here during the Iron Age. While this may be a problem of archaeological visibility, it supports the idea that the older Bronze Age monuments played an important role as sacred places, by virtue of their antiquity and mythological associations. Archaeological evidence is limited; however, the potential for research is illustrated by the excavation of a small wedge tomb at Altar in coastal west Cork (O'Brien 1993; 1999). Radiocarbon dating of a small pit inside the tomb entrance suggests activity between 356 BC–AD 68 (two-sigma calibration range), while an adjacent shell deposit is dated to 2 BC–AD 230. The fill sequence of a large pit towards the rear of the chamber (Figure 10.4) is dated to AD 120–336. This pit contained marine shell and fish remains, with evidence of *in situ* burning.

Also relevant here is a recently excavated ritual monument at Ballycarty, near Tralee, Co. Kerry (Connolly 1999). This consists of a subcircular stone cairn with a funnel-shaped entrance on the western side, and a short passage leading to a circular chamber area. While dating and cultural affinities have not been clarified, this monument is probably a local variant of the passage-tomb tradition (Cycle 1) in south-west Ireland. There are few details as to use-history; however, a series of radiocarbon dates does raise interesting questions as to the later significance of this monument. A single date for charcoal inside the entrance passage, calibrated to 96 BC–AD 75, suggests activity here in the Iron Age. The orientation of this monument to the west, possibly to the setting sun at the vernal equinox (Connolly 1999, 64), invites comparison with the use of wedge tombs like Altar in this period.

There is little evidence of Iron Age activity in the stone circles and related monuments of this region. However, once again this may be due to lack of survival and recognition. Recent excavation at Lissyviggeen stone circle near Killarney, Co. Kerry, has radiocarbon-dated a fire event to the 1st century AD (Figure 10.7; O'Brien 2000b). Also of interest is the presence of Ogham inscriptions of 4th–6th century AD date on a small number of Bronze Age monuments in this region (Moore 1998, fig. 4.1). Examples here include the stone pairs at Dromlusk and Derrygarrane South in Co. Kerry, and a rock-art outcrop at Knockbrack near Milltown, Co. Kerry. It is also likely that secondary Ogham inscriptions are present on several Bronze Age standing stones in this region, one imposing example being that at Faunkill in the Beara Peninsula, Co. Cork.

What understanding did the Iron Age people of south-west Ireland have of these older Bronze Age monuments? There is little evidence that they tried to destroy, desecrate or block access to these monuments, in an obvious display of antipathy or fear. However, the archaeological record is often equivocal in this regard, as seen in the case of the wedge tomb at Kilmashogue, Co. Dublin, where the main chamber was partly filled with stone fragments from a partial destruction of the monument. Charcoal from this fill has been dated to the Iron Age (Brindley and Lanting 1991/92, 24), raising the possibility that this particular monument was subject to malicious interference in that period. There may have

Figure 10.7 Lissyviggeen stone circle, Killarney, Co. Kerry. Setting for an Iron Age fire ceremony dated to the first century AD?

been widely differing interpretations of these older monuments in Iron Age societies across Ireland.

Most Iron Age communities were probably impressed by the antiquity of these megaliths, the achievement of their construction, and by various historical or mythological associations that survived in folk memory and religious belief. Early mythology suggests that these sites were seen as the dwelling places of spirits and ancestors, supernatural powers who were central to religious belief and cosmology. For this reason access to the 'ancient stones' was probably controlled by social convention and religious taboo.

A recent study of the Orkney passage tombs considers that their reuse in Iron Age times was in order to create a conscious link with the past. They may 'have been redefining the tradition of past constructions in their own terms' – in 'an attempt to project the identity of the lineage through an association with the ancestors' (Hingley 1996, 241). Whereas Iron Age people in Atlantic Scotland may have viewed older tombs as ancestral, different attitudes may have prevailed in south-west Ireland. The lack of domestic debris in wedge tombs and stone circles points to these monuments as liminal space, and contrasts sharply with the treatment of the Scottish tombs. These former monuments were mythologised to such a high degree that they were not considered appropriate for either human burial or artefact offerings. However, individual sites had their own unique histories, the contrasting use of the neighbouring Altar and Toormore wedge tombs in west Cork being a good example (O'Brien 1999). This raises a question as to why some Bronze Age megaliths held greater significance than others in the Iron Age.

Landscapes of the mind

The building of a monument creates a new sense of time and place at a given location – a natural place is transformed for ever in human consciousness. Many monuments were built in natural places that had already acquired a special significance, but it is also true that monuments can be part of a process whereby natural places subsequently gain their importance. This process is particularly obvious in the case of the 'sacred mountains' of the south-west where older monuments were drawn into a mythologised understanding of landscape. One obvious example is the Paps of Anu in Co. Kerry where a mountain landscape with prehistoric cairns is associated with the mother goddess of pre-Christian Ireland.

This is also evident at Altar wedge tomb in west Cork, already seen to have been the setting for ritual offerings in the Iron Age. This monument is precisely aligned on Mizen Peak (232m OD), a pyramidal shaped hill some 13 kilometres away across an open bay (Figure 10.8). Mizen Peak is believed to be Carn Ui Néit, a place connected in early legends with the Tuatha Dé Danann people. One figure associated with this mountain is Balar, a mythical tyrant with a blazing eye that destroyed all on which he looked. O hOgáin (1991, 43) refers to a comparable figure, Bolerion, associated with Land's End, Cornwall, who is also

Figure 10.8 Altar wedge tomb, Co. Cork, with alignment across Toormore Bay on distant Mizen Peak.

represented by solar imagery. Balar is linked in early mythology to the second Battle of Moytirra, when the Tuatha Dé Danann under the command of the god Lugh defeated the demonic race known as the Fomhoire of whom Balar was a leader. In one version Balar of the Evil Eye was subsequently pursued to the south-west of Ireland where he was beheaded by Lugh at Carn Ui Néit (O hOgáin 1991, 144). Lugh ('The Shining One') is also represented as a major sun deity in early Irish mythology.

From this, we can understand why the wedge tomb at Altar held a special significance for Iron Age people in the locality (Figure 10.9). This Bronze Age monument was drawn into their religious beliefs, possibly as a burial place of ancestors, but more probably as an abode of supernatural powers and portal to an otherworld now conceptualised as Tech Duinn. The marine food offerings made here in the Iron Age may have been linked to this idea of an otherworld beyond the sea, the latter regarded as the genesis of all life in early Irish mythology (Loffler 1983, 303). The placing of this fish and shellfish at Altar can also be linked to the lighting of a fire in the large chamber pit (O'Brien 1999, figs 51–3). As the earthly counterpart of the sun and symbol of life and rejuvenation, it is likely that fire held a special place in these religious beliefs.

The Altar tomb may have been particularly significant owing to its visual association with the sacred mountain of Carn Ui Néit. This alignment was possibly of greater significance, as the sun sets behind this mountain in early February and early November, the latter corresponding to Samhain, the ancient Celtic festival of the dead. This raises the interesting question whether the idea of an ancient Celtic calendar, involving an eightfold division of the year, is relevant to an understanding of Bronze Age megalith orientation. Ruggles (1999a; 1999b) has considered this in the light of the Altar alignment and is sceptical of any such association. However, he does acknowledge that this may explain the special significance of the Altar monument in the Iron Age, as this is the only Bronze Age megalith in this region to demonstrate that particular alignment on Mizen Peak.

In conclusion, from a consideration of archaeological evidence and early mythology we see how Iron Age rituals at Altar, involving a fire ceremony and marine offerings inside the chamber, may have been linked to a solar calendrical event marking the festival of Samhain. The deliberate alignment of the monument on the sacred mountain of Carn Ui Néit served to heighten the atmosphere on those particular occasions. This is a good example of an older monument being drawn into a cosmological understanding of the landscape in later times.

The triumph of Christianity

For this sun which we see rises daily for us because He commands so, but it will never reign, nor will its splendour last; what is more, those wretches who adore it will be miserably punished. Not so we, who believe in, and worship, the true sun – Christ – who will never perish.

(St Patrick, *Confessio*)

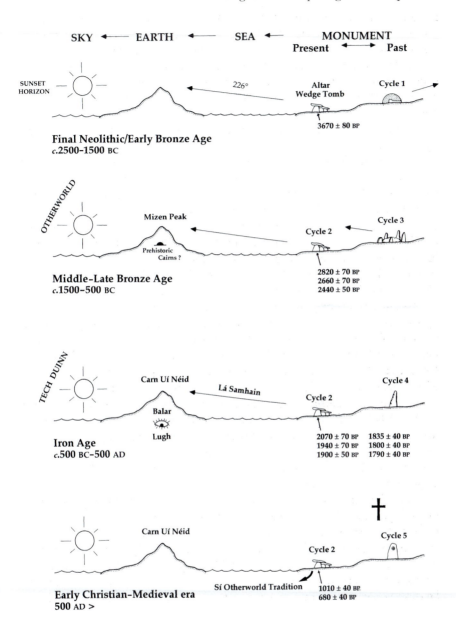

Figure 10.9 Sacred sites, sacred geographies: Altar wedge tomb in its landscape setting through time.

The 5th and 6th centuries saw the rapid spread of the Christian faith across Ireland, through zealous mission work that inevitably involved a clash with the older pagan beliefs. This conflict is recalled in the 7th-century biography of St Patrick, most famously in his lighting of the paschal fire on the Hill of Slane in opposition to the fire of the Druids on nearby Tara. So deep-rooted was the pagan cult of the sun in late prehistoric Ireland that it provided a major challenge to the early Christian mission (O hOgáin 1999, 190). The eventual triumph of Christianity saw these older beliefs submerged into a folk tradition that has survived down to modern times.

It would be interesting to examine the attitude of the first Christian missionaries to any active use or lingering tradition surrounding the Bronze Age megaliths of the south-west region. There are no historical sources to shed light on this, but it is certain that these 'pagan' monuments required a new interpretation as Christianity took hold. Though rejected by the established religion, the ancient stones continued to have certain associations for good or evil for local communities down to the modern era. Like other prehistoric monuments, wedge tombs and stone circles were regarded as otherworldly, the abodes of the Sí or fairies who inhabited the countryside as a parallel otherworld community (O hOgáin 1991, 185).

Archaeological evidence of this development is weak; however, it is clear that these monuments have no significant ritual use from early in the Christian era, and are certainly not used for human burial. The strength of the Sí tradition does raise questions as to the perception of these 'pagan' monuments. Recent archaeological finds are of interest here. A shell deposit at the entrance to Altar wedge tomb has been dated to the 10th or 11th century (O'Brien 1999, 138). At the nearby Toormore wedge tomb a deposit containing wheat, barley and rye, fish and bird bone placed at the tomb entrance, possibly in a cloth bag, has been radiocarbon-dated to AD 1425–1640 (O'Brien 1999, 180–1). Radiocarbon dates from Ballycarty passage tomb in Co. Kerry point to activity here between AD 547–655 and AD 1020–1379 respectively, contemporary with two bronze ringed pins found in close proximity on the cairn surface (Connolly 1999, 92). These, and comparable finds from other megalithic tombs in Ireland, point to a possible survival of pagan beliefs in local folklore traditions that surrounded these ancient sites down to modern times.

The Iron Age in south-west Ireland

The process of 'becoming Iron Age' in Ireland is generally associated with a significant transformation in social organisation and landscape perception, changes in settlement that had their origins in the Late Bronze Age. This may also be true for the south-west region where the appearance of hill-forts in the 1st millennium BC suggests fundamental changes in society. The question then arises whether this involved a rejection of Bronze Age beliefs, or rather that the older monuments carried their significance into the Iron Age, albeit with new interpretations.

I suggest that the distinctive character of the Iron Age in this region derives from its Bronze Age substrate and the way that people living here in the late 1st millennium BC interpreted this heritage. This is supported by the fact that the south-western lacuna in the La Tène distribution in Ireland corresponds geo-graphically (at least in part) to the social landscapes of the Bronze Age marked by wedge-tomb and stone-circle distributions (compare Figures 10.1 and 10.2). What we are looking at here is essential settlement continuity from Bronze Age to Iron Age times. There is no La Tène metalwork in south-west Ireland because people living there during the Iron Age subscribed to different cultural values that emanated directly from their Bronze Age heritage. They belonged to a world that owed its origins to an indigenous past.

This world, however, was not immune to external influence. The Hallstatt finds from Aughinish, Co. Limerick, Cappagh and Kilmurry in Co. Kerry, are evidence of contact between local Bronze Age communities and Continental Celts around the 6th century BC (Raftery 1998). The discovery of Roman material in the south-west is evidence of external links at a later date that would ultimately transform this Iron Age society. I agree with Warner (1998) when he argues that the resistance of the south-western region to Celticisation in the La Tène period was due to the presence of a strong local aristocracy since Late Bronze Age times. Whether through acculturation or, as Warner argues, Romanised intruders, this resistance eventually collapsed in the early centuries AD when the south-west region was finally Celticised, by population groups whose familiarity with Latin literacy saw them go on to develop the Ogham script.

Continuity and change in ritual and belief

While the symbolic dimension of megalithic monuments is widely recognised, many researchers have been slow to accept that fervent religious beliefs lay behind these ritual practices. Certain shared beliefs and values underlie the physical reality of these monument traditions. These core beliefs can be long-enduring, to be reinterpreted by different monument traditions as society evolved. In the successive megalith 'traditions' in south-west Ireland we can see how one such religious belief endured and was redefined in the face of changing social values and circumstances.

The appearance of stone circles and related monuments in this region by 1500 BC has generally been seen as marking an emphatic break with the past, through the arrival of a new people or new ritual practices. However, we can also see certain shared elements of belief, most notably in the common orientation of wedge tombs and stone-circle monuments. This continuity of belief is further emphasised by the complementary regional distribution of these monuments, suggestive of stable settlement patterns in the long term.

By the Middle Bronze Age it can be argued that worship of the sun was to the fore of religious beliefs in south-west Ireland. It is likely that the principal deity was a sun god, a forerunner of the great Daghdha of Celtic mythology, whose worship now focused on new monument types that embraced solar symbolism. The appearance of stone circles and stone rows was a development from the sun-worship beliefs that lay behind the building of wedge tombs. With the appearance of stone circle monuments we see a marked strengthening of the solar cult, while other elements of wedge belief, most notably the place of ancestors, are diminished. It appears that by the Middle Bronze Age the wedge tomb was no longer appropriate to the new social orders emerging in south-west Ireland. This new society grew out of the wedge-tomb communities that populated this region in the Early Bronze Age who passed on a set of timeless values that their descendants reinterpreted through new ritual foci in the landscape.

In the Iron Age we see a further transformation of religious belief, as the older monuments come to represent a mythical past. While Bronze Age megaliths may have physically endured into the Iron Age, it does not follow that the beliefs and cosmology they represented also continued. However, the reuse of these monuments during the Iron Age was probably based on some understanding of their early significance. This is likely given the strength of the oral tradition seen in early Celtic mythology. In the Tech Duinn myth, and in the excavation record from sites like Altar, we see how elements of an older Bronze Age belief system were incorporated into an Iron Age cosmology that attached special significance to the 'ancient stones' on the landscape. Elsewhere in Ireland we see further evidence for continuity in religious belief from earlier times. Many burial rites of the Iron Age reflect Bronze Age practices, while Raftery (1981, 199) argues that the paucity of burials from both periods of prehistory is a further indication of cultural continuity in the 1st millennium BC. This supports the suggestion that significant elements of Bronze Age religious belief survived into the Iron Age.

In conclusion, there has been a tendency to interpret different monument traditions in terms of different religious beliefs and cosmologies. By accepting that religious belief can transcend monument form, we see how the past reaches into the present to create the mythologised landscape.

An archaeology of inhabitation

When we explore the interface between archaeology and early Irish mythology there are indications of a mythologised landscape in the south-west region, encompassing elements of the natural landscape and monuments from the 'ancient' past. This term 'mythologised landscape' embraces both the sacred and non-sacred components of landscape, and also emphasises the incorporation of past worlds into these sacred geographies. In this paper I have argued that the south-west horizon was invested with cosmological and mythic significance by Iron Age people as an interpretation of their Bronze Age heritage. For these people, the older monuments were symbolically charged components of a mythologised landscape that they helped to create (Figure 10.9).

This is what Barrett is referring to when he talks about an 'archaeology of inhabitation', namely an understanding of place according to certain traditions and conventions, to which people contribute through their own practices. It is where human groups occupy a landscape of the past and assign new or altered meanings to that landscape. The inhabited place is known with reference to past experiences and by actions there that are played off against a wider 'reality' of social continuity and order. Inhabitation is not simply about occupying a place, 'it is a process of understanding the relevance of actions executed at some place by reference to other times and to other places' (Barrett 1999, 260). He concludes that the Iron Age was the product of the Bronze Age, but not as process of social evolution. 'Instead, the Bronze Age created the Iron Age because it made available the conditions by which Iron Age communities were themselves able to read of and to recognise the mythical histories by which they made themselves' (Barrett 1999, 264).

In this paper I have explored how changing attitudes to older monuments, reflected in new patterns of use and interpretation, were an important part of the process of 'becoming Iron Age' in south-west Ireland. The 'ancient stones' were proof of the enduring nature of this supernatural power, as articulated within the cosmology of Tech Duinn. This is the landscape in which the Iron Age people lived, surrounded by visible reminders of their ancestral religion to which they formed a strong spiritual connection.

References

Barrett, J., 1999. The mythical landscapes of the British Iron Age, in W. Ashmore and B. Knapp (eds), *Archaeologies of Landscape: Contemporary Perspectives*. Malden: Blackwell, 253–64.

Bradley, R., 1993. *Altering the Earth*. Edinburgh: Society of Antiquaries of Scotland.

Brindley, A., and Lanting, J.N., 1991/92. Radiocarbon dates from wedge tombs. *The Journal of Irish Archaeology* 6, 19–26.

Connolly, M., 1999. *Discovering the Neolithic in County Kerry: A Passage Tomb at Ballycarty*. Dublin: Wordwell.

De Valera, R., and O Nualláin, S., 1982. *Survey of the Megalithic Tombs of Ireland. Volume IV: Cork, Kerry, Limerick and Tipperary*. Dublin: Stationery Office.

Gwynn, E., 1924. *The Metrical Dindshenchas*, vol. V. Dublin: Dublin Institute for Advanced Studies.

Hingley, R., 1996. Ancestors and identity in the later prehistory of Atlantic Scotland: the reuse and reinvention of Neolithic monuments and material culture. *World Archaeology* 28, 231–43.

Loffler, C.M., 1983. *The Voyage to the Otherworld Island in Early Irish Literature*. Salzburg: Institut für Anglistik und Amerikanistik, Universität Salzburg.

Lynch, A., 1982. Astronomy and stone alignments in south-west Ireland, in D. Heggie (ed.), *Archaeoastronomy in the Old World*. Cambridge: Cambridge University Press, 205–13.

Moore, F., 1998. Munster Ogham stones: siting, context and function, in M. Monk and J. Sheehan (eds), *Early Medieval Munster: Archaeology, History and Society*. Cork: Cork University Press, 23–32.

Muller-Lisowski, K., 1948. Contributions to a study in Irish folklore. *Bealoideas* 8, 142–99.

O'Brien, W., 1993. Aspects of wedge tomb chronology, in E. Shee Twohig and M. Roynane (eds), *Past Perceptions: The Prehistoric Archaeology of South-west Ireland*. Cork: Cork University Press, 63–74.

O'Brien, W., 1999. *Sacred Ground: Megalithic Tombs in Coastal South-west Ireland*. Galway: Bronze Age Studies 4, National University of Ireland, Galway.

O'Brien, W., 2000a. Megalithic tombs, metal resources and territory in prehistoric south-west Ireland, in A. Desmond, G. Johnson, M. McCarthy, J. Sheehan and E. Shee Twohig (eds), *New Agendas in Irish Prehistory*. Dublin: Wordwell, 161–76.

O'Brien, W., 2000b. Lissyviggeen, in I. Bennett (ed.), *Excavations 1998: Summary Accounts of Archaeological Excavations in Ireland*. Dublin: Wordwell, 94–5.

Okasha, E, and Forsyth, K., 2000. *Early Christian Inscriptions of Munster*. Cork: Cork University Press.

O'Leary, P., 1989. A passage tomb on Clear Island in West Cork? *Journal of the Cork Historical and Archaeological Society* 94, 124–6.

O'Leary, P., and Shee Twohig, E., 1993. A possible Iron Age pillar stone on Cape Clear, Co. Cork. *Journal of the Cork Historical and Archaeological Society* 98. 133–40.

O Nualláin, S., 1975. The stone circle complex of Cork and Kerry. *Journal of the Royal Society of Antiquaries of Ireland* 105, 83–131.

O Nualláin, S., 1984. A survey of stone circles in Cork and Kerry. *Proceedings of the Royal Irish Academy* 84C, 1–77.

O Nualláin, S., 1988. Stone rows in the south of Ireland. *Proceedings of the Royal Irish Academy* 45C, 83–181.

O hOgain, D., 1991. *Myth, Legend and Romance: An Encyclopaedia of the Irish Folk Tradition*. London: Prentice Hall Press.

O hOgain, D., 1999. *The Sacred Isle: Belief and Religion in Pre-Christian Ireland*. Cork: The Collins Press.

Raftery, B., 1981. Iron Age burials in Ireland, in D. O Corráin (ed.), *Irish Antiquity: Essays and Studies presented to Professor M.J. O'Kelly*. Cork: Tower Books, 173–204.

Raftery, B., 1984. *La Tène in Ireland: Problems of Origin and Chronology*. Marburg: Vorgeschichtliches Institut.

Raftery, B., 1994. *Pagan Celtic Ireland*. London: Thames & Hudson.

Raftery, B., 1998. Observations on the Iron Age in Munster. *Emania* 17, 21–4.

Richards, J., 1999. Conceptual landscapes in the Egyptian Nile Valley, in W. Ashmore and B. Knapp (eds), *Archaeologies of Landscape: Contemporary Perspectives*. Oxford: Blackwell, 83–100.

Roberts, J., 1996. *The Stone Circles of Cork and Kerry: An Astronomical Guide*. Skibbereen: Key Books.

Ruggles, C., 1999a. *Astronomy in Prehistoric Britain and Ireland*. New Haven: Yale University Press.

Ruggles, C., 1999b. The orientation of Altar and other wedge tombs in the Mizen Peninsula, in W. O'Brien (ed.), *Sacred Ground: Megalithic Tombs in Coastal South-West Ireland*. Galway: Department of Archaeology, National University of Ireland, 315–17.

Thomas, J., 1991. *Rethinking the Neolithic*. Cambridge: Cambridge University Press.

Warner, R., 1998. Is there an Iron Age in Munster? *Emania* 17, 25–30.

Woodman, P., 1998. The Early Iron Age of Munster: not so different after all. *Emania* 17, 13–21.

Part IV

Scandinavia

Introduction

The Scandinavian peninsulas mark the northernmost limit of Atlantic Europe, and of the territory occupied by prehistoric farming communities. The shell-midden and cemetery sites of the Ertebølle group indicate that southern Scandinavia had a well-established Mesolithic population before farming arrived. Mesolithic burials at Vedbaek and Skateholm indicate the importance placed on individual identities and suggest complex multidimensional social organisation. Substantial monuments, however, did not appear until the Neolithic transition, around 4000 BC. The first Scandinavian monuments take the form of non-megalithic long mounds covering timber funerary structures, and of closed megalithic chambers under long or round mounds. The importance of the economic change may be disputed, but the Neolithic transition in south Scandinavia clearly coincided with an ideological transformation through which prehistoric communities became engaged with their surroundings in a different way, creating new landscape features as well as continuing to respect natural landmarks such as rocky outcrops, islands, or lakes.

The significance of the landscape – and in particular rivers, sea and shore – is revealed by the locations chosen for Neolithic monuments. Some of these Scandinavian Neolithic tombs dominated their surroundings by their sheer scale and monumentality; others were intentionally subservient to their visual setting. In areas such as Skåne and Bohuslän, many of the megalithic tombs were located on the crests of ridges or in other locations giving views of rivers or the sea. The megalithic tombs of Våstergotland, on the other hand, were arranged in straggling north–south rows, following the natural topography of the landscape. These may have encoded myths of origin, from a time when early farmers populated the region from the south (Tilley 1996).

A recurrent feature of Scandinavian prehistory is the special significance of watery places. In inland lakes and bogs, this is manifest in deposits of elaborate metalwork such as the Trundholm sun chariot, or more evocatively still, by 'bog bodies' such as Tollund and Grauballe – individuals who appear to have met violent ends, probably within a ritual context. Travel by water, too, had important symbolic associations from an early period, and traces of dug-out canoes have been found in a number of Mesolithic graves (Skaarup 1995). Sea and shore play a particularly prominent role in the recorded hunter-gatherer belief systems of northern Europe, which might encapsulate elements of very ancient landscape understandings. Thus the Saami people of northern Scandinavia considered the coast to be the meeting place of sky, earth and underworld, the underworld being associated with the dead. The shore is a contact zone between these worlds and was thus the most appropriate and powerful place for ritual communication with spirits or the ancestors, a significance which may be reflected in the placement of prehistoric rock art (Helskog 1999; Bradley 2000).

During the Bronze Age, the significance of the sea is highlighted by the prominence of ship depictions in rock carvings and on bronze razors. Bronze Age burial mounds are clustered along the coast and on coastal islands, as if to emphasise the special appropriateness of liminal locations, at the edge of the terrestrial world, for the deposition of the dead. Where burial mounds were placed on hills away from the coast, these hills were carved with ship motifs perhaps intended to represent the sea, and hence metaphorically to transform these inland locations to coastal islands (Bradley 2000).

This theme is taken up by the last of the regional studies in this volume, a study by Karin Ericson Lagerås of the distribution of Early Bronze Age burial mounds in one region of southern Sweden. By applying viewshed analysis to a sample of 400 mounds she is able to identify and to quantify preferences for particular types of location in the siting of these mounds. Locations offering views over the sea appear particularly to have been favoured, and this preference may relate to the cosmological beliefs of Bronze Age communities. The monuments may have resembled features of the landscape – the turf-covered mounds could easily have been assimilated with natural grassy hummocks – but they also send another message, indicating and identifying those places within the landscape which were held of special significance by the prehistoric communities who built them.

References

Bradley, R., 2000. *An Archaeology of Natural Places*. London: Routledge.

Helskog, K., 1999. The shore connection. Cognitive landscape and communication with rock carvings in northernmost Europe. *Norwegian Archaeological Review* 32, 73–94.

Skaarup, J., 1995. Stone-age burials in boats, in O. Crumlin-Pedersen and B.M. Thye (eds), *The Ship as Symbol in Prehistoric and Medieval Scandinavia*. Copenhagen: National Museum of Denmark, 51–8.

Tilley, C., 1996. *An Ethnography of the Neolithic. Early Prehistoric Societies in Southern Scandinavia*. Cambridge: Cambridge University Press.

11 Visible intentions?

Viewshed analysis of Bronze
Age burial mounds in western
Scania, Sweden

Karin Ericson Lagerås

Bronze Age burial mounds are without question a key category of monument in the investigation of Scandinavian Bronze Age society. They are characterised by their carefully chosen locations, their large numbers and their substantial size. Particular importance is claimed to derive from the fact that they were frequently placed in prominent positions in the landscape, but this observation raises a number of questions. Was visibility the main reason why the mounds were so often placed high in the landscape? What role was played by topography, proximity to the sea and direction of view? Was high visibility the primary aim, or can other intentions be traced from the location of these mounds? Intentionality is, in itself, hard to assess. In particular, it may be difficult, if not impossible, to draw a distinction between sacred and profane in the actions of prehistoric societies. The building of burial mounds is no exception, and one could ask if a division between the two spheres is meaningful today, or was ever intended during prehistoric times (Barrett 1991, 5). The present study seeks nonetheless to explore landscape perceptions and cognitive issues through the viewshed analysis of these Bronze Age burial mounds.

Viewshed analysis using GIS has rapidly attracted a great deal of attention within archaeology. The technique is especially well suited to investigate questions such as those raised some twenty years ago concerning the location of megalithic monuments on Orkney (Renfrew 1979; Fraser 1983), and since the end of the 1990s, a number of European researchers have devoted themselves to the development and application of viewshed analysis in archaeology. A special focus of interest has been the possibility of combining viewshed analysis with the investigation of territorial, social and cognitive aspects of the landscape. This is sometimes extended to include the study of astronomical features (Ruggles *et al.* 1993; Ruggles and Medyckyj-Scott 1996; Gaffney *et al.* 1995, 1996; Lock and Harris 1996; Wheatley 1995, 1996).

There have hitherto been few investigations in Sweden in which viewshed analysis of monuments has been a key feature, though a small number of such studies have been undertaken. One of these focused on megalithic graves in west Scania (Hårdh 1982); another concerned the large Bronze Age burial cairn at

Kivik in east Scania (Larsson 1993); while a third study analysed Bronze and Iron Age burial cairns in the Mälaren region near Stockholm (Petré 1981). Mention should also be made of an investigation in south-central Sweden where visual contact between Bronze Age mounds and medieval churches was examined (Sahlqvist 2000). None of these studies used GIS, however, and all of them (save Sahlqvist) included only a relatively small number of sites.

Investigating the visual aspects of a large number of objects in real life is very time-consuming, and can often only be undertaken within a digital setting. Furthermore, in some regions problems of infrastructure are difficult to overcome on the ground, and here GIS can serve as a helpful tool. When GIS is used for viewshed analysis it yields data that make it possible to quantify what is meant by 'large' and 'small' areas of visibility, and this constitutes a significant advantage when dealing with what are essentially elusive assessments. There has nonetheless been some discussion of the negative aspects of GIS on archaeological research. For example, Fisher and colleagues (1997) criticised several applications of viewshed analysis for failing to combine the analysis with statistical testing of the results (for instance Madry and Crumley 1990; Gaffney and Stančič 1991a, 1991b; Gaffney *et al.* 1995). Statistical testing of viewshed material is essential to strengthen arguments as to why a specific direction or range of view appears to have been preferred in any individual case. One method is to use a randomising test to assess whether there is a significant difference between the results given by the archaeological sites under study and those given by a randomly chosen sample of terrain points.

GIS analysis has also been criticised for being too limited to mappable features like topography, soils, geology or hydrology. A drawback of the technique may indeed be that it is unable to deal in an appropriate way with features such as settlements, religious centres and socially and culturally determined ways in which the world is perceived. These factors may either be unknown, or very difficult to map (Gaffney and van Leusen 1995, 367ff). It is nonetheless the case that of the different GIS applications available, viewshed analysis is the most suitable for combining GIS analysis with cognitive or phenomenological approaches. It is for this reason that viewshed analysis has been relatively widely adopted (Kvamme 1999, 177f, 183).

The following study employs viewshed analysis to consider visual aspects of almost 400 Early Bronze Age burial mounds in the province of Scania in southern Sweden (Figure 11.1). In this region, the Bronze Age as a whole extends in calibrated radiocarbon years from 1500 BC to 500 BC. The majority of the burial mounds date to the earlier part of this period and were built of turf, though stones were sometimes part of the construction. Viewsheds were created for these mounds so that with the aid of a digital terrain model it was possible to investigate what areas of the landscape were visible or invisible from any given point. The procedure was also reversed and the results used to assess from which areas within the landscape the mounds themselves could be seen. In order to test the hypothesis that Bronze Age burial mounds were situated at points in the landscape where especially wide vistas were available, a randomising test was

Figure 11.1 Location of Scania in southern Sweden.

conducted involving a randomly sampled group of terrain points. A cumulative viewshed analysis (Wheatley 1995) of the complete group of almost 400 mounds was also undertaken.

One problem with viewshed analysis is what has been called the rim-effect (Fisher *et al.* 1997, 587). This means that views which would have extended beyond the limits of the digital terrain model are not included in the result. Nor does the viewshed provided by the computer take into consideration poor eyesight, or a cloudy or rainy climate. There is also the problem of the vegetation, and the possibility that trees interfere with a given view. A computer-generated viewshed takes no special account of vegetation, but provides a result as if the spectator were standing in the middle of a desert. Wherever possible, knowledge of regional or local vegetation characteristics should be taken into consideration. Several pollen analyses from Scania reveal that the landscape during the later part of the Bronze Age was characterised by relatively open pastures. This was also true for parts of the landscape during the Early Bronze Age when it is thought that a majority of the burial mounds were erected (Berglund *et al.* 1991; Regnell, in press). This general knowledge of the Bronze Age landscape is as close as we can expect to get, and we must accept the lack of more precise details.

Study area and material

The area of the investigation is on the south-west coast of Scania (Figure 11.2), facing towards Denmark which lies less than twenty kilometres distant. This is a hummocky landscape, crossed by a number of streams that have their outlets in the Oresund (the narrow strait separating Sweden and Denmark) and run mainly in a west–east direction. The study is part of a larger Bronze Age project undertaken by the Department of Archaeological Excavations of the Swedish National Heritage Board (Jensen, in press).

The analysis is based upon a total of 391 mounds, in varying states of preservation, registered in the Central Register of Ancient Monuments. The material ranges from groups of burial mounds located at heights between 50–100 metres above sea level to single mounds located only a few metres above sea level. The area of investigation measures some 20 kilometres long from north to south and about 15 kilometres from east to west. The mounds included in the inventory do of course fall far short of the original total, since a large number must have been destroyed by cultivation. Nonetheless, the general pattern of distribution may be expected to be representative, even though the overall density nowadays is lower than in prehistoric times (Riddersporre 1987).

The majority of the burial mounds in the region are believed to have been erected in the early part of the Bronze Age, during periods II and III (Lundborg 1972; Håkansson 1985). Secondary graves are known to have been inserted in existing mounds during the rest of the Bronze Age. These secondary burials were sometimes associated with modification to the mound itself which means that many mounds might have gained both height and monumentality which they did not possess from the beginning. There is also the possibility that some of the mounds are Neolithic, and cover invisible megalithic graves, or are of Iron Age date (Säfvestad 1993, 162). Furthermore, Late Bronze Age burial mounds are known in north-west Scania, in the southern part of the neighbouring province of Halland, and on the south-west part of the Danish island of Fyn (Thrane 1993, 79ff; Andersson 1999, 9ff). For the purposes of this study, however,

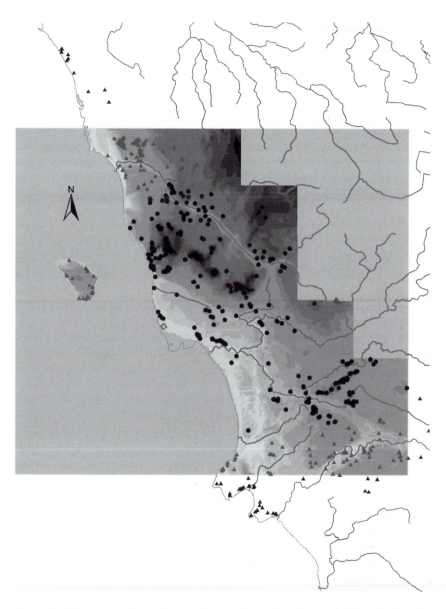

Figure 11.2 Study area in south-west Scania, facing the Oresund. Filled circles indicate burial mounds included in the analysis, triangles those excluded.

the assumption has been made that the majority of the mounds were erected
during a fairly limited time interval in the Early Bronze Age.

Methodology

In order to conduct a viewshed analysis it is necessary to have a digital terrain model as a background. Height data were provided in digital form by the National Land Survey of Sweden, where height values are given every 50 metres. Using this data a digital terrain model was built, in this case a grid-based terrain model in which each cell measured 20×20 metres.

To test the results, a group of randomly chosen terrain points were viewshed-analysed under the same conditions as the burial mounds. For each viewshed analysis, both for the mounds and the terrain points, it was decided that the digital spectator had an eye-level fixed at 1.5 metres above sea level. It was not possible to establish if height data from the National Land Survey in the vicinity of mounds originated from the highest level of an existing mound, or from a point just beside it. This uncertainty over the exact point of measurement prohibited the addition of a general assumed height to any of the mounds in the analysis. This means that the viewsheds calculated in this analysis have their outlook not from the top of a given mound (whether extant or destroyed), but from ground level at the edge of the mound. Each cell was defined as visible (1) or not visible (0) from the defined point of outlook. The number of cells visible or not visible was thereafter recalculated to give a total in square kilometres, and it is on this basis that the results are presented.

The focus was directed to two questions. First, was it possible to establish whether the Bronze Age mounds had been located in more conspicuous positions than a randomly sampled test group of terrain points? In order to assess this, these randomly sampled terrain points were viewshed-analysed in the same way as the burial mounds, so as to investigate whether the burial mounds differed in a significant way from the test group of terrain points. The randomising test in this study was conducted by Torbjörn Ahlström (Department of Archaeology, University of Lund, Sweden). For each individual viewshed, the digital terrain model was adjusted for the effect of the curvature of the earth (van Leusen 1998).

The second question concerned cumulative viewsheds (Wheatley 1995). Is it possible, from groups of mounds, to determine which areas are distinguished as particularly view-intense? The technique of the cumulative viewshed could be described as many single viewsheds put on top of one another, and enables the researcher to establish whether certain localities are particularly view-intense, or conversely, whether no monuments at all are visible from some localities. The cumulative viewshed technique has been proposed as a suitable tool for the investigation of social or cognitive aspects of landscape perception during prehistoric times (Wheatley 1996; Ruggles and Medyckyj-Scott 1996).

Four different terrain models were used, each of them corrected from survey points situated either at elevated locations or on the coast. It should be noted that in the cumulative viewshed analysis, technical limitations made it impossible to use a terrain model that was corrected for earth curvature.

Random sample testing

The results from the viewshed analysis of the burial mounds were tested by comparison with a random sample. The results are displayed in histogram form (Figure 11.3). The upper histogram shows the areas visible from a random selection of 200 burial mounds; the lower histogram shows the visible areas for a random selection of 200 terrain points. The mean average value for each group is marked by a line, and it is clear from these diagrams that the larger mean value is attached to the mound group. The difference in mean average value of visible area between the mounds and the terrain points is 111 km². It is nonetheless necessary to determine whether this difference is sufficiently large to support the claim that the mounds were not placed randomly in the landscape. Two hypotheses were assessed:

1   the null-hypothesis: that the mounds are randomly placed in the landscape;
2   the alternative hypothesis: that the mounds are not randomly placed in the landscape, but were located with respect to visibility.

In the randomising test, data from the mound group and the terrain-point group were put together, and new differences in mean value were calculated. This

Randomly sampled material

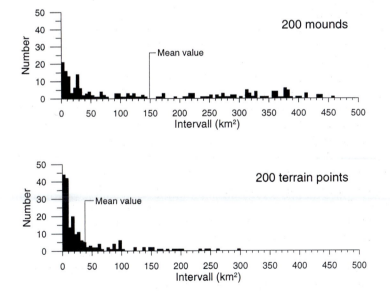

Figure 11.3 Viewshed areas of 200 terrain points (below) and Bronze Age mounds (above).

procedure was conducted 10,000 times, and new mean values were calculated each time and compared with the original value of 111 km^2. In no case did mean values from these randomising tests equal or exceed the original mean value of 111 km^2. If the difference in mean value had been distributed to both sides of 111 km^2, it would not have been possible to demonstrate that there was a significant difference in location between the mounds and the random terrain points. The result that was actually obtained, by contrast, provides very strong support for the hypothesis that the locations of the mounds were not random in terms of visibility in the landscape.

Mounds with a view

The carefully chosen location, the size, and the large number of Bronze Age burial mounds is testimony to a massive labour investment and large-scale cultural activity. The construction of mounds has been argued to be the reflection of everything from settlement patterns and territorial claims to world images in the form of religious beliefs. By comparison with Neolithic monuments, which are expected to reflect a more collectively orientated social structure, Bronze Age monuments have been interpreted as the result of a more individual- or family-centred society. Only a small percentage of the population were buried under a mound, but that mound served to manifest for ever their presence and dominance in the landscape. The high visual prominence of burial mounds has generally been regarded as of particular importance in this context. But could other significant motives be found for their prominence? Each of the individual viewshed analyses was based on the outlook from the mound itself, and tells us what areas can be seen, or not seen, from that mound. But a mound also has a visual impact on the surrounding landscape. It is therefore necessary to consider both aspects of visibility – the view towards and the view away from – in order to reach a deeper understanding of the motivations of Bronze Age society.

A number of questions must be addressed. Is it self-evident that the mounds were built mainly to be seen from the outside, from a distance, for instance as territorial markers? Or should the focus of attention lie upon the burial place itself? Should the location of a burial mound in a location commanding extensive views be interpreted to mean that the people who were buried there look out upon the life that goes on around them? An important consideration in this discussion is whether the distinction between the view towards a mound and the view away from a mound was significant for those who built it, or whether that distinction is simply the result of what has been called a Western, horizontally orientated world-view (Tuan 1990, 129ff); a view that does not see the world as a unified cosmic space, but as a landscape laid out in front of our feet.

Through a cumulative viewshed analysis that included all 391 mounds, a picture was created that indicates from which areas of the landscape many mounds, few mounds, or no monuments at all are visible (Figure 11.4). This analysis reveals that it is from the sea, and more specifically from one particular area of sea, that there is the highest chance of seeing a large number of mounds.

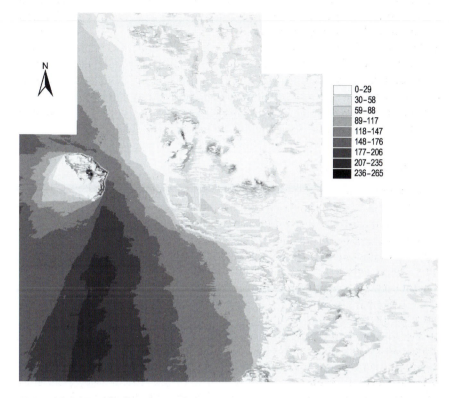

	0–29
	30–58
	59–88
	89–117
	118–147
	148–176
	177–206
	207–235
	236–265

Figure 11.4 Viewshed analysis of the 391 Bronze Age mounds in the study area. Shading illustrates the number of mounds theoretically visible from each cell of the digital terrain model: dark areas indicate high values (many mounds visible) and light areas low values.

At the same time, it identifies the visual characteristic that unifies more than half the mounds: more than half of them look out over this same area of sea, located not close to the coast but out in the Oresund. The fact that the highest view-density area is located some distance from the coast probably reflects the fact that mounds at higher altitudes have a larger viewshed over the sea, whereas mounds placed at low altitude closer to the coast have a more restricted maritime viewshed. What is equally clear from this analysis is that the inland streams do not stand out as particularly view-intense. There are thus no grounds for arguing that mounds along inland streams were built as visible territorial markers for people travelling upstream.

Many of the mounds that are visible from the sea lie at some distance inland. Most of them, in fact, lie more than three kilometres from the coast. Even in an open landscape it may have been difficult to discern single mounds or even groups of mounds at such distance, given in particular the hummocky nature of the landscape. For many of the mounds, it is obvious that it would have been much easier to observe the sea from the mound than to observe the same mound from the sea. Thus it is most likely that it was the view *from* a mound towards different parts of the landscape – sea, pastures, fields and settlement sites – that played the leading role.

In some of the mounds in this region, seaweed was used as part of the mound material. The same practice is also attested in Late Neolithic single graves found in the vicinity of Bronze Age mounds (Jensen, in press). This practice might reflect a way of establishing an extra link with the sea and all the things it stood for. The prominent role played by the sea and by boats during the Bronze Age is manifest in many ways: as boat motifs in rock carvings, as ship-shaped stone settings in graves, and in the depiction of ships on small cult objects such as bronze razors. This evidence can be interpreted to mean that boats, and the sea itself, served as links to other parts of the world, in both the physical and the spiritual sense. It may also have been that eye-contact with the sea established a claim to fishing rights in an area (Olausson 1992, 261).

Vicki Cummings (this volume, ch. 7) discusses the possibility that a culture–nature dualism was absent from the Neolithic world-view. Constructions such as chambered tombs in south-west Wales and south-west Scotland are themselves related to distinctive and symbolic natural features. These monuments play with the dualism of what is created and what is humanly built. A similar dualism may apply to the Bronze Age mounds of south-west Scania. These are mainly built of turf, in such a way that at one and the same time they both blend with the surrounding landscape and distinguish themselves from it. Organic in nature, it was only a matter of time before the surface of the mounds regained its original green colour and vegetation of grass, trees and shrubs. This process of development cannot have been completely unknown to people during the Bronze Age. But to what extent did it matter, and to what extent did they care? Were the turfs placed upside down to delay regrowth, or were they placed green side upwards in order to stimulate it? We know very little of these matters, and of how vegetation was handled within a grave-setting. Was it for instance an accepted behaviour to let livestock graze on burial mounds in order to keep them clear of bushes, and ensure that they remained visible (Olausson 1992, 261)?

Monuments, as human constructions, fall somewhere between the natural and the created. Turf, soil, large and small stones, put together will create shapes and expressions that sometimes show similarities to natural features within a hummocky landscape, and at other times stand out like exclamation marks. Towards what particular features in the prehistoric landscape the Bronze Age burial mounds were related as visual impressions remains a relatively unexplored field of research. That a visual intention lies behind the location of the burial mounds is in my view beyond doubt, however, and GIS applications offer us an opportunity to study aspects of that visibility. Some things are more easily placed in a grave than others, and some things are more easily detected by archaeologists. To us, the grave itself with body and grave goods are obvious remnants. But how do you put a piece of heaven and a piece of sea in a grave? Perhaps by placing the graves in locations that offer a wide vista.

Acknowledgement

I wish to thank Torbjörn Ahlström, Ulf Bodin, Per Lagerås and Karin Lund from the Swedish National Heritage Board, Department of Archaeological Excavations in Lund and The Archaeological Institute at the University of Lund for their help. I owe them all a big thank you, though at the same time I wish to emphasise that any mistakes are entirely my own.

Note

The formula used to calculate the effect of earth curvature was taken from the following paper published at the CAA 98 homepage (Computer Applications and Quantitative Methods in Archaeology): M. van Leusen, 1998, 'Viewshed and Cost Surface Analysis Using GIS (Cartographic Modelling in a Cell-Based GIS II)', Groningen Institute of Archaeology, Netherlands.

The adaptation to incorporate the Spatial Analyst extension was undertaken by Ulf Bodin at the Swedish National Heritage Board.

References

Andersson, M. 1999. Högens betydelse som socialt och religiöst monument. En studie över gravhögar från yngre bronsålder i nordvästra Skåne och södra Halland, in M. Olausson (ed.), *Spiralens öga. Tjugo artiklar kring aktuell bronsåldersforskning.* (Avdelningen för arkeologiska undersökningar skrifter nr. 25.) Stockholm: Riksantikvarieämbetet, 9–25.

Barrett, J.C., 1991. Towards an archaeology of ritual, in P. Garwood (ed.), *Sacred and Profane: Proceedings of a Conference on Archaeology, Ritual and Religion, Oxford 1989.* Oxford: Oxford University Committee for Archaeology, 1–9.

Berglund, B.E., Larsson, L., Lewan, N., Olsson, G.A., and Skansjö, S., 1991. Ecological and social factors behind the landscape changes, in B.E. Berglund (ed.), *The Cultural Landscape during 6000 years in Southern Sweden – The Ystad Project.* Ecological Bulletins 41. Copenhagen: Munksgaard, 425–50.

Fisher, P., Farrelly, C., Maddocks, A., and Ruggles, C., 1997. Spatial analysis of visible areas from the Bronze Age cairns of Mull. *Journal of Archaeological Science* 24, 581–92.

Fraser, D., 1983. *Land and Society in Neolithic Orkney.* Oxford: British Archaeological Reports.

Gaffney, V., and Stančič, Z., 1991a. *GIS Approaches to Regional Analysis: A Case Study of the Island of Hvar.* Ljubljana: Znansteveni Institut Filozofske Fakiltete.

Gaffney, V., and Stančič, Z., 1991b. Diodorus Siculus and the island of Hvar, Dalmatia: testing the text with GIS, in G. Lock and J. Moffett (eds), *Computer Applications and Quanatitative Methods in Archaeology 1991.* Oxford: Tempus Reparatum, 113–25.

Gaffney, V., Stančič, Z., and Watson, H., 1995. The impact of GIS on archaeology: a personal perspective, in G. Lock and Z. Stancic (eds), *Archaeology and Geographical Information Systems: A European Perspective.* London: Taylor & Francis, 211–29.

Gaffney, V., Stančič, Z., and Watson, H., 1996. Moving from catchments to cognition: tentative steps toward a larger archaeological context for GIS, in M. Aldenderfer and H.D.G. Maschner (eds), *Anthropology, Space and Geographic Information Systems.* New York: Oxford University Press, 132–54.

Gaffney, V., and van Leusen, M. 1995. Postscript – GIS, environmental determinism and archaeology, in G. Lock and Z. Stančič (eds), *Archaeology and Geographical Information Systems: A European Perspective*. London: Taylor & Francis, 367–82.

Håkansson, I., 1985. *Skånes gravfynd från äldre bronsålder som källa till studiet av social struktur*. (Acta Archaeologica Lundensia Series in 8⁰, nr. 14.) Malmo: Gleerup.

Hårdh, B. 1982. The megalithic grave area around the Lödde-Kävlinge river. A Research Programme. *Meddelande från Lunds Universitets Historiska Museum 1981–1982*. Stockholm: Almqvist & Wiksell International, 26–47.

Kvamme, K. L., 1999. Recent directions and developments in Geographical Information Systems. *Journal of Archaeological Research* 7, 153–201.

Jensen, B.L. (in press). *Kring de heliga backarna*.

Larsson, L. 1993. Relationer till ett röse–några aspekter på Kiviksgraven, in Larsson. L., (ed.), *Bronsålderns gravhögar*. Rapport från ett symposium I, Lund 15.XI–16XI 1991. University of Lund Institute of Archaeology Report series no. 48. Lund: Institute of Archaeology, 135–49.

Lock, G. R., and Harris, T. M., 1996. Danebury Revisited: an English Iron Age hillfort in a digital landscape, in M. Aldenderfer and H.D.G. Maschner (eds), *Anthropology, Space and Geographic Information Systems*. New York: Oxford University Press, 214–240.

Lundborg, L., 1972. *Undersökningar av bronsåldershögar och bronsåldersgravar i södra Halland: Höks, Tönnersjö och Halmstads härader under åren 1854–1970*. Hallands museums skriftserie 2. Halmstad: Hallands Museum.

Madry, S.L.H., and Crumley, C.L., 1990. An application of remote sensing and GIS in a regional archaeological settlement pattern analysis, in K.M.S. Allen, S., Green and E. Zubrow (eds), *Interpreting Space: GIS and Archaeology*. London: Taylor & Francis, 364–80.

Olausson, D., 1992. The archaeology of the Bronze Age cultural landscape – research goals, methods and results, in L. Larsson, J. Callmer and B. Stjernquist (eds), *The Archaeology of the Cultural Landscape. Fieldwork and Research in a South Swedish Rural Region*. (Acta Archaeologica Lundensia Series in 4⁰, no. 19.) Stockholm: Almqvist & Wiksell International, 251–82.

Petré, B. 1981. Relationen mellan grav gård och omland – exponering och kommunikation som funktion i förhistoriska gravar, med exempel på Lovö. *Bebyggelsehistorisk tidskrift*, no. 2. Uppsala: Swedish Science Press, 11–16.

Regnell, M. (in press). *History of Human Environment – A Voyage through Landscape and Time*.

Renfrew, C., 1979. Investigations in Orkney. *Reports of the Research Committee of the Society of Antiquaries of London* 38. London: Society of Antiquaries.

Riddersporre, M., 1987. Retrogressiv analys av äldre lantmäterihandlingar. Det dolda kulturlandskapet. Metodkonferens 1985. *Riksantikvarieämbetet Rapport 1987:2*.

Ruggles, C.L.N., and Medyckyj-Scott, D.J., 1996. Site location, landscape visibility, and symbolic astronomy. A Scottish case study, in H.G.D. Maschner (ed.), *New Methods, Old Problems. Geographic Information Systems in Modern Archaeological Research*. (Center for Archaeological Investigations, Occasional Paper, no. 23.) Carbondale: Southern Illinois University at Carbondale, 127–46.

Ruggles, C.L.N., Medyckyj-Scott, D.J., and Gruffyd, A., 1993. Multiple viewshed analysis using GIS and its archaeological application: a case study in northern Mull, in J. Andresen, T. Madsen and I. Scoller (eds), *Computing the Past. Computer Applica-*

tions and Quantitative Methods in Archaeology. CAA92. Aarhus: Aarhus University Press, 125–32.

Säfvestad, U., 1993. Högen och bygden – territoriell organisation i skånsk bronsålder, in L. Larsson (ed.), *Bronsålderns gravhögar.* Rapport från ett symposium I, Lund 15.XI–16XI 1991. University of Lund Institute of Archaeology Report Series, no. 48. Lund: Institute of Archaeology, 161–69.

Sahlqvist, L. 2000. *Det rituella landskapet. Kosmografiska uttrycksformer och territoriell struktur.* Aun 28. Uppsala: Uppsala Department of Archaeology and Ancient History.

Thrane, H., 1993. From mini to maxi. Bronze Age Barrows from Funen as illustrations of variation and structure, in L. Larssson (ed.), *Bronsålderns gravhögar.* Rapport från ett symposium I, Lund 15.XI–16XI 1991, ed. L. Larsson. University of Lund Institute of Archaeology Report Series, no. 48. Lund: Institute of Archaeology, 79–90.

Tuan, Y.-F., 1990. *Topophilia: A Study of Environmental Perception, Attitudes, and Values.* New York: Columbia University Press.

van Leusen, M., 1998. Viewshed and Cost Surface Analysis Using GIS (Cartographic Modelling in a Cell-Based GIS II). Groningen Institute of Archaeology, Netherlands.

Wheatley, D., 1995. Cumulative viewshed analysis: a GIS-based method for investigating intervisibility, and its archaeological application, in G. Lock and Z. Stančič (eds), *Archaeology and Geographical Information Systems: A European Perspective.* London: Taylor & Francis, 171–85.

Wheatley, D., 1996. Regional variation in earlier Neolithic Wessex, in H.D.G. Maschner (ed.) *New Methods, Old Problems. Geographic Information Systems in Modern Archaeological Research.* (Center for Archaeological Investigations, Occasional Paper, no. 23.) Carbondale: Southern Illinois University at Carbondale, 75–103.

12 Conclusion: long conversations, concerning time, descent and place in the world

Alasdair Whittle

The contributions to this volume offer a striking demonstration of diversity over time and diversity from place to place through what we now recognise as 'Atlantic Europe'. From early standing stones separated from their natural sources on the Central Alentejan plain, and Iberian rock art set in impressive locations but with restricted views, to walled and bastioned constructions in northern Portugal placed for all to see and for those within to look out far and wide, there was clearly no one way of doing things. As such, these studies already begin to answer the question set by Christopher Tilley (1999, ch. 3), about the usefulness of common terms like 'megalith'. It is not just the term 'megalith' that is potentially problematic, but practically all others in general archaeological usage, including 'monument', 'monumentality' and 'landscape' themselves. 'Enclosures' are another case in point (cf. Oswald *et al.* 2001). Our general language is rather clumsy and probably inadequate, but as the papers included here move to their specific studies rooted in times and places, this difficulty appears to fall away. Everywhere, so it seems, there was not just diversity, or different ways of doing things, but – as several of the authors bring out clearly, particularly with reference to the beginnings of the Neolithic – diversity in the form of a play between what was local practice and other ideas of wider currency. These contributions can be read as part of much longer debates about diversity from region to region and from sequence to sequence. The Iberian situations already cited, for example, can obviously be fitted into much wider contexts, and the same can be said of all the other studies here.

In this concluding chapter, I want to ask (but will not necessarily answer) two questions. First, is the diversity I have already claimed to be seen only as a function of the passage of time and the separations of space? And, second, can we make any sort of sense, as outside observers, of the diversities visible at any one time and through time, in any one place and from place to place? Possible answers may seem to be partly contradictory. I anticipate that we shall be able to find far more diversity at a given time and in a given place (however we define *that* problematic term), and that it will be marked by recurrent multiplicity, ambiguity and possible contradiction, and by no means confined to the sphere of the kinds of construction under review in this volume. On the other hand, without having the room here adequately to deal with spatial or geographical variation, it may still be legitimate to sketch an outline of some general and recurrent developments through time. An escape from possible contradiction may be available if we take more account of diversity in explanations of long-term change.

Diversities

Empirically, it certainly looks as though there were different ways of doing things and different understandings of the world in simultaneous operation. Just from the studies included in this volume, there is an intriguing separation (which deserves perhaps rather more comment) between, on the one hand, Early Neolithic settlements on the Central Alentejan plain sited close to rocky out-crops, and on the other, the single and grouped granite standing stones (assuming these do indeed have an early date) placed away from their geological source. There are also noteworthy variations among the architectural constructions of the north Brittany coast, to say nothing of contrasts to what was normal practice along (or perhaps more accurately just back from) the south-west Brittany coast, notably in the Morbihan. In both contexts, there may have been further variation in terms of the descent of populations and the dominant trends of subsistence. In both areas the question of 'slighting the sea' (Schulting 1998; cf. Calado this volume, ch. 2) has been raised. Further studies may suggest that in south-west Brittany, at least, there were significant variations within the local Late Mesolithic both in terms of diet preference and in the rate at which subsequent changes were effected (Schulting and Richards 2001). And if we were, rather artificially, to separate three relevant aspects of 'monuments' of the kind under discussion in this volume – their setting, their form, and their contents, where that is architecturally appropriate – it would not be hard to find further examples of variation in each aspect. All the contributors discuss the settings, and a few the architectural forms of the 'monuments' or constructions in question. There is, however, rather little on 'contents' or things placed within, beside or near them. We do not have very far to look for significant variation in treatments of human bone placed within such constructions (e.g. Wysocki and Whittle 2000). But my main interest in diversity in the present instance is a more theoretical one.

In discussing whether, in addition to possessing a concept of static or cyclical time, any people really lack a durational or linear sense of time, the anthropologist Maurice Bloch referred to evidence from Bali, and to 'the long conversation that is Balinese society', in which 'at some time, one notion of time is used, and others, another . . .' (Bloch 1977, 284). He suggested that static or cyclical time was something most often expressed in ritual contexts, whereas linear, durational time was encountered in the practical spheres of agriculture, village and politics. He has since elaborated the idea of multiple and overlapping workings-through of the same and related ideas, as well as that of the style and sequence of their presentation, drawing mainly on evidence from Madagascar (in a series of essays collected in Bloch 1998). It is clear that 'monument' studies in Neolithic archaeology have themselves already partially captured a sense that these many and varied constructions are projections, idealisations, or presentations made for particular purposes. Some time ago it was proposed that the large deposits of human bone that are frequently encountered served to promote an ideology of collective identity at odds with a reality of much more restricted and sectional interests (Shanks and Tilley 1982). In another analysis megaliths served as 'instruments of conversion' for agriculturalists seeking to bind indigenous people into a new lifestyle and way of thinking, particularly about subsistence and the commitment of labour (Sherratt 1995). More general accounts (Bradley 1993; Whittle 1996) have also shared much of this overall approach, though differing in detailed interpretations, seeing monuments as something which first changed minds before new forms of subsistence could be adopted. This is perhaps far too teleological, as though the desired end was foreseen long before the means to bring it about had been applied and sustained. But from this tradition may be retained a sense of different kinds of conversation going on, a sense of multiple, overlapping ways of presenting one kind of understanding of people's place in the scheme of things.

Three issues seem to recur in the studies in this volume: possible distinctions between nature and culture; ways of seeing as a sense of place; and a sense of time that embraces ideas of human descent and origins. Without further apology, I want to use a few ethnographic examples to illustrate the argument, dwelling especially on the latter point, about time and descent. In all three themes, considerable diversity and ambiguity among Neolithic people should be expected, and the challenge facing continuing monument studies is to capture rather more than has so far been achieved of the many-sidedness of how people saw themselves and their worlds.

It has become commonplace to deny the universality of the Western conception of a distinction between nature and culture (e.g. Descola and Pálsson 1996). Ingold conveniently draws together a number of examples of indigenous conceptions, according to which no radical distinction appears to be drawn between people and their environment (Ingold 2000, especially ch. 5, 81–4). The examples are largely to do with gardeners and cultivators, people who tend plants in wooded and forested settings within which humanity is embedded. The same kind of argument can be extended to animals (Ingold 2000, ch. 4), with relations of trust long preceding relations of domination. There are, however, both counter-examples and other, ambiguous examples. Rival (1993, 648) has noted that while the Huaorani of Ecuador are reluctant gardeners, cultivating manioc mainly for use in feasts, many other native Amazonians do dichotomise the world by opposing nature to culture. Howell (1996) has discussed how the forest Chewong of Malaysia, hunters and gatherers and part-time cultivators, do not make a rigid distinction between 'nature' and 'culture', but do differentiate between 'them' and 'us':

> The continuity, or extension, of humanity is, as it were, moving in and out and around the numerous named and enumerated beings and objects in their

environment – in the many worlds that they maintain exist in the forest. What is of interest, however, is that such boundaries are far from absolute, and 'us' is a fluid category. Moreover, reality is not divisible into material and spiritual, into mind and body, emotion and intellect. Rather, it is perceived as being made up of endlessly mutually interacting and fluid beings and qualities.

(Howell 1996, 142)

While cultivation may have been on a restricted scale in many early Neolithic contexts, the husbandry of animals was arguably a much more common practice, with all that raises in terms of issues of control and killing (Whittle *et al.* 1999), particularly if there was indeed some kind of turning away in coastal areas from the resources of the sea. It is possible that Vicki Cummings (this volume, ch. 7) is right in maintaining that the general outlook and world-view of people across the Mesolithic–Neolithic transition may have been little altered. It would seem, however, that something had changed, since relationships previously not addressed in such ways had become an issue. The assertion of a continued closeness to what we might call 'nature' could have been part of a continuing discourse that involved, in part, coming to terms with very different ways of treating animals and other constituents of the world.

From this perspective, any new placing of stone or other material, any new building, may have involved both continuity and change: continuity because of the way practice was perhaps normally grounded in existing belief, and change because construction involved attention to and drawing attention to matters that had previously been implicitly understood, taken for granted or unquestioned. Constructions close to rocky outcrops in south-west Wales, or the enhanced footings given to long cairns in western France, might most obviously be taken as evidence of continuity, while stones moved around might indicate dislocation and disruption, but both may have been ambiguous. Constructions set near the sea are another case in point. They could have served or been thought of on the one hand as portals giving access to a special place, or on the other as barriers denoting denial and restriction; alternatively they might have been conceived of as existing in a special kind of liminality, both temporal as well as spatial.

It is hard to penetrate these mental worlds. One possible way in is by the kinds of visibility offered by all the sorts of site under discussion in the studies here. These are very varied and may often have been highly selective. The landscapes of everyday routine were presumably extremely well known, intimately or at least passably familiar to those who inhabited them, knowledge of even relatively distant places being passed on by what has been called 'topographical gossip' (Widlok 1997). It is hard to think of landscapes the parts of which were not named, either in association with myths of creation as in the Dreamtime, or as among the western Apache connected to past events and people, narratives about whom provided a moral framework for subsequent generations (Basso 1984; 1996). Buildings and placings, and by extension the kinds of seeing that went with them, might be thought of as a kind of naming process. This may regularly, however, have been a selective business. The kinds of seeing that went with special places and constructions may not always have been the kinds of seeing that operated in daily life. It might be tempting at this point to have recourse to some grand explanatory scheme, reminiscent perhaps of Lévi-Strauss's distinction between 'hot' and 'cold' societies, and their allegedly differing use of history and myth, or the difference argued by Paul Connerton (1989) between inscribed and incorporated practices, the former relying on frequent and open repetition and exegesis, and the latter operating through less explicit performance, less open to question and more dependent on emotion. In this way a general distinction between open and closed, easily visible and more hidden away, might be proposed, and this might have some resonance with the data presented in most of these studies. But it is unlikely that such a notion would be illuminating everywhere, without further attention to the details of each context and setting. The Melanesian example of *malangan* objects suggests that what is not seen is not necessarily forgotten, and issues of seeing are not easily divorced from questions of the style and character of memory (Küchler 1987; 1993).

Another challenge for continuing monument studies in Atlantic Europe will therefore be to capture more of the sense of contrast between what was seen (and remembered) in daily lives on the one hand, and in special times and places on the other. By way of high-level generalisation, which might have some value to generate hypotheses, we could contrast the early situations in the wooded valley settings of central and western Europe during the LBK, where longhouse settlements provided the principal and dominant focus for a whole range of concerns, with the much greater separation seemingly visible, in varying ways, throughout Atlantic Europe. Explanation of this could be varied. There might be a connection with greater mobility or at least bigger ranges in the lifestyle of Atlantic Europe. Questions of access to land, and the retention of memory in a landscape where occupations and settlements may have come and gone over time (cf. Küchler 1993, 90–1), could have been major issues. Any one building or placing, and the kind of seeing that went with it, may potentially have been a claim to retention of tenure or a maintenance of memory. These reflections are very general. What could be extended (cf. Bradley 1997) is a series of systematic comparisons between the settings of the everyday and the placing of monuments.

Questions of nature and culture, and of special kinds of seeing and memory, lead on to matters of time. Following Bloch (1977), it would not be particularly daring to suggest that many if not most of these constructions existed in and for a ritualised time, as one part of the 'long conversations' about it all. But what kind of time or times? Until recently, a very common answer would have been the time of ancestors. This single answer has had two major and rather different sources, which might in itself be a matter for unease (Whitley 2000). On the one hand, there have been ancestors as legitimation, suggested by such diverse cross-cultural generalisers as Meillassoux, Saxe modified by Goldstein, and others (cf. Morris 1991). On the other hand, there have been ancestors as conceptual and emotional underpinning, produced by engagement with monument studies and also by selective reading of ethnography. One of the clearest formulations of the latter kind of answer has relied on explicit analogy with parts of Madagascar to suggest that Stonehenge was part of the domain of the ancestors, symbolised in stone, separated from the realm of the living that was represented by wood (Parker Pearson and Ramilisonina 1998; Parker Pearson 2000). Even if this particular case were to be accepted, it would hardly extend in the same form to earlier situations. To cope with those, I have suggested elsewhere (Whittle 1996) the idea of 'abstract ancestors', which itself should be refined in the light of the very considerable diversity of forms of remembering and descent which are evident throughout the ethnographic record (Barrett and Fewster 1998; Whittle 1998).

I would like briefly to consider three situations from ethnography to illustrate further diversity and possibilities. In a generalising discussion of their religion and metaphysics, Guenther (1999, 426) has suggested that 'hunter–gatherers regard nature as pervasively animated with moral, mystical and mythical significance'. He notes the prevalence among them of shamanism as a way of 'entering and conceptualizing such a universe and . . . relating to, channeling and transforming its beings and forces for the benefit of humans'. Ecstasy and transformation pervade shamanic ritual, cosmology and cosmogony; mythical beings from the past such as the Trickster enable and also subvert creation, in a layered and temporally fluid universe (Guenther 1999, 427–30). In description of a specific hunter–gatherer group, the Nyaka of southern India, Bird-David (1999, 259–60) has noted belief in the coexistence alongside themselves of non-human persons including the deceased, former inhabitants of their area but of different identity, mythical ancestors, naturalistic spirits and non-Nyaka deities. Contact is kept with these both simply by being in the forest and by annual rituals of possession. In the different setting of four mobile groups in Africa, however, Woodburn (1982) found little concern for the deceased as a continuing force, once immediate emotional ties had been broken by death and disposal.

Another world is represented by the Lugbara across the Congo–Uganda border (Middleton 1960). This society described as composed of tribes, clans, territorial sections and lineages can be seen at different levels – from the linking relations of authority of those who hold statuses in these 'units', to the immediate world of family and inner lineage, which regularly regards the surrounding world as hostile (Middleton 1960, 230, 236). The wider social network is conceived of in terms of clans, and clans are conceived of in terms of myth (Middleton 1960, 231). These go back in a line of descent from ancestors recognised in genealogies, which may often change (Middleton 1960, 12), to the founders of clans, who were the sons of a pair of hero-ancestors, who were the descendants of a line of siblings put on earth by God the creator. Middleton stressed that such a scheme was never related as a single narrative (1960, 232), and it was certainly flexible enough to include the historical appearance of Europeans. The scheme slides from genealogy to myth, and from human figures to not-quite-human figures such as the hero-ancestors and their predecessors. In the intimate world of the family and lineage, genealogy is a principal focus of concern, men, especially, manipulating the cult of the dead as the means to authority. Lineages are the agnatic (or uterine) core of a territorial section, and the means to think of that as unchanging, whereas in reality there is change all the time within and between lineages and territorial sections (Middleton 1960, 7–13). Within the lineage, different kinds of ancestors are recognised (Middleton 1960, 32–4; note that the difficulties of translating indigenous conceptions into English are fully recognised). On the one hand there are all forebears, including on occasion the living, who form a collectivity in which individuals are not important. On the other hand there are individual forebears, who are recognised as direct and significant ancestors (or 'ghosts' in the terminology which Middleton adopts) by agnatic descendants, with whom they are in personal and responsible contact, through the provision of individual shrines. The living make offerings to the varying categories of dead at shrines, since the dead may send sickness to express displeasure with actions considered to weaken or disunite the lineage. The shrine and the cult of the dead become the focus of central values to do with lineage and kinship (Middleton 1960, 34–5).

Lugbara shrines are varied, though they often take the form of simple arrangements of stones, and they are situated in a range of settings from within the settlement to outside it. Although ancestry as defined here is so important in Lugbara life, there appears to be no rite of collective burial as described for parts of Madagascar (e.g. Bloch 1971; Mack 1986). The world of the dead lies 'somewhere beneath the surface of the world' (Middleton 1982, 150). The dead are feared as well as revered (Middleton 1960, 201; 1982), and as so often elsewhere, funerals are occasions for gatherings, licence and the important business of realignment (Middleton 1960, 202–4; 1982). The dominant rite seems to be individual inhumation within houses, compounds and elsewhere. Some elders are given burial trees – figs planted at the head of their graves – which become sacred and are referred to in the same term which is translated as collective ancestor (Middleton 1960, 66; 1982).

In radical contrast, history for the Jivaro of Amazonian Ecuador is forgetting (Taylor 1993). Along with many other people of Amazonia, they have no ancestor cults, and have only simple funerary rites, and shallow genealogical memory. Forgetting the dead involves transforming them into something quite different, whose otherness helps to define values and relationships among the living. Through concepts of continuity of soul and singularity of face and name, the dead remain important as the source of the identity and destiny of the living, for if one person does not die, someone else cannot be born, but according to these conceptions they must be transformed from specific memories as alive to a mental representation as deceased (Taylor 1993, 655) and be reduced to an 'abstract singularity'. The death of men may cause houses to be abandoned, with bodies left in them or elsewhere to hasten the dissolution of the corpse. Separation and erasure are here central concepts, but the deceased appear to remain a potent force. 'Being nowhere in particular . . . [the dead] are, potentially, everywhere all the time' (Taylor 1993, 653).

This has taken us far from Atlantic Europe but even these three situations open up many relevant interpretive possibilities, some of which I will note here briefly.

The idea and memory of the past are not confined to agriculturalists, and legitimation of the present by means of the past, as abundantly seen among the Lugbara, may be as much about authority as it concerns resources, scarce or otherwise. Bloch (1998, 81) has claimed that there is no universal need to remember, and the Jivaro example certainly underlines the possibility and the importance of forgetting. If, however, memory is in part a way of making sense of things, forgetting is not that different. The memory and reworking of the past in terms of mythical and genealogical descent can be extremely varied even within one society, as the Lugbara example has underlined. Ingold (2000, 140–2) has given brief examples of further variety, covering creators, mythic beings, and spirit inhabitants, as well as human forebears. The use of concepts of ancestry and descent can be fluid, situational and tactical. To the Lugbara case noted here can be added many others from African and other ethnographies (e.g. Bohannan 1952; Fortes 1959). While lineage is central for the Lugbara, cognatic systems are also significant elsewhere, and the 'descent group' may not be a group as such (Scheffler 1966). These are issues to deal with at greater length elsewhere. The Lugbara example suggests that there may often be no single, linked narrative or account of such matters. Middleton's account implies that there is latent overall coherence, but following Bloch (1998), it is possible that this is not always so, in which case diversity and divergence are most probably inherent characteristics. What is important may be recognised or worked materially in quite simple ways (such as Lugbara shrines), while forgetting and separation may be the focus of considerable effort, with significant material consequences, such as house abandonment. These examples, together with those noted by Ingold (2000, 140–2) indicate the clear possibility of continuity and overlap in senses of time and descent among hunter-gatherers, horticultural foragers, and agriculturalists.

In this respect, myth may be of particular significance. Myth can be powerful and pervasive, with a 'hovering closeness' in Bellah's striking phrase (Bellah 1965; quoted in Guenther 1999, 426). As argued in another context, that of the Foi of Papua New Guinea, myth can be seen not as simply a charter for the status quo, but as a creative and fluid way in which different views of the world can be presented, contested and reworked (Weiner 1988; 1991). Lugbara myth was flexible enough to incorporate the coming of Europeans, and the Nyaka world-view permeable enough to integrate aspects of Hindu belief (Middleton 1960; Bird-David 1999). It has been argued often and accepted widely that memory and transformation of past practices were significant sources of monumental tradition in Neolithic western Europe. The likely links between longhouses and long mounds/cairns and between different kinds of ditched enclosure are perhaps the two instances most widely discussed (Bradley 1998). The creative fusion of different kinds of belief, including the powerful world of myth, may have been another significant source of changing practice at the Mesolithic–Neolithic transition in western Europe. I have discussed this elsewhere both in broad terms and with specific reference to motifs on the menhirs of the Morbihan area of Brittany (Whittle 1996; 2000). The studies in this volume serve usefully to remind us that there were wider phenomena at this time, which cannot all be linked to and derived from the 'Danubian' world of the LBK. This is not to claim some coherent underlying unity from the Atlantic coast of Iberia right up to Scandinavia via Ireland and Britain. But there may have been dispersed commonalities of belief, among on the one hand scattered indigenous forager populations and on the other the dispersed but linked communities of herders and incipient cultivators, some perhaps of external origin. It remains possible that the latter at least had a common, Indo-European language (Renfrew 2000a; 2000b). Indeed, new and shifting discourse about the fundamentals of life and death could have been one of the principal forms of communication which fostered the proposed spread of Indo-European at this time.

One long view

The studies in this volume between them cover long periods of time as well as a broad geographical area. In the discussion above I have concentrated mainly on situations and possibilities early in Neolithic sequences. I would like to end by outlining a scheme of recurrent trends through time, though these may not be found in all areas and diversity can be stressed within as well as between regions at any one time. Though very general, this scheme may be helpful, because many discussions (including my own) have probably been guilty of conflating the characteristics of a series or sequence of situations into one general model. To retain a sense of flexibility and diversity, I have deliberately avoided putting timescales on the following tentative phases.

In an *early* phase, there may recurrently have been much looking back, to the longhouses and ditched enclosures of the LBK on the one hand, and to the beliefs and myths of the indigenous world of western Europe on the other. Some people at least may have been physically orientated to their notional point of origin (e.g. Bradley 2001), and perhaps all were constantly aware of significant features of the surrounding physical world, from which many may not have distinguished or separated themselves at a conceptual level. Major concerns may have been with mythical beginnings and descents, and relations with the world of spirits, mythical ancestors and the like. Many early monuments, recurrently of simple rather than elaborate construction, may not have been specifically or centrally connected with the human dead as their principal focus. At the same time, however, a number of constructions may have been used in part for the disposal of very specific persons, perhaps better thought of as charismatics, spirit leaders, clan founders or the like rather than as the incipient or emergent elites more familiar from much of the archaeological literature. Small family groups may have been another early focus. Many monuments may have been placed quite carefully in specific locations in the landscape, often with relatively restricted or with particular views in and out.

In a *middle* phase, looking back continued, but was diversified. Some of the looking back concerned the monumental tradition itself. Memory began to refer to earlier events in the cycle of constructions and commemorations, as well as to the mythical times and fusions of the early phase. Architectural elaboration was recurrent, especially in the forms of cairns, mounds, chambers and other cognate structures. There was not only monumentality from place to place, but also diversity and sometimes quite rapid experimentation with different styles and ways of doing things. Where they occur, ditched circular and linear monuments complemented the cairn and mound traditions. The human dead were more often drawn into these constructions, especially but not exclusively those of mounds and cairns. Following the Lugbara model, there may have been the beginning of a shift from mythical to some kind of genealogical reckoning, though it is not necessary to see every collective deposit of human remains as representing 'the ancestors'. Many of them may have been formed by successive individual deposits, and the collectivities thus created may have been in part to do with coalitions and alliances among the living, including among kin groups but by no means restricted to them. Some of the more elaborate constructions of this middle phase may have been placed so as to have wider views, and to be more easily seen by those looking in; the example of Knocknarea in this volume (ch. 9) shows how not only views but whole tracts of land may have been physically brought into this kind of world-view.

In a *late* phase, senses of time may have diversified further. At least three kinds of time might be suggested to have been operating simultaneously. There may still have been a sense of looking back to the timeless world of ancestors and spirits, as argued for example in the case of Stonehenge (Parker Pearson and Ramilisonina 1998; Parker Pearson 2000). There may also have been a greater sense of looking to the future in a cycle of past, present and future in which the idea of rebirth may been important (Whittle 1997). Stonehenge may provide one example of this, and Bradley's study in the present volume (ch. 8) offers good arguments for a kind of looking forward and anticipation, connected to a group of monuments that appear not to be early in their regional sequence and setting. Thirdly, genealogical reckoning may have become much more prominent, generally expressed in smaller monuments and graves separate from the monumental tradition itself. Genealogical reckoning may later have become the basis for a greater degree of social differentiation than before; in my view it does not in itself constitute evidence for the immediate appearance of significant social differentiation, and this was also like so much else very varied from region to region. Some if not many of the major monuments of the late phase may have had very little direct connection with the remains of the human dead; they may have in part drawn in and drawn upon their surrounding landscapes to represent the whole world. There may not have been single, unified or coherent narratives covering all these disparate themes, though in some instances a sense of genealogical seniority, concern for the future, and access to remote ancestors could have been linked together to enable certain persons to claim or assert pre-eminence among their peers. Whether this was the world-view of those looking out from the monumental Copper Age sites of northern Portugal, to cite but one of the studies in this volume, remains to be seen.

The contributions to this volume and this brief coda both indicate how much remains to be discussed, re-examined and discovered in this central topic, the business of trying to listen-in on diverse long conversations, which so often seem just out of earshot.

References

Barrett, J., and Fewster, K., 1998. Stonehenge: *is* the medium the message? *Antiquity* 72, 847–52.

Basso, K.H., 1984. 'Stalking with stories': names, places, and moral narratives among the Western Apache, in E.M. Bruner (ed.), *Text, Play and the Story: The Reconstruction of Self and Society*. Washington, DC: American Ethnological Society, 19–55.

Basso, K.H., 1996. Wisdom sits in places: notes on a western Apache landscape, in S. Feld and K.H. Basso (eds), *Senses of Place*. Santa Fe: School of American Research Press, 53–90.

Bellah, R.N., 1965. Religious evolution, in W.A. Lessa and E.Z. Vogt (eds), *Reader in Comparative Religion* (3rd edn). New York: Harper and Row, 36–50.

Bird-David, N. 1999. The Nyaka of the Wynaad, south India, in L.B. Lee and R. Daly (eds), *The Cambridge Encyclopedia of Hunters and Gatherers*. Cambridge: Cambridge University Press, 257–60.

Bloch, M., 1971. *Placing the Dead: Tombs, Ancestral Villages and Kinship Organization in Madagascar*. London: Seminar Press.

Bloch, M., 1977. The past and the present in the past. *Man* 12, 278–92.

Bloch, M., 1998. *How We Think They Think: Anthropological Approaches to Cognition, Memory and Literacy*. Boulder, CO: Westview.

Bohannan, L., 1952. A genealogical charter. *Africa* 22, 301–15.

Bradley, R., 1993. *Altering the Earth: The Origins of Monuments in Britain and Continental Europe*. Edinburgh: Society of Antiquaries of Scotland.

Bradley, R., 1997. *Rock Art and the Prehistory of Atlantic Europe*. London: Routledge.

Bradley, R., 1998. *The Significance of Monuments: On the Shaping of Human Experience in Neolithic and Bronze Age Europe*. London: Routledge.

Bradley, R., 2001. Orientations and origins: a symbolic dimension to the long house in Neolithic Europe. *Antiquity* 75, 50–6.

Connerton, P., 1989. *How Societies Remember*. Cambridge: Cambridge University Press.

Descola, P., and Pálsson, G. (eds), 1996. *Nature and Society: Anthropological Perspectives*. London: Routledge.

Fortes, M. 1959. *Oedipus and Job in West African Religion*. Cambridge: Cambridge University Press.

Guenther, M. 1999. From totemism to shamanism: hunter-gatherer contributions to world mythology and spirituality, in L.B. Lee and R. Daly (eds), *The Cambridge Encyclopedia of Hunters and Gatherers*. Cambridge: Cambridge University Press, 426–33.

Howell, S., 1996. Nature in culture or culture in nature? Chewong ideas of 'humans' and other species, in P. Descola and G. Pálsson (eds), *Nature and Society: Anthropological Perspectives*. London: Routledge, 127–44.

Ingold, T., 2000. *The Perception of the Environment: Essays in Livelihood, Dwelling and Skill*. London: Routledge.

Küchler, S., 1987. Malangan – art and memory in a Melanesian society. *Man* 22, 238–55.

Küchler, S., 1993. Landscape as memory: the mapping of process and its representation in a Melanesian society, in B. Bender (ed.), *Landscape: Politics and Perspectives*. Providence and Oxford: Berg, 85–106.

Mack, J., 1986. *Madagascar: Island of the Ancestors*. London: British Museum Publications.

Middleton, J., 1960. *Lugbara Religion: Ritual and Authority among an East African People*. London: Oxford University Press.

Middleton, J., 1982. Lugbara death, in M. Bloch and J. Parry (eds), *Death and the Regeneration of Life*. Cambridge: Cambridge University Press, 134–54.

Morris, I., 1991. The archaeology of ancestors: the Saxe/Goldstein hypothesis revisited. *Cambridge Archaeological Journal* 1, 147–69.

Oswald, A., Dyer, C., and Barber, M., 2001. *The Creation of Monuments: Neolithic Causewayed Enclosures in the British Isles*. Swindon: English Heritage.

Parker Pearson, M., 2000. Ancestors, bones and stones in Neolithic and Early Bronze Age Britain and Ireland, in A. Ritchie (ed.), *Neolithic Orkney in its European context*. Cambridge: McDonald Institute for Archaeological Research, 203–14.

Parker Pearson, M., and Ramilisonina, 1998. Stonehenge for the ancestors: the stones pass on the message. *Antiquity* 72, 308–26.

Renfrew, C., 2000a. At the edge of knowability: towards a prehistory of languages. *Cambridge Archaeological Journal* 10, 7–34.

Renfrew, C., 2000b. Archaeogenetics: towards a prehistory of languages, in C. Renfrew and K. Boyle (eds), *Archaeogenetics: DNA and the Population Prehistory of Europe*. Cambridge: McDonald Institute for Archaeological Research, 3–12.

Rival, L., 1993. The growth of family trees: understanding Huaorani perceptions of the forest. *Man* 28, 635–52.

Scheffler, H.W., 1966. Ancestor worship in anthropology: or, observations on descent and descent groups. *Current Anthropology* 7, 541–51.

Schulting, R.J., 1998. Slighting the sea: stable isotope evidence for the transition to farming in northwestern Europe. *Documenta Praehistorica* 25, 203–18.

Schulting, R., and Richards, M., 2001. Dating women and becoming farmers: new AMS and stable isotope evidence from the Breton Mesolithic cemeteries of Téviec and Hoëdic. *Journal of Anthropological Archaeology* 20, 314–44.

Shanks, M., and Tilley, C. 1982. Ideology, symbolic power and ritual communication: a reinterpretation of Neolithic mortuary practices, in I. Hodder (ed.), *Symbolic and Structural Archaeology*. Cambridge: Cambridge University Press, 129–54.

Sherratt, A., 1995. Instruments of conversion? The role of megaliths in the Mesolithic/Neolithic transition in north-west Europe. *Oxford Journal of Archaeology* 14, 245–60.

Taylor, A.C., 1993. Remembering to forget: identity, mourning and memory among the Jivaro. *Man* 28, 653–78.

Tilley, C., 1999. *Metaphor and Material Culture*. Oxford: Blackwell.

Weiner, J.F., 1988. *The Heart of the Pearl Shell: The Mythological Dimension of Foi Sociality*. Berkeley: University of California Press.

Weiner, J.F., 1991. *The Empty Place: Poetry, Space, and Being among the Foi of Papua New Guinea*. Bloomington and Indianapolis: Indiana University Press.

Whitley, J., 2000. Too many ancestors. Paper presented at the Theoretical Archaeology Group conference, Oxford.

Whittle, A., 1996. *Europe in the Neolithic: The Creation of New Worlds*. Cambridge: Cambridge University Press.

Whittle, A., 1997. *Sacred Mound, Holy Rings. Silbury Hill and the West Kennet Palisade Enclosures: A Later Neolithic Complex in North Wiltshire*. Oxford: Oxbow Books.

Whittle, A., 1998. People and the diverse past: two comments on 'Stonehenge for the ancestors'. *Antiquity* 72, 852–54.

Whittle, A., 2000. 'Very like a whale': menhirs, motifs and myths in the Mesolithic–Neolithic transition of northwest Europe. *Cambridge Archaeological Journal* 10, 243–59.

Whittle, A., Pollard, J., and Grigson, C., 1999. *The Harmony of Symbols: The Windmill Hill Causewayed Enclosure, Wiltshire*. Oxford: Oxbow Books.

Widlok, J., 1997. Orientation in the wild: the shared cognition of Hai||om Bush-people. *Journal of the Royal Anthropological Institute* 3, 317–32.

Woodburn, J., 1982. Social dimensions of death in four African hunting and gathering societies, in M. Bloch and J. Parry (eds), *Death and the Regeneration of life*. Cambridge: Cambridge University Press, 187–210.

Wysocki, M., and Whittle, A., 2000. Diversity, lifestyles and rites: new biological and archaeological evidence from British Earlier Neolithic mortuary assemblages. *Antiquity* 74, 591–601.

Index